# Nineties Knowledge

# Nineties Knowledge

*Editor*
David Crystal

EDINBURGH   NEW YORK

Published 1992 by W & R Chambers Limited
43—45 Annandale Street, Edinburgh EH7 4AZ

© W & R Chambers Ltd 1992

**British Library Cataloguing in Publication Data**

A catalogue record for this book is
available from the British Library

ISBN 0-550-17254-8

Editorial Manager  Min Lee
Illustrations by John Marshall and George Kilgour
Transparency for jacket  Tony Craddock/Science Photo Library
Cover design by Caleb Rutherford
Typeset by Selwood Systems, Bath
Printed in England by Clays Ltd, St Ives, plc

# Contents

# Preface

The idea for this book arose from a mock-interview experience I had in 1989. (I was giving the interview, not receiving it.) The Rotary Club of Holyhead routinely offer sixth-formers from the local comprehensive school the chance to have an interview relating to the career they have in mind, and I was asked to talk to several who were envisaging university entrance. I always devoted the first part of the interview to technical matters to do with their subject and the application form, and then broadened the topic to whatever happened to be going on in current affairs or modern thought. The experience which sticks in my mind is asking someone about the possibility that Nelson Mandela might be released. She did not know who Mandela was. I asked her what she thought of the situation in South Africa. She couldn't tell me. I asked her what apartheid was. She couldn't say.

I began to keep notes on the kinds of topic which my candidates seemed to be unaware of, or which they found difficult. I hasten to add that some of the interviewees were magnificent in the precision and clarity of their answers – but the majority were not. Over the following weeks, I jotted down 'balance of payments', 'greenhouse effect, 'ACAS', 'backbencher', 'cantata' 'market forces', 'Rococo', 'Solidarity' and 'prices and incomes policy'. During the conversations, I was also surprised to find how difficult it was to be precise myself, suddenly faced with the task of explaining these notions to someone who did not know. To explain one concept required the introduction of another, and that one required a third. I came to realize that I did not know as much about them as I thought. Faced with the task of explaining 'Baroque', I could hear myself waffling. In talking about the experience to friends and colleagues, it emerged that everyone was having difficulty with many of these notions. It dawned on me that a plainly written guide to essential concepts in current affairs and modern thought might be of value to a much wider audience than the one I had first encountered.

The present book is the result – an expansion and systematization of those first experiences. It is in no sense a complete guide to modern thought – but I think the selection of concepts provides a representative sample of the issues which young people (and old) will routinely encounter in the media and in conversation (especially formal conversations, of which the interview remains the classic example.) I have included just over 700 concepts, and presented them alphabetically (organized on a letter-by-letter basis). I have added pronunciation guides in places, a fairly large number of cross-references between entries, and a separate index of the people referred to in the entries –

which incidentally makes interesting reading in its own right. The information comes from the database which I compiled for the *Cambridge Encyclopedia*, but I have substantially expanded and rewritten the material to suit the more discursive level required, and had all the entries checked by specialists, to ensure that the move in the direction of plain English does not introduce unacceptable kinds of simplification.

I hope the book helps to solve at least some of the problems of those having to come to terms with the increased breadth of modern syllabuses or the increased range of modern educated discussion. My own next problem, I imagine, is what to do with an interviewee who turns up next year armed with a copy of *Nineties Knowledge*.

David Crystal
Holyhead
*March 1992*

# Acknowledgements

The entries in *Nineties Knowledge* have been checked by specialists:

Art and Architecture   Kitty Michaelson
Economics and Business   Donald Rutherford
Education   Kathryn Dean
Environment   Rob Edwards
History and Politics   Stewart Ross
Law   Nicolas Lockhart
Medicine and Nutrition   Raymond Mills
Music   Marion Main
Philosophy and Logic   Robert Calder
Psychology   Robert Grieve
Religion   William McDonald
Science   Peter Brand
Sociology   David McCrone

**abdication**   A situation which occurs when the ruler of a country gives up the throne or other high office. Most abdications take place under duress: the ruler is forced to abdicate following a wartime defeat, a revolution, or a constitutional crisis. Napoleon Bonaparte was forced to abdicate twice — once in 1814, then (following his attempt to regain power) in 1815. Edward VIII of England was forced to abdicate in 1936, after 11 months in office, because of public disapproval of his proposed marriage to a divorcee,

Some famous abdications

| Ruler | Born-Died | Status and country | Year of abdication |
|---|---|---|---|
| Amanullah Khan | 1892–1960 | Ruler of Afghanistan | 1929 |
| Charles X | 1757–1836 | King of France | 1830 |
| Constantine I | 1868–1923 | King of Greece | 1917 |
| Cromwell, Richard | 1626–1712 | Lord Protector of England | 1659 |
| Edward II | 1284–1327 | King of England | 1326 |
| Edward VIII | 1894–1972 | King of England | 1936 |
| Farouk I | 1920–1965 | King of Egypt | 1952 |
| Juliana | 1909– | Queen of the Netherlands | 1980 |
| Louis-Philippe | 1773–1850 | King of France | 1848 |
| Mary | 1542–1587 | Queen of Scots | 1567 |
| Michael | 1921– | King of Rumania | 1947 |
| Napoleon I | 1769–1821 | Emperor of France | 1814, 1815 |
| Nicholas II | 1868–1918 | Emperor of Russia | 1917 |
| Sihanouk, Norodom | 1922– | King of Cambodia | 1955 |
| Umberto II | 1904–1983 | King of Italy | 1946 |
| Wilhelm II | 1859–1941 | Emperor of Germany | 1918 |
| Wilhelmina | 1880–1962 | Queen of the Netherlands | 1948 |

Mrs Wallis Simpson. On the other hand, some rulers choose to abdicate, sometimes because of illness or age, or simply because they feel they have ruled for too long. Queen Wilhelmina of the Netherlands voluntarily abdicated in 1948, as did her daughter, Queen Juliana, in 1980. ▷ **constitution**

**abortion**   The expulsion of a foetus from the womb before it can survive independently of the mother. A spontaneous abortion (usually called a *miscarriage*) occurs in about 20% of apparently normal pregnancies, and may not be recognized. It may arise from defects in the mother's body or problems which arise in the maternal environment, such as accidents and certain kinds of illness. These days, the term *abortion* usually refers to the deliberate removal of the foetus from the mother, either by the use of drugs or by surgical procedures. There are several reasons given for an induced abortion (often called a *termination of pregnancy*) — to prevent the birth of a physically or mentally handicapped child, to prevent the birth of a child resulting from rape or incest, to safeguard the health of the mother, or to exercise birth control. Unless permitted by the Abortion Acts of a country, induced abortion is a criminal offence. Much depends on the time limit legally recognized by a country at which a foetus is deemed to be capable of independent survival. In the UK, this limit since 1968 was the 28th week of pregnancy, although some foetuses expelled before then may survive. In the USA and in some European countries, the time limit recognizes this fact, and is set some weeks earlier. Proposals to reduce the time limit in the UK often received controversial hearing, but in 1990 Parliament approved a measure to reduce it to 24 weeks. Those in favour of keeping or extending the time limit usually argue for the woman's 'right to choose'. Those in favour of reducing the limit argue for the baby's right to life — and some groups (notably, the Roman Catholic Church) assert that induced abortion is in principle morally unjustified, for this reason. ▷ **ethics**

**abstract art**   A form of art which does not attempt to represent objects, persons, or other features of the real world, but relies instead on lines, colours, and shapes for its aesthetic appeal. It seems to have emerged around 1910, partly as a reaction against the 19th-century styles of art which presented objects in a realistic way (▷ **Realism** and **Impressionism**). Early abstract artists included Russian painter Vasily Kandinsky (1866–1944), Spanish painter Joán Miró (1893–1983), and Rumanian sculptor Constantine Brancusi (1876–1957). Abstract tendencies have been present in one form or another in most cultures. It is possible to distinguish two broad trends. First, there is an approach which simplifies or distorts natural appearances — what is sometimes called 'semi-abstract' art. This can be seen in many kinds of modern art (▷ **Cubism** and **Expressionism**), and also in much figurative art from earlier periods, which always has its starting-point in the real world. Second, there is an approach which totally rejects any dependence on natural appearances — what is sometimes called 'pure' abstract art. Such works establish their own 'reality' and are intended to appeal in their own right. Only the latter should, strictly speaking, be called 'abstract', but the term is often used imprecisely to cover a wide range of 20th-century art. ▷ **action painting; art; figurative art; modern art**

**abstract expressionism**   ▷ **action painting**.

**ACAS**   The abbreviation, pronounced **ay**-kas, of **Advisory, Conciliation and Arbitration Service** — a body set up by the British government in 1975. The chief function of ACAS is to provide facilities for mediation in industrial disputes between employers and trade unions, especially where a trade union is taking industrial action. There are offices in London where representatives of both sides can meet, and advisers who can talk to each side separately, to see whether there is a basis for settlement. ▷ **industrial action; trade union**

**acid rain**   A term first used in the 19th century to describe polluted rain in Manchester, UK, and now used generally for polluted rainfall associated with the burning of fossil fuels. Acid pollution can be wet (rain, snow, mist) or dry (gases, particles). A number of gases are involved, particularly sulphur dioxide ($SO_2$) and oxides of nitrogen ($NO$). Reactions in the atmosphere lead to the production of sulphuric acid ($H_2SO_4$) and nitric acid ($HNO_3$). In Europe about 85% of $SO_2$ in the air comes from the burning of fossil fuels, and chemical plants which remove the sulphurous emissions are being

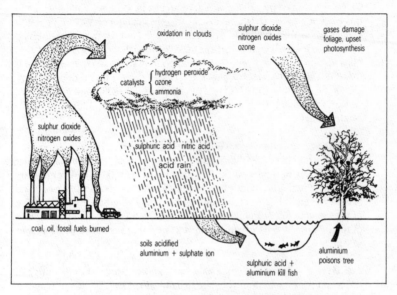

*Acid rain – The chain from pollutants to acidified lakes and dying trees*

fitted to some power stations. The main emissions of oxides of nitrogen, including ($NO$) and ($NO_2$), are from fossil-fuel power generation and the internal combustion engine. Acid rain is implicated in damage to forests and the stonework of buildings, and increases the acid content of soils and lakes, harming crops and fish. In 1985, 19 countries formed the 'Thirty Percent Club', agreeing to lower their emissions of $SO_2$ by 30% by 1993, using 1980 emissions as the baseline. ▷ **fossil fuels; greenhouse effect**

**acquired immune deficiency syndrome**  ▷ **AIDS**.

**Act of Parliament**  A bill which has passed through all the required stages of debate in both houses of the UK parliament, and received the royal assent. At that point it also becomes known as a *statute*. *Statute law* consists of all the Acts passed by Parliament, the earliest dating from 1235. The same kind of procedure applies in other parliamentary systems, although the specific stages through which a bill passes may vary. ▷ **bill, parliamentary; legislature**

**action painting**   A form of abstract art which first became fashionable in the USA in the late 1940s. At first, the style of painting was called 'abstract expressionism', but this was felt to be a rather clumsy and inexact phrase, so it was replaced by a name which more vividly captures what goes on in this kind of art. The style emphasizes the physical act of applying paint to canvas, rather than the finished picture. The paint may be thrown or dribbled onto the canvas, which might be tacked to the floor. People might ride bicycles across the wet surface, or roll about on it. The movement's leader was the US artist Jackson Pollock (1912–56), who often produced huge works: his painting called 'One' is five metres (17 feet) long. In France, a similar movement was called *Tachisme* (from *tache*, 'blot, mark'). ▷ **abstract art**

**activism**   Anyone who favours vigorous and direct action in support of a cause — especially a political cause. Activism is usually found at the core of a political party, and is particularly prominent in any kind of revolutionary movement. Activists who strongly support fundamental change in a political system are often referred to as **militants**. Many activists, especially those of the extreme left or right, are ready to invoke the use of force in support of their goals. ▷ **left wing; Militant Tendency; pressure group; right wing**

**additives**   Chemicals which have been added to food or drink during its processing or preparation. They are usually added for a particular purpose. For example, *preservatives* reduce the chances of food going bad through the action of bacteria. *Anti-oxidants* prevent fats from becoming rancid. *Emulsifiers* permit a stable mixture of oil and water. *Colourants* give a more definite or attractive colour. *Flavouring agents* (also called *flavouring enhancers*) improve the taste. Some of these additives occur in nature, but many are made artificially (synthetically). In most countries there are laws controlling the use of food additives: they should be there only for the best of reasons, and they need to be safe. Usually, information about the use of additives is printed on a packet, bottle or tin. Nonetheless, in recent years many people have come to fear synthetic additives, and they will often buy food only if it contains natural additives — or no additives at all. ▷ **E-number**

**adult education**   The provision of further or continuing educational opportunities for people over the minimum school-leaving age; also known as **continuing education** or **community education**. Frequently this takes place in institutions specially set up to cater for mature learners, but it is

POST CARD

$\mathcal{E}$ MERALD

**THOMSON** *Cruises*

also common for schools and colleges and other centres of learning to be used. In addition to the formal opportunities offered by institutions, there are numerous informal sources of adult education, such as broadcast programmes on radio and television, as well as correspondence and distance-learning courses, for people who wish to or must learn at home or as part of their job. ▷ **distance learning; further education**

**Adventists** Christians who believe that the second coming of Jesus Christ on earth is close at hand. The term *advent* comes from the Latin word for 'arrival'. Forms of adventism are found in most periods of Christian history, and in many Protestant denominations, but the most influential movement in recent times began in the USA, when an American farmer, William Miller (1781–1849), predicted Christ's return and the end of the world in 1843–4. His followers eventually formed a denomination known as the Seventh Day Adventists, who believe that the second coming of Christ is delayed only by a failure to keep the Sabbath (Friday to Saturday evening). They are very strict in their observance of the Sabbath, as well as of Old Testament dietary laws. ▷ **Christianity; millenarianism**

**adversary politics** A political situation which exists in two-party electoral systems (such as in the UK) where the policies of the parties and government are polarized between right and left. This results in significant reversals in policy when government changes. Because the electoral system works against successful challenges from third parties, the views of the majority of the electorate occupying the 'middle ground' tend to be under-represented. ▷ **coalition; left wing; opposition; proportional representation; right wing**

**Advisory, Conciliation and Arbitration Service** ▷ **ACAS**.

**aerobics** A system of physical training in which exercises such as walking, swimming, and running are pursued for a sufficiently long period to increase performance. The increases can be assessed using a point scoring system available on charts for different ages and types of effort. In the 1980s, the term was particularly used for movement exercises in time to music, which became popular among keep-fit groups at all ages. The use of oxygen by muscles in carrying out any form of physical activity is known as *aerobic metabolism*. ▷ **calisthenics**

**aeronautics** The broad body of scientifically-based knowledge describing aeroplanes as objects subject to the laws of physics. The term is usually taken to mean knowledge which focuses upon the vehicle itself, rather than upon the associated commercial or operational usage, although in practice

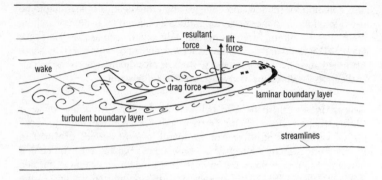

*The flow of air over an aircraft*

such a definition is not rigidly adhered to. Thus, aeronautics is taken to cover such topics as the generation of lift to make the aeroplane fly, the physical factors affecting manoeuvring, the production of thrust through the use of propellers and jets, the strength of the structure, and the way these various elements are combined to produce a functioning vehicle.

**aerosol**   A suspension of microscopic particles or liquid droplets dispersed through the air, usually by forcing a liquid through a fine nozzle under pressure. Natural examples include mist, fog, and smoke. The term is also used for the implement (usually a can with a push-button device) which produces an aerosol spray. These sprays are useful as a means of depositing fine even layers of material, such as in paint sprays, insecticides, and perfume dispensers. There is now evidence that the fluorocarbon propellants which have been used in these sprays have damaged the ozone layer around the earth, and moves to ban the propellants have taken place in many countries. ▷ **CFCs; ozone layer**

**aesthetics**   The philosophical investigation of art, in a wide sense, including the visual arts (painting, sculpture, photography, film), music, literature, drama, and dance. The subject may be traced back to ancient Greece, and has co-existed with the making of works of art. The name dates from the 18th century, when the *Critique of Judgment* of the German philosopher Immanuel Kant (1724–1804) was perhaps the most notable work on the subject. Aesthetics deals with a wide range of questions. What is it to perceive an object or a performance as a work of art? What does it mean to say that something is beautiful? What features, if any, are important or essential to it? Are there any objective standards for saying that a work is 'artistic' or 'good'? To what degree is beauty to be found in a work itself or 'in the eye of the beholder'? And what meaning and function can be ascribed to art criticism? ▷ **art; philosophy**

**affirmative action**   A term, particularly associated with the USA, describing policies which give preferential treatment to certain kinds of minority group, considered to be disadvantaged with regard to employment or educational opportunity. They require institutions to act 'affirmatively' in their practices, avoiding discrimination on grounds of race, ethnic origin, or sex. The policies include a wide range of possible actions, from generally encouraging the employment of minorities to the actual setting of quotas of minorities to be employed. President John F Kennedy first gave legal status to the notion in the early 1970s. Although widely implemented, the policies are controversial, their opponents arguing that they are themselves unjust and discriminatory. ▷ **ethnicity; racism; sexism**

**African National Congress (ANC)**   The most important of the Black South African organizations opposed to White rule and the policy of apartheid in South Africa. It began life in 1912 as the South African Native National Congress and, under the influence of the Indian nationalist leader Mahatma Gandhi (1869–1948), organized passive resistance to White power. After World War II, Oliver Tambo (1917–  ) and Nelson Mandela (1918–  ) organized its youth wing. It was active in the 1950s, leading opposition to the measures of the Afrikaner Nationalist government, but was banned by the government in 1961, and Mandela was imprisoned in 1964. Other members of its leadership went into exile. The ANC then began a campaign of industrial and economic sabotage through its military wing. This campaign was not particularly successful, so in the 1980s the ANC began attacking persons as well as property. Based in Zambia for several years, it grew into a force of around 6000 guerrillas. Following political progress in the late 1980s, the ANC was unbanned and Mandela released in February 1990, and it suspended its armed struggle in August of that year. ▷ **apartheid**

**agnosticism**   A person who believes that the existence of God can neither be known (as theists believe) nor denied (as atheists believe). The basic notion is a very ancient one — there is, for example, a reference to people believing in an 'unknown god' in the New Testament (in *Acts of the Apostles*, 17.23). The modern term comes from the Greek word for 'knowledge' (*gnosis*), and was first used in 1869 by the English biologist T H Huxley (1825–95). Agnostics were contrasted with 'gnostics', or metaphysicians. Agnosticism was later extended to include the view that knowledge must be restricted to what is available to the senses, and that anything not so available (including therefore religion and God) is irrelevant to life today. ▷ **atheist; empiricism; theology**

**agricultural policy**   ▷ **Common Agricultural Policy**.

**AID/AIH** ▷ **artificial insemination**.

**AIDS** An acronym of **acquired immune deficiency syndrome**, the result of infection with a human immune deficiency virus (HIV). Groups at high risk of acquiring the disease are homosexual or bisexual men, individuals with a history of intravenous drug abuse, sufferers from haemophilia who have received many transfusions of blood or factor VIII prior to 1986, persons who have had casual sexual relationships especially in sub-Saharan Africa, San Francisco, or New York, and sexual partners and children of any of those. The origin of HIV virus is unknown, but it is possible that it originated from a group of African monkeys, themselves immune to the disease. In humans, transmission is by direct blood or seminal contact. The virus enters cells of the immune system, and slowly destroys the defence of the body against infection. Infected individuals may remain free from symptoms and show HIV antibodies only in the blood. With the passage of months or years, infections from organisms that usually do not cause illness develop, along with a rare form of skin cancer. A high incidence of death follows. ▷ **factor VIII**

**alcoholism** A harmful state which develops when someone comes to be mentally and physically dependent on alcohol — but the term is used in a variety of ways. Some people use the term simply in a joking or insulting way, referring to the abnormal behaviour which comes when people regularly drink too much. Most however now see alcoholism as an illness, with alcoholics suffering from such symptoms as loss of memory, delusions, personality changes, and damage to the liver, heart and brain. The level at which someone is viewed as an alcoholic also varies greatly between countries and social groups, with some accepting higher levels of drinking ('social drinking') than others. Treatment may involve the use of drugs alongside a long period of carefully-planned withdrawal, under medical supervision. Alternatively, an alcoholic may join a self-help group, the most famous being Alcoholics Anonymous (AA). AA was founded in the USA in 1935, and now has over a million members in over 90 countries. It consists of local groups where members (identified only by their first names) meet to give each other support.

**alexia** ▷ **dyslexia**.

**algorithm** A set of precisely determined rules, which if applied to a complex problem will yield a solution or optimal results. For example, when playing second in noughts and crosses, 'Occupy the centre position immediately, if it is empty' is part of an algorithm which will result in your never losing. Try it. Because they are precisely defined and their application requires no insight, algorithms can be programmed into computers. ▷ **heuristic**

**alien**   A person living in a country who is not a citizen of that country. A citizen of one country is usually an alien in another, and vice versa, but the law may permit certain exceptions. In the UK, for example, citizens of the Republic of Ireland are not regarded as aliens, nor are Commonwealth citizens. Citizens of member states of the European Community also enjoy certain privileges: they enjoy full economic rights, and may not be discriminated against in the economic field. The rights of aliens vary from country to country: in the UK, they may hold most kinds of property, but may not vote or hold a public office. ▷ **Commonwealth; European Community**

**allegory**   A story in verse or prose in which a deeper level of meaning exists alongside the obvious events and characters of the narrative. Myths and fables (such as Aesop's fables) are both allegorical. When the fox is defeated in one of Aesop's stories, there is a message for everyone about how crime does not pay. Allegory may therefore be understood as a kind of continuous figure of speech, always inviting interpretation. Nothing can be taken at face value. Allegories are often found in works with a religious or political bearing, where the characters symbolize different attitudes or concepts. Famous examples include John Bunyan's *Pilgrim's Progress* (1678) and George Orwell's *Animal Farm* (1945). ▷ **literature**

**allergy**   An abnormal reaction of the body to contact with certain foreign substances. These substances, known as *allergens*, are harmless in themselves, but in sensitive individuals they react with proteins produced within the body by cells of the immune system. These proteins, called *antibodies*, would normally destroy foreign substances entering the body. But in the case of allergens, the reaction with the antibodies results in damage to the body cells and tissues. A large number of substances found in nature (such as dust, fur, pollen, and certain foodstuffs) are actual or potential allergens, and can lead to a wide range of illnesses, such as asthma and various kinds of skin disease. Pollen, for example, is a well-established cause of hay-fever during the summer. Certain kinds of drug can now be used to reduce sensitivity in some cases.

**alternative energy**   Any source of energy which does not rely on the burning of fossil fuels (chiefly coal, gas and oil) or nuclear power. Fossil fuels cause problems because they are a major cause of pollution; they are also in limited supply, and some countries have none at all. Nuclear power is a controversial energy source, as many people doubt its safety. As a result, there has been a growing interest in finding other sources of energy, such as the sun (solar power), heat from within the earth (geothermal power), water movement (tidal power, wave power, or hydroelectric power), and

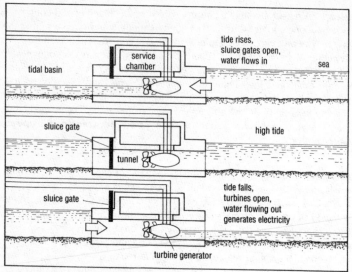

*The generation of elecricity by tidal power*

wind. These sources are particularly important in countries which do not have fossil fuels, but they attract interest everywhere because they avoid most of the problems of pollution. However, alternative energy schemes can be criticized on other grounds. To develop a large hydroelectric power scheme, for example, it may be necessary to flood a valley and for people to be rehoused. Wind power requires tall towers with large wind-driven propellors, which may be a visual intrusion. A barrage built across a river estuary, to harness tidal power, will alter the balance of living things in the estuary. ▷ **energy; hydroelectric power; nuclear reactor; renewable resources**

**alternative medicine**   Any approach to the treatment of illness using procedures other than those recommended by medical science. The demand for this kind of treatment has increased in recent years, generated by individuals who have not been relieved of their complaints by orthodox methods. Sufferers from cancer, depression, asthma, back problems, allergies, and other such 'problem' diseases are especially likely to look to alternative medicine for help. There are over 50 different approaches, including acupuncture, aromatherapy, autosuggestion, bioenergetics, biomagnetic therapy, Christian Science, chiropractic, fasting, hypnosis, herbalism and dietotherapy, homeopathy and holistic medicine, hydrotherapy, ion therapy, massage, meditation, naturopathy, and osteopathy. For the most part, these procedures are based on theories of disease for which there is scant evidence, and some invoke principles that many people recognize as bizarre. On the other hand, there are widespread anecdotal reports of the success of courses of treatment on individuals. The problem, then, is how to distinguish the genuinely effective from superstition. Almost none of the therapeutic methods used as alternative medicine have been or are readily capable of being rigorously assessed, using standard scientific techniques. Until such assessments are made, the medical establishment will remain critical. However, a more positive attitude is now frequently found among medical practitioners, fuelled partly by increased information about successful alternative medical practices in other countries (such as acupuncture in China). ▷ **holistic medicine; homeopathy**

**altruism**   The view that people sometimes intentionally promote the interests of others without considering their own interests. Anyone who gives help without expecting anything in return can be said to be acting altruistically. Some, such as the English political philosopher Thomas Hobbes (1588–1679), have argued that supposedly altruistic actions are always really self-interested — a view disputed by his opponents. ▷ **ethics**

**ambassador**   The highest-ranking diplomat, resident abroad, who officially represents his or her country in relations with foreign governments. Ambassadors are to be distinguished from **consuls**, whose chief functions are to protect citizens abroad, and to guard the commercial interests of these citizens. There is only one ambassador (living or working in an *embassy*) assigned to a country, but there may be a consul (living or working in a *consulate*) in each of several chief cities.

**Amnesty International**   A human rights organization founded in London in 1961 largely by the efforts of Peter Benenson, a Catholic lawyer. It is based in the UK, but there are several groups in other, mainly industrialized, countries. The fundamental concern of Amnesty is to seek the immediate and unconditional release of prisoners of conscience, as long as they have not advocated violence. It also campaigns against torture and the death penalty, and tries to produce independent, authoritative reports on countries' abuses of human rights. The organization was awarded the Nobel Peace Prize in 1977. Its logo is a burning candle within barbed wire. ▷ **human rights**

*Amnesty International logo*

**Anabaptists**   The name given to various left-wing groups of believers who came out of the Protestant Reformation in the 16th century; they were also known as **Rebaptizers** because converts allowed themselves to be baptized again (held to be a crime punishable by death, at that time). They refused to recognize infant baptism (including their own), and believed in the baptism of believing adults only. They emphasized adherence to the word of scripture, strict Church discipline, pacifism, and the separation of Church and state. They refused to swear civil oaths. Because they were prepared to criticize the state, they often suffered fierce persecution. The movement originated in Zürich in 1625, and spread throughout Switzerland, Germany, and the Low Countries, moving later to the USA. Leading Anabaptists of the time were the German preacher Thomas Müntzer (c.1489–1525) and the Dutchman Jan Mattys (died 1534). A later development was the Mennonite sect, named after the Dutchman Menno Simons (1496–1559), which now has over a million believers in the USA. In many ways Anabaptists were also the forerunners of the modern Baptists. ▷ **Baptists; Reformation**

**anarchism**   A general term for political ideas and movements which reject the state and other forms of authority and coercion (eg by the police or military) in favour of a society based exclusively upon voluntary cooperation between individuals. The word comes from Greek *anarkhos*, meaning 'without ruler'. To anarchists the state, whether democratic or not, is always seen as a means of supporting a ruling class or elite, and as an impediment to social relations. However, they differ in their view of the nature of their future society: proposals range from a communist society based on mutual aid to one based on essentially self-interested voluntary exchange. They reject involvement in political institutions, and often support civil disobedience action against the state, and on occasions political violence. Anarchist movements were most prevalent in Europe in the second half of the 19th and early 20th centuries, but virtually died out apart from fringe groups after the Spanish Civil War. Famous anarchist theorists include the English political writer William Godwin (1756–1836), and Russian revolutionaries Mikhail Bakunin (1814–76), and Prince Peter Kropotkin (1842–1921). ▷ **nihilism**

**Anglican Communion**   A worldwide fellowship of Churches which all share a close relationship with the Church of England in matters of religious doctrine and practice. Most of them are found in the British Commonwealth, and owe their origins to the missionary activities of the Church of England in the 19th century. (An important exception is the Episcopal Church in the USA, which was fostered by the Scottish Episcopal Church.) Churches from non-Commonwealth countries are also part of the Anglican Communion, such as those in Brazil, China and Japan. The Communion is based on cooperation, as there is no single worldwide authority, but every 10 years the Archbishop of Canterbury invites bishops throughout the Communion to take part in the **Lambeth Conference** to consider matters of common concern. The 1968 Conference also set up an Anglican Consultative Council to act during the 10-year intervals. There were over 72 million Anglicans in 1990. ▷ **Christianity**

**Anglo-Catholicism**   A movement within the Church of England, dating from the 1830s, which looks for continuity and community between the Church of England and the wider Catholic Church, especially Roman Catholicism. It stresses the importance of the sacraments, formal statements of belief (as in a Creed), and traditional liturgical practices, such as the use of incense and vestments.   ▷ **Anglican Communion; Roman Catholicism**

**annual percentage rate**   ▷ **interest**.

**annulment**   A legal declaration that something previously agreed in law (such as a contract, a court decree, or the decision of a public body) is no longer valid.  The effect of an annulment is that the rights and duties which were recognized before are now treated as if they never existed. The notion is often encountered with reference to marriage. A null marriage is one which has never existed in law. Examples would include a marriage where one or both partners were too young, or were insane, or were close blood relatives, or were already married. A distinction should be drawn with a **divorce**, where the marriage was perfectly valid, but it has now been legally ended.

**anthropology**   The study of the human race, especially seen in relation to the history and variety of individual races, physical features, environments, and cultures. In its broadest definition, its scope includes archaeology, social and cultural anthropology, physical anthropology, and aspects of linguistics. The primary concern of archaeologists is 'digging up history' — recovering and documenting the material remains of past communities. Cultural and social anthropologists study particular living societies, and attempt through comparison to establish the range of variation in human, social, and cultural institutions, and the reasons for these differences. Physical anthropologists study local biological adaptations and the evolutionary history of human beings. Anthropological expertise has also been applied in the USA (and to some extent elsewhere) in dealing with problems of multi-ethnic communities, nowadays particularly with regard to medicine and education. Such developments fall under the heading of *applied anthropology*. ▷ **ethnicity; linguistics; sociology; Three Worlds theory**

**antibody**   ▷ **allergy**.

**anti-oxidants**   ▷ **additives**.

**antisemitism**   Hostility or prejudice towards Jewish people — an attitude which has been present ever since Jews began to settle in Europe in the first century. Its origins are complex, being partly religious (early Christianity held Jews to blame for the death of Jesus Christ), partly cultural (dislike of the distinctive Jewish dress and ritual), partly economic (many Jews earned hostility through their role as a class of money-lenders and middlemen in the Middle Ages). Antisemitism became strong in Europe in the 19th century, as nationalism grew, and from the 1880s there were pogroms (organized massacres) of Jews in Eastern Europe, which caused many to flee, especially to the USA. Hitler's racial policies were the most blatant form of antisemitism, beginning in the 1930s and culminating in the Holocaust. The phenomenon still exists in certain countries, often in more subtle forms, and since the establishment of Israel has been reinforced by Arab anti-Zionism. ▷ **Holocaust; Zionism**

**apartheid** The policy of separate racial development found in the Republic of South Africa, supported traditionally by the Nationalist Party, and more recently by other right-wing parties. The word is Afrikaans, meaning 'apartness'. Under the policy, different races are given different rights; but in practice the system is one of White supremacy, Blacks having no representation in the central state parliament. The provisions of apartheid primarily relate to labour, land segregation (Blacks being placed in special reserves, called *Homelands* or *Bantustans*), segregation in towns and cities, social and educational separation, and an exclusive White right to vote, but there are also many smaller-scale provisions relating to the use of transport, beaches, lavatories, park benches, and so on. The whole system, legally introduced in South Africa since 1948, is backed by extensive repression, evidenced by the Sharpeville Massacre in 1960 and the Soweto student riots in 1976. Its principal architect, prime minister Hendrik Verwoerd (1901–66), was assassinated in 1966. Widespread international condemnation of the system led to the withdrawal of South Africa from the Commonwealth in 1961; there were several international sanctions on sporting and cultural events in the 1960s and 1970s; and there were moves towards economic sanctions in the 1980s. Well-known individual opponents to apartheid include Nelson Mandela (1918– ), Archbishop Desmond Tutu (1931– ), and Steve Biko (1946–77). For many years, world opinion seemed to have little effect, but since the late 1980s there have been dramatic changes, with a series of reforms, introduced by prime minister F W de Klerk (1936– ), resulting in the progressive dismantling of the apartheid system. ▷ **Black Consciousness; civil rights; right wing**

**apologetics** A branch of theology which gives a reasoned justification for Christian faith in the light of specific criticisms or charges. The word comes from Latin *apologia*, meaning 'defence', and has been used in this way since the second century, when writers such as St Justin Martyr wrote apologies for their beliefs. St Augustine (fourth century) and St Thomas Aquinas (13th century) were other famous apologists. The term should not be confused with the common modern sense of the word 'apology', which means an expression of regret for an error one has committed. ▷ **Christianity; theology**

**apostasy** ▷ **heresy**.

**applied arts** ▷ **decorative arts**.

**arbitration** A process which takes place when an independent party (the **arbitrator**) is brought in to settle a dispute; known in Scotland as an **arbiter**. Commercial contracts often say that disputes must be settled in this way, in an attempt to avoid lengthy and costly proceedings in the courts. There are specialist trade tribunals engaged in settling business disputes, such as the London Maritime Arbitrators Association and the Grain and Feed Trade Association. In industrial disputes, also, a case may be submitted to arbitration — in the UK, often involving the government conciliation service, ACAS. The notion of arbitration is a very broad one, including (at one extreme) solutions to personal arguments and (at the other) the res-olution of international conflicts, such as over the location of a frontier. An example of an international arbitration body is the Permanent Court of Arbitration, which sits in The Hague. ▷ **ACAS; tribunal**

**archaeology/archeology** The study of past peoples and societies through the systematic analysis of their material remains. It originated as an aspect of the revival of interest in classical culture during the Renaissance, and was, until the study of human antiquity was established in the 1860s, an almost exclusively European and antiquarian pursuit, interpreting chance survivals of monuments and artefacts with reference to the biblical and classical background. The emphasis since has shifted firmly to the study of human development over the long period of more than two million years in which written records were non-existent (*prehistory*) or at best rudimentary (*protohistory*), and to the recovery of new data through excavation, field survey, laboratory study, and computer analysis. Radiometric dating methods (determining the age of an object by measuring the amount of a radioactive element present within it) established the discipline on a new and firmer footing in the 1950s and 1960s. Politically too the subject has an often potent role to play in the modern world, its finest monuments standing at once as symbols of ancient culture and contemporary nation-hood. ▷ **anthropology; Three Age System**

**archetype** An original or typical example of something (an event, character, attitude, theme), which gives rise to many instances or copies throughout history or everyday life. The word (pronounced **ah**-*kee-tiyp*) comes from Greek, meaning 'original pattern'. One implication, deriving from the work of the Swiss psychiatrist Carl Jung (1875–1961), is that these concepts are present in the unconscious mind of all people, and will be recognized by everyone, regardless of which culture they belong to. Archetypal themes include the fundamental facts of human existence, such as birth, growing up, family bonds, love, and death. Archetypal situations include the conflict between good and evil, jealousy between siblings, and the quest for vengeance. Archetypal personalities include the great mother, the wise old man, the rebel, the witch, the conquering hero, the local lad who makes good, and the damsel in distress. Archetypes are a fertile source of images in art and literature — the skull, for example, is an archetypal image of death.

**architecture**   The art or science of building — especially the task of designing buildings, as opposed to physically constructing them. In this respect, there has been great division of opinion as to what exactly constitutes architecture. The most usual standpoint is typified by the English author John Ruskin (1819–1900), who said in *The Seven Lamps of Architecture* (1849): 'Architecture is the art which so disposes and adorns the edifices raised by man, for whatsoever uses, that the sight of them may contribute to his mental health, power, and pleasure'. The German art historian Nikolaus Pevsner (1902–83) put it more succinctly in *An Outline of European Architecture* (1943): 'A bicycle shed is a building; Lincoln Cathedral is a piece of architecture'. Traditionally, therefore, the study of architecture has tended to concentrate on aspects of higher culture and especially art — looking at ennobling buildings, such as the Parthenon (Athens) or the Pantheon (Rome), and at great figures, such as Christoper Wren (1632–1723). Nevertheless, the practice of architecture since the 19th century has increasingly involved a larger number and variety of often complex skills and disciplines. It now takes into account technical considerations of structural engineering, environmental services, and energy conservation, as well as functional considerations of room layout, interior design, and human comfort. Correspondingly, there has been a greater acceptance of the wider concerns and domain of architecture as anything which has been consciously, or even unconsciously, designed and built for the use of people. A recent phrase is 'inhabited sculpture'. ▷ **Baroque; classicism; Gothic; orders of architecture**

**Armageddon**   A place (pronounced *ah-muh-**ge**-duhn*) mentioned in the New Testament in the *Revelation to St John* (16.16) as the site of the final cosmic battle between the forces of good and evil in the last days of the World. The name means 'the mountains of Megiddo', the site of a defeat in Old Testament times of King Josiah (2 *Kings* 23).

**arms control**   A policy of restraint exercised by one or more countries over the level, type, deployment, and use of their armaments. Countries may make an agreement to reduce their arms levels (a *multilateral* agreement), or one country may decide to act alone (*unilaterally*). The aim of arms control is to reduce the possibility of war and/or reduce its consequences. It is based on the notion that states can reduce arms to their mutual benefit, including that of reducing the burden of costs, without weakening their defensive position. Originating in the USA in the 1950s, it has gained increasing acceptance as a policy: several major agreements have been reached about nuclear missiles, as well as about biological and chemical weapons. An example is the first Soviet–American agreement, made in 1972, to limit anti-ballistic missiles, known as SALT 1 (Strategic Arms Limitation Talks and Treaty). ▷ **arms race; disarmament**

**arms race** A situation which arises when countries increase the numbers and capacity of their military weapons, and the size of their armed forces, in the belief that only by maintaining a superiority will they be able to guarantee their national security. The race may take place on a relatively small scale, such as between the countries of the Middle East, or on a large scale, such as the nuclear arms race between the USA and the Soviet Union in the 1950s and 1960s. Many maintain that the continual growth in weapons itself becomes a threat to security, by increasing international tension and distrust — a view which has helped promote the alternative concept of arms control. ▷ **arms control**

**art** Originally, 'skill' (of any kind), a meaning the word still has in many everyday contexts. A contrast was often drawn with 'nature', as in one of Dr Johnson's definitions: 'The power of doing something not taught by nature and instinct: as to *walk* is natural, to *dance* is an art'. Modern usage referring especially to painting, drawing, or sculpture emerged by around 1700, and during the following century the modern sense of 'Art' (often spelled with a capital 'A') and of an artist as a creative genius of a special kind began to develop. The artist came to be seen as someone distinct from the artisan, or skilled manual worker. By the 19th century, art was normally (instead of occasionally) associated with the imaginative and creative production of objects for abstract contemplation, with no useful function. 'Objects' here referred particularly to the 'visual arts' (painting, drawing, sculpture, etc), and also more generally, to include such 'fine arts' as literature, music, and drama. The definition of art has become controversial again in the 20th century. New forms, such as film, television, street theatre, pop music, and happenings, are claimed by some to be art, by others not. ▷ **abstract art; Art Deco; Art Nouveau; Baroque; collage; Cubism; decorative arts; Divisionism; Expressionism; figurative art; fresco; genre painting; Gothic; Impressionism; modern art; Naturalism; Rococo; Romanticism; still life; Surrealism; watercolour**

**Art Deco**   An abbreviation of the name of the international exhibition of modern decorative and industrial arts, held in Paris in 1925: the Exposition Internationale des Arts Décoratifs et Industriels Modernes. It is pronounced *aht-de-koh*. It has come to refer to the decorative arts of the 1920s and 1930s generally, and the 'modernistic' style associated with them. Typical features included a fondness for strident colours, artificial substances (such as plastics), geometrical lines and shapes, and the kind of streamlining found in aircraft and automobile design, but used non-functionally for household objects such as wireless sets, tables, and teapots. The style can be seen in the design of many large cinemas of the period. It was revived for a while in the late 1960s. ▷ **art; decorative arts**

**artificial insemination (AI)**   A method of enabling couples to have a baby who are prevented from doing so in the normal way, perhaps because of some anatomical deformity or because the male is infertile or has difficulty engaging in normal sexual intercourse. It is an instrumental technique which introduces seminal fluid into the vagina at a time in the female cycle when there is a good chance that conception will take place. When the semen is that of the husband, the technique is called **AIH** ('artificial insemination by husband'). When it is that of some other male — as would be necessary if the husband were infertile — the technique is called **AID** ('artificial insemination by donor'), the identity of the donor usually remaining unknown. Although the technique has long been used in relation to the breeding of livestock (especially cattle), it has been part of human medicine for only a few years, and is not always successful. The AID technique has also been controversial, raising questions of a moral or legal kind.

**artificial intelligence (AI)**   A term applied to the study and use of computers that can simulate some of the characteristics normally ascribed to human intelligence, such as learning, deduction, intuition, and self-correction. The subject encompasses many branches of computer science, including natural language processing, pattern recognition, and robotics. Progress has been made in several areas, notably problem-solving, language comprehension, vision, and locomotion. Computers can now be programmed with the knowledge and decision-making ability to perform a wide variety of tasks which, if carried out by a human, would be said to involve intelligence — such as playing chess, making a medical diagnosis (on the basis of responses given by a patient), and finding the best way through an obstacle course. However, it is a continuing source of debate whether the term 'intelligence' is the most appropriate way of describing what computers can do. ▷ **cognitive science; cybernetics; heuristics**

**Art Nouveau**   A French term (pronounced *ah-noo-voh*) meaning, literally, 'new art'. It is a style which flourished from about 1890 to about 1905, mainly in the decorative arts, characterized by natural-looking plant

and flower motifs, and writhing patterns of sinuous, curling lines. It was named after a Paris shop, and went under several different names in the rest of Europe: it was called *Jugendstil* in Germany, *Sezessionstil* in Austria, and *Stile Liberty* (after the shop in Regent St, London) in Italy. Typical products include the drawings of the English illustrator, Aubrey Beardsley (1872–98), the jewellery of French designer René Lalique (1860–1945), and the Paris Metro station entrances of French architect Hector Guimard (1867–1942).
▷ **art; decorative arts**

**asceticism** The practice of a rigorous kind of self-discipline for a spiritual or religious end; pronounced *a-se-ti-si-zm*. It involves avoiding or rejecting ordinary bodily and sensual pleasures. Ascetic practices include fasting, meditation, a life of solitude, the renunciation of possessions, the denial of sexual gratification, and, in the extreme, the seeking out of discomfort or pain. Ascetics are found in many religions, especially among those following a monastic way of life.

**associated state** A former British colony which has entered into a free and voluntary arrangement with Britain, as the former colonial power. The state enjoys the right of self-government, but recognizes the British sovereign as head. Britain is responsible for external relations and for defence. The concept was introduced for states wishing to be independent, but economically unable to support themselves. The island of Antigua in the Caribbean was the first to be given this status, in 1967 (though it became independent in 1981). ▷ **imperialism**

**astrology** A system of knowledge which claims to understand human nature in terms of the heavens. It relies upon precise measurement and a body of symbolism which has come to be associated with each of the signs of the zodiac and the planets (including the Sun and Moon). It rests on a foundation of ancient philosophy, particularly on the idea that the force which patterns the heavens likewise orders humanity. Events in the heavens influence events on earth. The astrologer casts a *horoscope*, based on the exact date and hour of the subject's birth, when the positions of the various heavenly bodies can be ascertained. The subject's personality, history, and future are then interpreted in the light of the traits of character ascribed to these heavenly bodies. As with religion, astrology is a source of both trivial superstition and profound insight. The most significant stages in the development of the subject took place in the first millenium BC in Mesopotamia and Greece. From there it spread worldwide, developing distinct branches and great variation in method. It blossomed most in those periods representing peaks of cultural achievement — Classical Greece, Renaissance Europe, and Elizabethan England. Today it thrives in several Eastern countries, and in the West is undergoing something of a rebirth, though the modern emphasis is on self-knowledge rather than on predicting events — as can be seen in the astrology columns of many popular newspapers and magazines. Equally, a great deal of scepticism is directed towards the subject, both by many who believe in conventional religion as well as by those who deny the validity of any kind of influence which goes beyond what is recognized by conventional science. Astrology is the mother of astronomy, although the two parted company in the 17th century. ▷ **zodiac**

**astrometry** ▷ **astronomy**.

**astronomy**   The study of all classes of celestial object, such as planets, stars, and galaxies, as well as interstellar and intergalactic space, and the universe as a whole. The branch of classical astronomy concerned with the precise measurement of the positions of celestial objects is known as **astrometry**. The first known systematic observers were the Babylonians, who compiled the first star catalogues in about 1600BC. Modern astronomy began 450 years ago with the Polish scientist Nicolas Copernicus (1473–1543), who set the scene for the overthrow of the classical cosmology, asserting that the Sun, not the Earth, is at the centre of the Solar System. Isaac Newton described gravitational theory in the 17th century, and thenceforth planetary astronomy became an exact science. From Newton's time, professional observatories were established, records properly kept, and mathematics was applied to understanding the heavens. Techniques to build large telescopes were developed, and observatories constructed on mountain sites in the USA, such as the Mount Wilson Observatory. **Radio astronomy** emerged after World War II, followed in the 1960s by ultraviolet, X-ray, infrared, and submillimetre astronomies. Opening these new windows on the cosmos produced many unexpected discoveries, such as quasars, pulsars, active galactic nuclei, X-ray binary stars, and the microwave background. Amateurs are also still able to contribute data to astronomy, for example by observing new comets, supernova explosions in distant galaxies, and the visual appearance of the planets. ▷ **astrology; astrophysics; big bang; cosmology**

**astrophysics**   The application of physical laws and theories to stars and galaxies, in order to explain their behaviour. The biggest triumph of this subject has been its explanation for energy production inside stars. There have also been notable successes in explaining the properties of galaxies and quasars. ▷ **astronomy**

**asylum** ▷ **political asylum**.

**atheist**   Someone who does not believe in the existence of a god or gods. It includes both the rejection of any specific belief in God, and the view that the only reasonable approach to claims about divine existence is to be totally sceptical about them. Some atheists say, simply, 'There is no god'.

Others say that the human mind is not capable of discovering that there is a god. Others say that theism is incompatible with science or psychology, or that advances in these subjects have made belief in God unnecessary. Others say that it is not possible to demonstrate, on the basis of experience, that God exists, or that the evidence of the senses (such as the existence of evil) actually suggests that God does not exist. Communist states are officially atheistic. Even certain religions can be viewed as atheistic — Buddhism, for example, does not require belief in a supreme being. ▷ **agnosticism; humanism; scepticism; theist**

**authoritarianism** A form of government, or a theory advocating such government, which is the opposite of democracy, in that the consent of society to rulers and their decisions is not necessary. A dictator is an authoritarian ruler. Voting and discussion are not usually employed, except to give the appearance of democratic legitimacy to the government, and such arrangements remain firmly under the control of the rulers. Authoritarian rulers draw their authority from what are claimed to be special qualities of a religious, nationalistic, or ideological nature, which are used to justify their dispensing with constitutional restrictions. Their rule, however, relies heavily upon force. ▷ **democracy; totalitarianism**

**autocrat** ▷ **dictator**.

**automation** The control of a technical process without using a human being to intervene to make decisions. The result of one operation is fed back to control the next. Central heating is a simple automatic system: the thermostat is a sensor, feeding information back to the heater, which then adjusts automatically, switching on and off as necessary. Computers are the most widespread example of automation, controlling systems which humans would find too time-consuming. A widely-known example is in aviation, where the automatic pilot system ('George') relieves the pilot of the routine tasks of flying. ▷ **computer science; cybernetics**

**avant garde** A term first used to describe the radical artists of mid-19th-century France and Russia, often with political associations; the word comes from French, meaning 'advance guard', pronounced **a-**_von_ **gahd**. Since then it has been applied to the innovative, experimental artists of any time, described by the English poet W H Auden as 'the antennae of the race'. ▷ **art; literature**

**backbencher** A member of the British parliament who sits on the 'back benches' in the House of Commons. These are the places where MPs sit who do not hold a government office or post in the official opposition party. Ministers sit on the front benches. ▷ **cabinet; opposition**

**background radiation**   Naturally-occuring radioactivity, of very low intensity, which can be detected at any place on Earth. It results from cosmic rays reaching the Earth from outer space, and from the radioactive decay of minerals in the soil. When measuring the radiation from a substance, the background radiation must be separately determined, so that it can be discounted.

**Baha'i**   A religious movement arising out of the Persian Islamic sect Babi in the 1860s; pronounced *ba-hiy*. Mirza Husayn Ali (1817–92), known as Baha Allah ('Glory of God'), declared himself the prophet foretold by the founder of the Babi movement, Mirza Ali Mohammed (1819–50). Baha'ism teaches the oneness of God, the unity of all faiths, the inevitable unification of humankind, the harmony of all people, universal education, and obedience to government. It has no priesthood, and its adherents are expected to teach the faith. Local assemblies meet for informal devotions in homes or rented halls. There is little formal ritual, but there are ceremonies for marriage, funerals, and the naming of babies. Its headquarters is in Haifa, Israel. There were over five million adherents in 1990. ▷ **religion**

**bail**   A sum of money (or other form of security) left with the police or the courts, as a guarantee that someone temporarily freed from custody will return to stand trial when required to do so. A person who is bailed is obliged to appear in court on the date set or else forfeit the sum of money stipulated by the court. Frequently other persons are required as *sureties*, who guarantee the appearance of the accused in court. The idea behind bail is to give an accused person every opportunity to prepare a defence, and also to avoid inflicting unnecessary punishment on someone who may subsequently be found innocent. A judge or a magistrate decides whether a person may be bailed, and if so, for what amount. Normally, a person is given bail, unless there are grounds for not doing so (such as the likelihood that the person will commit a further offence). However, the bail procedure varies a great deal between the different legal systems of the world — for example, there are several differences between the systems used in England and in Scotland.

**balance of payments**   The difference between what a country earns and what it spends, as a result of its international trading and investment activities. Two types of calculation are made. The *current account* handles the country's income from selling goods and services abroad (exports), offset by its expenditure on goods and services received (imports). The difference between these two totals is the *trade balance*. Also included in this total are 'invisible' services bought and sold abroad, such as air transport, banking, insurance, shipping, and tourism. The *capital account* deals with private and corporate investment abroad, borrowing and lending, and government financial transactions. If a country spends more than it earns, there is said to be a balance of payments *deficit*. This situation drains a nation's reserves of convertible currency and gold, and can lead to a devaluation of its currency. ▷ **devaluation; gross domestic product; invisibles**

**ballistics**   The study of what takes place when a projectile is fired from a firearm. Ballistics has three aspects: (1) *internal*, concerning the way the object is thrown into the air; (2) *external*, investigating the way it moves in flight; (3) *terminal*, analysing its impact on the target. **Forensic ballistics** helps in the investigation of gun crimes.

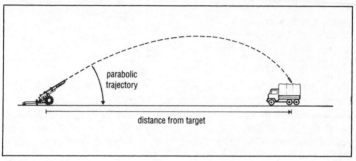

*Ballistics*

**bankruptcy**   In everyday language, the state of being reduced to financial ruin. More technically, it is the legal procedure which is used to decide the value of the property a person has, and how this is to be distributed among the people who are owed money (the creditors). In law, this procedure is commonly referred to as **sequestration**. The bankruptcy proceedings are started when a creditor presents a bankruptcy petition to a court. The court has to decide whether a person may be made bankrupt, and if so, how much of the person's property is to be distributed, which creditors are to be paid, and how much they are to be paid. The corresponding concept of **liquidation** applies to companies. Liquidation may be compulsory (as when a company is unable to pay its debts) or voluntary (as when its members have decided to cease trading).

**Baptists**   A worldwide communion of Christians, who believe in the baptism (through bodily immersion in water) only of adult believers prepared to make a personal confession of faith in Jesus Christ. They have certain links with the 16th-century Anabaptists, but mainly derive from early 17th-century England and Wales, where Baptist churches spread rapidly, and in the USA, where a very rapid increase took place in the late 19th century. Strongly biblical, the emphasis in worship is on scripture and preaching. Individual congregations are self-governing, but usually linked together in associations or unions. The Baptist World Alliance was formed in 1905. In 1990 it included over 140 member denominations, representing over 35 million baptized members. ▷ **Anabaptists; Christianity**

**bar code** A pattern of black vertical lines, with information coded in the relative widths of the lines. It is a type of coding very widely used in the retail market, such as on food packages. The bar-coded labels can be read by special bar-code scanners, and the output entered into a computer to link the product with such factors as price and stock level. There are standards for bar codes, such as the European Article Numbering Code.

*Bar code*

**Baroque** A style of architecture, art, and music popular in the 17th century and the first part of the 18th century; pronounced either *ba-rok* or *ba-rohk*. The term was originally used by jewellers to describe a rough pearl. Baroque art was especially associated with Louis XIV of France, but spread over most of W Europe until it was transformed into another style, Rococo, in the early 18th century.

The Baroque style began in Italy, as a reaction against classical kinds of architecture. It is characterized by curvilinear forms and ornate decoration arranged in dramatic compositions, often on a large scale and in a complicated fashion. It can be seen in Britain in the work of Sir John Vanbrugh

*St Peter's, Rome*

(1664–1726), in such buildings as Blenheim Palace and Castle Howard, and in the designs of Sir Christopher Wren (1632–1723). In painting and sculpture the style can be seen in many vivid and detailed works expressing Catholic beliefs, representing Jesus Christ, the saints, or miraculous events. Baroque sculpture is well illustrated in the works of the Italian, Gian Lorenzo Bernini (1598–1680), who designed the colonnade in front of St Peter's Cathedral in Rome. In painting, the style can be seen in the dramatic patterns of strong light and shade (*chiaroscuro*) of the Italian, Caravaggio (1573–1610), such as his 'Christ at Emmaus' (in the National Gallery in London).

The term has also come to be used in music for the typically lively and often intricate works of many composers between about 1600 and 1750 — a period which includes the Italians Claudio Monteverdi (1567–1643) and Antonio Vivaldi (1678–1741), and the Germans Johann Sebastian Bach (1685–1750) and George Frideric Handel (1685–1759). A well-known example of Baroque musical exuberance is Vivaldi's *The Four Seasons*. ▷ **architecture; art; Rococo**

**battery farming** ▷ **factory farming**.

**behaviourism/behaviorism** The view that psychology is most effectively pursued by analysing the observable behaviour of people and animals, in preference to ideas, thoughts, feelings, and other hypothetical internal states. It was able to explain with some success the behaviour of animals under laboratory conditions, and has had an important influence on modern psychology. It was less convincing when applied to human behaviour and relationships, and is now rarely held in extreme form. ▷ **mentalism; psychology**

**Berlin Wall** A concrete wall built by the East German government in 1961 to seal off East Berlin from the part of the city occupied by the three main Western powers. It was built largely to prevent mass illegal immigration to the West, which was threatening the East German economy. It was the scene of the shooting of many East Germans who tried to escape from the Eastern sector. The Wall, seen by many as a major symbol of the denial of human rights in Eastern Europe, was unexpectedly opened in November 1989, following increased pressure for political reform in East Germany, and has since been demolished. ▷ **communism; Warsaw Pact**

**Bhopal** A city in Central India, the capital of Madhya Pradesh; pronounced *boh-pahl*. It was the scene of a major industrial disaster in December 1984, when poisonous isocyanate gas escaped from the US-owned Union Carbide factory, killing about 2500 people, injuring many more, and leaving 100000 homeless.

**bicameral system** A system of government which has two houses, or chambers; the word comes from Latin, meaning 'two rooms'. The two houses usually have different methods of election or selection. The United Kingdom has a bicameral system: the Houses of Parliament comprise the House of Commons and the House of Lords. In some countries the two chambers enjoy equal powers; but commonly one chamber enjoys supremacy over the law-making process, with the other enjoying powers of revision and delay (as in the UK). The bicameral system began in England in the 16th century, and arose out of the previously established distinction between the nobility and clergy, on the one hand, and the common people, on the other. Supporters of the system claim that it is more likely to prevent hasty or unfair legislation, by ensuring that laws are given a thorough discussion. Its critics point to the duplication of effort involved in running such a system, and to the way real power may be located in only one of the two chambers. A single-chamber system of government is said to be **unicameral**. ▷ **Congress; parliament**

**big bang**   The popular name given to a hypothetical model of the way the universe was created. It postulates that all matter and energy were once concentrated into an unimaginably dense state, or primeval atom, from which it has been expanding since a creation event between 10 and 20 thousand million years ago. The main evidence favouring this model comes from cosmic microwave background radiation, detected in 1965, thought to be a remnant of the big bang; and the electromagnetic energy monitored from galaxies (*redshift*), which indicates that they are moving away from us. The theory of an expanding universe is now generally accepted. ▷ **background radiation; cosmology**

**bilateralism**   ▷ **multilateralism**.

**bill, parliamentary**   A draft of a proposed new law for consideration by a legislature. The procedures vary considerably from country to country. In the UK, bills may be 'public' or 'private' in origin. Public bills are introduced by the government, or by an individual member of parliament. Private bills come from outside parliament. Some bills contain both private and public elements. The bill is given a formal 'first reading' in one chamber of parliament, then printed and debated, and given a 'second reading'. It is then referred to a committee (the 'committee stage'), which may introduce amendments. The amended bill is put before the house (the 'report stage'), and given a 'third reading'. It then goes to the other chamber, where a similar procedure is put into operation. After both houses have passed the bill, it receives the royal assent and becomes an Act of Parliament. ▷ **Act of Parliament; legislature**

**bill of rights**   A list of citizens' rights set out in constitutional documents. Usually accompanying the document is an elaboration of the institutional means and powers by which such rights may be enforced. The best-known example is the first ten amendments to the US Constitution, adopted in 1791. This protected the liberties of private citizens in relation to the federal and (later) state governments, including freedom of the press, speech and religion, the right to a fair and public trial, the right to bear arms, and protection against unlawful search and seizure. It was adopted because of popular pressure during the campaign to ratify the Constitution (1787–8), and its meaning has been expounded in many cases decided by the Supreme Court. ▷ **constitution**

**binary code**  A code derived from a number system which uses only two digits, 0 and 1, in comparison with the decimal system which has ten digits, 0 to 9. The binary system has a particular advantage when working with digital computers, in that only two electronic states, off and on, are required to represent every possible binary digit. All digital computers operate using various binary codes to represent numbers and other characters. ▷ **byte**

| Arabic | Binary Numbers | Arabic | Binary Numbers |
|--------|----------------|--------|----------------|
| 1 | 1 | 19 | 10011 |
| 2 | 10 | 20 | 10100 |
| 3 | 11 | 30 | 11110 |
| 4 | 100 | 40 | 101000 |
| 5 | 101 | 50 | 110010 |
| 6 | 110 | 60 | 111100 |
| 7 | 111 | 70 | 1000110 |
| 8 | 1000 | 80 | 1010000 |
| 9 | 1001 | 90 | 1011010 |
| 10 | 1010 | 100 | 1100100 |
| 11 | 1011 | 200 | 11001000 |
| 12 | 1100 | 300 | 100101100 |
| 13 | 1101 | 400 | 110010000 |
| 14 | 1110 | 500 | 111110100 |
| 15 | 1111 | 1 000 | 1111101000 |
| 16 | 10000 | 5 000 | 1001110001000 |
| 17 | 10001 | 10 000 | 10011100010000 |
| 18 | 10010 | 100 000 | 11000011010100000 |

**biodegradable substance**  Any substance that can be decomposed by natural processes, particularly as a result of bacteria or fungi, so that its constituents can be used again by other organisms. Many modern materials (such as plastics) are non-biodegradable, and accumulate in the ecosystem. ▷ **ecosystem**

**bioengineering** The application of engineering theories and techniques to biological or medical science; also called **biomechanics**. It is particularly concerned with the design of equipment for keeping people alive or improving the quality of life, such as the development of artificial limbs and of life-support systems for astronauts.

**biological rhythm** The rhythmical change in a biological function of a plant or animal; also called **biorhythm**. The frequency of rhythms varies from short (eg less than a second) to long (eg more than a year). Many rhythms arise from within organisms; others are entirely dependent upon external environmental factors (such as the alternation of light and dark). Internal rhythms are usually synchronized to follow periodic changes in the environment. Examples of biological rhythms in humans are breathing and sleeping, which are controlled by the brain. A biological rhythm which has a periodicity of about one day is called a **circadian rhythm** (from Latin *circa* 'about' and *dies* 'day'). It is this rhythm which is most affected by disturbances in sleeping pattern and exposure to daylight, after rapid travel through several time zones ('jet lag'). ▷ **physiology**

**biomechanics** ▷ **bioengineering**.

**biorhythm** ▷ **biological rhythm**.

**biosphere** That part of the Earth's surface and atmosphere in which living organisms are found, and with which they interact to form the global ecosystem. The word was formed on analogy with 'atmosphere'. ▷ **ecosystem**

**biotechnology** The application of biological and biochemical science to large-scale production. Isolated examples have existed since early times, such as brewing; but the first modern example was the large-scale production of penicillin in the 1940s. Other pharmaceutical developments followed. Research in genetic engineering is prominent in current studies. ▷ **genetic engineering**

**black comedy** A form of comedy which derives its often bitter humour from exposing and facing up to the grotesque accidents and meaningless misfortunes to which human life is liable. It shows human beings in such a hopeless or pointless situation that there is little else for an audience to do other than laugh. The French dramatist Eugene Ionesco (1912– ) called life a 'tragic farce'. Such views are prominent in the so-called 'theatre of the absurd'. They can be expressed either in narrative or in dramatic form. Examples include Evelyn Waugh's *Black Mischief* (1932), Nathanael West's *The Day of the Locust* (1939), and Joe Orton's *Loot* (1965). ▷ **literature**

**Black Consciousness** An attitude, found particularly in the USA, which asserts that Blacks, by virtue of their ethnicity and history, possess a cultural tradition distinct from the wider population. It rejects the notion that Blacks have been totally absorbed into White society, distinguishable only by colour. Proponents of Black consciousness aim to raise the awareness of Blacks by espousing and publicizing their cultural traditions and values. In South Africa, the **Black Consciousness Movement** was formed by Steve Biko in 1969, which developed into an organization seeking to create cooperation in social and cultural fields. Most of its leaders were imprisoned in 1977, and Biko died in police custody. The film *Cry Freedom* (1988) was based on these events. ▷ **apartheid; ethnicity**

**black economy** Any economic activity which is not officially recorded, and usually not taxed. It arises when work is carried out, or wages paid, but where no record is made of the transaction for income tax or value-added-tax purposes. The recipient thus illegally avoids paying tax. ▷ **taxation**

**black hole** A region of space-time from which matter and energy cannot escape. In origin, it is matter (such as a star or galactic nucleus) that has collapsed in on itself to the point where its escape velocity exceeds the speed of light. Its boundary is known as the *event horizon*: matter or light generated inside the event horizon can never escape. Black holes are believed to exist on all mass scales. Some binary stars which strongly emit X-rays may have black hole companions.

**black market** An illegal trade in goods or currencies. The practice is well-known in countries where there is rationing or restriction on the availability of of food, petrol, clothing, and other essential commodities. These may be difficult or impossible to obtain using legal channels, but may be available (at a much higher price) 'on the black market'. In countries where strict currency exchange controls exist, there is invariably a black-market economy which can make foreign currency available above the official rate. ▷ **exchange rates**

**blood sports** Sports which involve the hunting and killing of animals as a recreation; often referred to as **field sports**. Examples include fox hunting, stag hunting, hare coursing, and bull-fighting. Cock-fighting, once popular in Britain, and still practised illegally in certain parts of the country, is a popular sport in many continental countries and in Asia. Bull-fighting is popular in Spain. In the UK, several of these activities have been made illegal — for example, bull-baiting since 1835, and badger-baiting since 1973. Blood sports have come under increasing attack in recent years from those concerned with animal welfare, notably the League against Cruel Sports.

**boat people**   The popular name for the Vietnamese who fled Vietnam by boat after the communist victory in 1975, travelling to Australia, Hong Kong, Japan, and several other parts of SE Asia. Many died on the long voyages, or were killed by pirates. Schemes to return these people to their home country gained momentum in 1989, and the first involuntary repatriation was carried out by the Hong Kong authorities in December of that year.

**Body Art**   A type of modern art which exploits the artist's — or someone else's — physical presence as a work of art in its own right. Artists may stand in a gallery like living statues, perhaps singing; photograph themselves performing some banal action, such as smiling; or may deliberately injure themselves. Such activities were fashionable in the 1960s, and are still occasionally encountered. ▷ **art; happening; Minimal Art; modern art**

**boiling water reactor**   ▷ **nuclear reactor**.

**boom**   A peak in economic activity. A boom is characterized by little or no unemployment, increased profits, and high levels of investment. Businesses are buoyant and confident. ▷ **depression; recession**

**bovine spongiform encephalopathy**   ▷ **BSE**.

**boycott**   A general refusal to have dealings — usually in relation to trade — with a person, company, or country. The word comes from the name of a British land agent in Ireland, Charles Cunningham Boycott (1832–97), who in 1880 opposed the policies of an Irish organization seeking land reforms (the Land League), and was socially ostracized — local people having nothing to do with him. The notion is now found in a wide range of contexts.   A trade union may boycott talks with a company as a negotiating ploy. Individuals may refuse to buy a country's goods as a gesture of political protest — for example, goods from South Africa, in protest against apartheid. Boycotts have also been used in international sporting events, such as by the USA at the 1980 Moscow Olympic Games. They are often effective only if legally enforced. ▷ **embargo; pressure group; sanctions**

**brain drain**   The loss through emigration of highly qualified people in a country, such as academics, lawyers, scientists, and doctors. Always present to some degree, the brain drain from Britain to the USA, Australia, and other countries has dramatically increased since the 1970s, as people look for better pay and working conditions overseas.

**brainstorming**   A method of problem solving which relies on intensive discussion between a group of people to spark off new ideas and creative thinking. People are encouraged to think aloud, without fear of criticism. All ideas are noted, no matter how silly or irrelevant they may appear to be, and given serious consideration at a later stage. ▷ **lateral thinking**

**breeder reactor**  ▷ **nuclear reactor**.

**British Commonwealth**  ▷ **Commonwealth**.

**brokerage**  ▷ **insurance**.

**BSE**  or **mad cow disease** The abbreviation for **bovine spongiform encephalopathy**, an invariably fatal disease of the central nervous system affecting mature cattle, currently restricted to the UK and Ireland. The disease appeared suddenly in 1985 and reached epidemic proportions by 1989. Affected cattle may show behavioural changes and incoordination. There is no known treatment or cure. BSE is probably caused by a group of viral agents, notorious for their resistance to high temperatures and disinfectants. The BSE agent is unique in that it may have crossed species, cattle having been infected by eating feed containing sheep products affected by the disease known as *scrapie*. It is feared that humans could contract BSE by eating meat products containing nervous tissue of contaminated cattle.

**Buddhism**  A tradition of thought and practice originating in India about 2500 years ago, and now a world religion, deriving from the teaching of Buddha (Siddhartha Gautama), who is regarded as one of a continuing series of enlightened beings. The title *Buddha* is Sanskrit for 'the enlightened one'. The teaching of Buddha is summarized in the *Four Noble Truths*, the last of which affirms the existence of a path leading to deliverance from the universal human experience of suffering. A central concept is the law of *karma*, by which good and evil deeds result in appropriate reward or punishment in this life or in a succession of rebirths. Through a proper understanding of this condition, and by obedience to the right path, human beings can break the chain of karma. The Buddha's path to deliverance is through morality, meditation, and wisdom. The goal is *Nirvana*, which means 'the blowing out' of the fires of all desires, and the absorption of the self into the infinite.

There are two main traditions within Buddhism, dating from its earliest history. *Theravada* Buddhism adheres to the strict and narrow teachings of the early Buddhist writings: salvation is possible for only the few who accept the severe discipline and effort necessary to achieve it. *Mahayana* Buddhism is more liberal, and makes concessions to popular piety: it teaches that salvation is possible for everyone. As Buddhism spread, other schools grew up, among which are Zen and Lamaism. Recently Buddhism has attracted growing interest in the West. Underlying the diversity of Buddhist belief and practice is a controlling purpose. The aim is to create the conditions favourable to spiritual development, leading to liberation or deliverance from bondage to suffering. This is generally seen as involving meditation, personal discipline, and spiritual exercises of various sorts. Over 1000 million people live in lands where Buddhism is a significant religious influence. ▷ **reincarnation; religion**

**budget**   An income and expenditure plan for a specified period of future time. Most commercial organizations of any size prepare budgets to forecast sales revenue, operating costs, capital expenditure, and cash flow. They may even be prepared several years in advance, and amended annually. A government budget is a statement of forecast expenditure in the following financial year, and of how the income needed will be raised (eg by taxation or borrowing). In the UK, the government's budget is presented to Parliament, invariably accompanied by great publicity ('Budget Day') in March of each year. Supplementary budgets may be presented at other times, especially when the economic situation is uncertain. ▷ **Chancellor of the Exchequer; taxation**

**buffer state**   A small state lying between two or more larger and potentially belligerent states, as a means of reducing border friction between them. It is often specially created for the purpose, though such creations are seldom successful. Belgium has sometimes been considered a buffer state, lying between Germany and France.

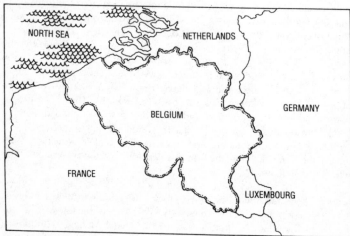

*Belgium (a buffer state)*

**business cycle**  ▷ **trade cycle**.

**byte**  A basic computing term, referring to a fixed number of bits (binary digits), and usually defined as a set of eight bits. An eight-bit byte can therefore take 256 different values corresponding to the binary numbers 00000000, 00000001, 00000010, through to 11111111. A *kilobyte* is one thousand bytes; a *megabyte* is one million bytes. ▷ **binary code**

**cabinet**  In a parliamentary system, a group of senior ministers usually drawn from the majority party; the corresponding group of ministers who are in opposition are called the **shadow cabinet**. Cabinet government began in Britain in the 17th century. It forms the link between the executive and legislative branches of government, as its members must be drawn from the legislature. Cabinets usually contain about 20 senior ministers, appointed by the prime minister to head the various departments of government. The British cabinet is bound by the doctrine of collective responsibility: ministers must publicly support decisions taken by the cabinet, or its committees, or else resign. Its minutes are secret, and may not be published until after 30 years (though several leaks and autobiographical publications in recent years have somewhat undermined this principle). The importance of the cabinet varies across political systems. A cabinet may also be found in a non-parliamentary system, such as that of the USA, where it provides the president with an additional consultative body. ▷ **Chancellor of the Exchequer; legislature; parliament; secretary of state**

*C*

**calculus**  A branch of mathematics which studies the nature of continuously varying quantities; the term comes from the Latin word for 'pebble', used in making calculations on an abacus. For example, calculus could be used to define the nature of an increase in speed or a variation in voltage in an electrical circuit. *Differential calculus* is a system of rules for making calculations of this kind: it considers small increments of a variable and works out the rate at which it is changing. *Integral calculus* deals with the way in which these continuously varying quantities can be added together. Because these techniques are dealing with progressively smaller quantities, their combined functions are said to comprise the *infinitesmal calculus*. The early development of calculus was associated with English mathematician Isaac Newton (1642–1727) and German mathematician Gottfried Wilhelm Leibniz (1646–1716), between whom there was a fierce controversy over who invented the notion.

**calisthenics**  The art and practice of bodily exercises designed to produce beauty and grace rather than muscular development. They are often performed with the aid of handheld apparatus, such as rings and clubs. Similar exercises were first seen in Germany in the 19th century. ▷ **aerobics**

**Calvinism**   The Christian teaching which ultimately derives from the 16th-century Protestant reformer, John Calvin (1509–64). It was adopted and developed by several Churches which arose after the Reformation, such as the state Church in the Netherlands, and the Church of Scotland. Calvinism has emphasized the sovereignty of God, the Bible as the sole rule of faith, the doctrine of predestination (only the 'elect' are to be saved), and justification by faith alone. There has been a Neo-Calvinist renewal in the 20th century under the influence of the Swiss theologian Karl Barth (1886–1968). ▷ **predestination; Presbyterianism; Protestantism; Reformation**

**cantata**   Music which is 'sung'. The Italian solo cantata of the 17th–18th centuries was a setting of secular (usually amatory) verses, alternating two types of presentation — recitative (in which words are delivered naturally and quickly, with a simple musical accompaniment) and aria (a song with an elaborate structure, for solo voice). The Lutheran cantatas (such as those of Bach) were church compositions for soloists, choir, and instruments. More recent cantatas, whether sacred or secular, are usually choral and orchestral pieces, with or without soloists; many are festival or commemorative pieces. ▷ **classical music; motet; sonata**

**capitalism**   A set of economic arrangements which developed in the 19th century in Western societies following the Industrial Revolution. The concept derives from the writings of Marx, and is based upon the private ownership of the means of production by the capitalist class, or bourgeoisie. The workers, or proletariat, own nothing but their labour, and although free to sell their labour in the market, they are dependent upon the capitalist class which exploits them by appropriating the surplus value created by their labour. Non-Marxist economists define capitalism as a system in which most property is privately owned and goods are sold freely in a competitive market, but without reference to exploitation, except where monopoly situations occur. Capitalism may be an ideological stance: Marx saw it as one stage in a historical process, finally being replaced by socialism. It has been the most productive economic system to date, though it has given rise to massive environmental (eg pollution) and social (eg unemployment) problems. ▷ **ideology; Marxism; socialism**

**capital punishment**   A sentence of death passed by a judicial body following a trial. Capital punishment for murder has been abolished in the UK, though proposals for its reinstatement are regularly debated by parliament, and it remains the penalty for treason and piracy. It is still available in several states of the USA, and in many other countries. When the sentence is available, it is not always carried out; a head of state or other authority can recommend a reprieve. Countries employ a variety of procedures in carrying out executions, including lethal injection, electrocution, hanging, gassing, and shooting. Those in favour of capital punishment argue that it is a better deterrent than life imprisonment, and avoids the risk of exposing prison staff, other prisoners, and eventually the public (if a prisoner were granted parole) to potentially dangerous people. Those against capital punishment question the morality of the act, and argue that it does not deter murderers any more than does life imprisonment, and that errors of justice do occur, leading to the death of innocent people.

**cartel**   An agreement by a number of companies in the same industry to fix the prices and/or quantities of their products, thus avoiding cut-price competition or over-production. It is often seen as not being in the public interest, since the prices fixed will be higher than those which would prevail in a free market. As a result, many countries (and the European Community) have made cartels illegal. To be successful, a cartel needs to involve all producers of a product, and to strictly control the production quotas assigned to each member. OPEC (the Organization of Petroleum Exporting Countries) has some of the features of a cartel; this organization was set up in 1960 to coordinate the petroleum policy of its members, in order to protect their interests. It controls the price of crude oil and the quantities to be produced.
▷ **OPEC**

**censorship**   The process of controlling the way people can spread or have access to ideas or material, especially on political or moral grounds. In its extreme form, it involves the wholesale banning of information, including works of fiction, enforced by the imposition of penalties against offenders. As such it is a characteristic of authoritarian states, which seek to regulate the flow of information, opinion, and expression. This is usually justified by reference to state security, the public interest, and good taste. In contemporary democracies, the term usually has wholly negative connotations, because such societies pride themselves on the freedoms enjoyed by their people, including the right of free expression, which is often enshrined in law (eg the First Amendment to the US Constitution). But censorship plays a part in even the most enlightened and progressive of societies, its legitimacy deriving from an assumed consensus on what is and is not acceptable at a particular time. Organizations of all kinds have certain secrets which they seek to protect for reasons of security, confidentiality, and personal privacy. Such information will be 'classified' to some degree, and be restricted to those authorized to receive it.

Art in all its forms has always been prone to censorship, often due to the desire of artists to extend the boundaries of taste and to challenge authority.

For example, in the British theatre it was not until 1968 that managements ceased having to submit manuscripts of plays for approval by the official censor, the Lord Chamberlain. Formal pre-censorship of this kind is uncommon today in the West. One major exception is film and video recordings, which are usually previewed by a board of censors, before being released for public consumption, with cuts if required. Since 1972 the monthly periodical Index on Censorship has campaigned against abuses of the fundamental right of free expression throughout the world. ▷ **media**

**census**   A count of the population resident in an area at a given time, together with the collection of social and economic data about the people, made at regular intervals. In many countries census data form the basis for the planning of service provisions (such as health and education), and a census is taken at regular intervals — in the UK, for example, every 10 years. The USA conducted its first national census in 1790, and France and the UK began to collect census data in 1801. In the UK, the task is in the hands of the Office of Population Censuses and Surveys. The United Nations has tried to ensure some comparability between the questions asked in different countries, and has been partially successful.

**centre, the**   The centre ground in political opinion and action, which avoids the extremism and idealism of right and left, and advocates compromise solutions to the problems of society. It is often characterized by practical responses — more concerned with 'getting things done' than with searching for the means of achieving ideal objectives. ▷ **left wing; right wing**

**CFCs**   The acronym for **chlorofluorocarbons**, also called **Freons**; derivatives of methane and ethane containing both chlorine and fluorine. They are inert, volatile compounds, used as refrigerants and aerosol sprays. Their decomposition in the atmosphere is thought to damage the Earth's ozone layer, and there have been international moves to limit their use. ▷ **ozone layer**

**chamber music**   Music for two or more players intended for performance in a room rather than a concert hall, with only one player to a part. The term is a translation of the Italian 'musica da camera', and applies only to instrumental music, and therefore mainly to music since about 1600. Until about 1750 the main type of chamber music was the trio sonata (typically for two violins and continuo). Since then the string quartet (for two violins, viola, and cello) has come to be the most typical form of chamber ensemble, but any wind, string, or keyboard instrument might be involved. Composers who wrote a great deal of chamber music include Haydn, Mozart, Beethoven, Schubert, and Brahms. ▷ **classical music; sonata**

**chamber of commerce** An association of business enterprises in a town or district, whose aims are to promote the area and its members' businesses; sometimes called a chamber of trade. The Chambers of Commerce of the USA (established 1912) represent, through member organizations, some five million business firms and individuals. The International Chamber of Commerce (ICC), based in Paris, was set up in 1920, and has the affiliation of over 40 national institutions. In the UK, and certain other countries, chambers of commerce are voluntary organizations.

**Chancellor of the Exchequer** The senior minister responsible for the UK Treasury, and a senior minister in the cabinet. The Chancellor takes responsibility for the preparation of the budget, and (unlike in most other countries) is economic as well as finance minister. This post should be clearly distinguished from the post of **Lord (High) Chancellor**, who is a lawyer appointed to head the judiciary, and who also presides over the House of Lords. ▷ **budget; cabinet; treasury**

**chaos** A state of disorder and irregularity in a system whose evolution in time, though governed by simple exact laws, is highly sensitive to starting conditions: a small variation in these conditions will produce wildly different results. Long-term behaviour of chaotic systems cannot be predicted. Chaos is an intermediate stage between highly-ordered motion and fully-random motion. For example, in fluid flow, a slowly-moving fluid exhibits perfectly regular flow; as the fluid velocity increases, the flow becomes chaotic; and as the velocity increases still further, the flow becomes fully turbulent (random). In a chaotic system, the values of some quantity at two points maintain their relationship as time passes, even though the exact value of each cannot be predicted in the future. In truly random motion, there exist no such relationships. Chaos is present in most real systems, such as in weather patterns and the motion of planets about the Sun; the stable classical motion widely accepted as the norm in physics is now known to be the exception rather than the rule. The underlying structure of chaos exhibits universal features, regardless of the system in question. The modern theory of chaos is based on the work of US meteorologist Edward Lorenz (1917– ) in 1963, arising from the study of convection in the atmosphere. Fractals feature in a comprehensive description of chaos. ▷ **fractals**

**charismatic movement** A movement of spiritual renewal, which takes a variety of forms in Roman Catholic, Protestant, and Eastern Orthodox Churches. *Charisma* is from a Greek word meaning 'favour', and refers to someone who has special charm or appeal — in the religious context, someone who has received a special power from God. The movement emphasizes the present reality and work of the Holy Spirit in the life of the Church and the individual. It is sometimes accompanied by speaking in tongues. ▷ **evangelicalism; faith healing; Pentecostalism**

**chauvinism**   An excessive or blind adherence to a point of view — originally in support of one's nation, later in support of any group, cause, or belief. The word comes from the name of Nicolas Chauvin, a French soldier who displayed extreme devotion to Napoleon. Its most common use today is in relation to those who defend or demonstrate male sexist attitudes ('male chauvinists'). ▷ **sexism**

**Chief Executive**   ▷ **executive**.

**chlorofluorocarbons**   ▷ **CFCs**.

**Christadelphians**   A Christian sect which teaches a return to primitive Christianity and that Christ will soon come again to establish a theocracy lasting for a millennium. The name means 'Brethren of Christ'. It was founded in New York in the 1840s by a British immigrant, John Thomas (1805–71), and is most strongly represented in the USA. Christadelphians are congregational in organization, and there are no ordained ministers. ▷ **Christianity; millenarianism**

**Christian Democrats**   Members of Christian Democratic political parties, most of which were formed in Western Europe after 1945, and which have since become a major political force. The Christian Democratic philosophy is based upon strong links with the Catholic Church and its notions of social and economic justice. It emphasizes the traditional conservative values of the family and church, but also more progressive, liberal values such as state intervention in the economy and significant social welfare provision. Christian Democrat parties emerged to fill the vacuum created by the general disillusionment with parties of the right and left after World War II, a major exception being the UK, which has no such party. Successful examples include the Christian Democratic Union in Germany (formerly West Germany) and the Christian Democratic Party in Italy. ▷ **conservatism; democracy; liberalism; Roman Catholicism**

**Christianity**   A world religion centred on the life and work of Jesus of Nazareth. The earliest followers were Jews who, after the death and resurrection of Jesus, believed him to be the Messiah or Christ, promised by the prophets in the Old Testament, and in unique relation to God, whose Son or 'Word' (*Logos*) he was declared to be. During his life he chose 12 men as *disciples*, who formed the nucleus of the Church as a society or communion of believers. By the end of the first century, the Gospel ('Good News') of Jesus was reduced to writing and accepted as authoritative as scriptures of the New Testament, understood as the fulfilment of the Jewish scriptures, or Old Testament. Through the witness of the 12 earliest leaders (*Apostles*) and their successors, the Christian faith quickly spread through the Greek and Roman world, and in 315 was declared by Emperor Constantine to be the official religion of the Roman Empire. It survived the break-up of the Empire and the 'Dark Ages' through the life and witness of groups of monks in monasteries, and formed the basis of civilization in the Middle Ages in Europe.

Major divisions, separated as a result of differences in doctrine and practice, are the *Eastern* or *Orthodox Churches*, the *Roman Catholic Church*, acknowledging the Bishop of Rome as head (the *Pope*), and the *Protestant Churches* stemming from the split with the Roman Church in the 16th-century Reformation. All Christians recognize the authority of the Bible, which is read at public worship at least every Sunday, the first day of the week, celebrating Christ's resurrection. Most Churches recognize at least two sacraments (Baptism, and the Eucharist, Mass, or Lord's Supper) as essential. The impetus to spread Christianity to the non-Christian world in missionary movements, especially in the 19th and 20th centuries, resulted in the creation of numerically very strong Churches in the developing countries of Asia, Africa, and South America. A powerful ecumenical movement in the present century, promoted by, among others, the World Council of Churches, has sought to recover unity among divided Christians. About a third of the world population is Christian — over 1750 million in 1990. ▷ **Adventists; Anabaptists; Anglican Communion; Anglo-Catholicism; Baptists; Calvinism; Christadelphians; Christian Science; Congregationalism; ecumenism; evangelicalism; Friends, Religious Society of; Lutheranism; Methodism; millenarianism; Mormons; Nonconformists; Orthodox Church; Pentecostalism; Presbyterianism; Protestantism; Reformation; Roman Catholicism; Salvation Army; World Council of Churches**

**Christian Science**  A religious movement which seeks to restore the original Christian message of salvation from all evil, including sickness and disease as well as sin. It was founded in the USA by Mary Baker Eddy (1821–1910). The first Church of Christ, Scientist, was established in 1879 in Boston, followed in 1892 by the present worldwide organization, with its headquarters at Boston. Eddy's *Science and Health with Key to the Scriptures* (1875) and the Bible are the principal texts of the movement. They believe that God is Spirit and the good creator; accordingly, sin, sickness, death, and matter itself seem real only to mistaken human belief. Health is restored, not by recourse to medical treatment, which they decline, but by applying practices in keeping with the principle of divine harmony. The internationally known newspaper, *The Christian Science Monitor*, is published by the society. ▷ **alternative medicine; Christianity**

**Church of England**  ▷ **Anglican Communion**.

**Church of Scotland**  ▷ **Anglican Communion**.

**circadian rhythm**  ▷ **biological rhythm**.

**CIS (Commonwealth of Independent States)** A body comprising 11 of the republics of the former Soviet Union, established after the dissolution of the Soviet state in December 1991. Its membership is Armenia, Azerbaijan, Belarus, Kazakhstan, Kirghizia, Moldova, Russia, Tadzhikistan, Turkmenia, Ukraine, and Uzbekistan. Georgia was the only USSR republic not to join, because of continuing civil unrest. The new supreme body, the Council of Heads of State, met in Minsk for the first time at the end of 1991. In the early months of 1992, major questions remained concerning the economy and the distribution of strategic forces, and tension was in evidence between several member states. The alliance was also threatened by internal dissension and violence in some of the republics, as ethnic minorities asserted their identity and in several cases put forward their own claims for independence. The continuing existence of the CIS remains uncertain, at the time of writing this entry (March 1992), though what form any alternative might take is itself unclear.

**civil disobedience** A strategy which aims to achieve political goals in a non-violent way by refusing to cooperate with a government or its agents. It is a mass illegal protest, intended to discredit the authority of the state. It was adopted by M K Gandhi and his followers in India in 1930, in opposition to Britain's imperial rule. The movement was banned, and many were arrested, including Gandhi; but a pact was reached in 1931, and the Indian National Congress then participated in the second Round Table Conference. The strategy was later used to good effect in the USA by Martin Luther King Jr in his civil rights campaign, and is a path sometimes advocated by opponents of nuclear weapons. ▷ **activism; civil rights**

**civil list** In the UK, since 1760, a payment made from public funds for the maintenance of the royal household and family (except the Prince of Wales, who receives the revenues of the Duchy of Cornwall instead). It covers the salaries of the household staff, travel, entertaining, and public engagements at home and abroad. A sum payable from the Treasury is fixed by Act of Parliament at the beginning of each reign; in exchange, the new sovereign surrenders to the Exchequer the revenues from the Crown Estate. During the reign of Queen Elizabeth II (1952– ), the original sum has had to be reviewed upwards several times because of inflation. In 1990, the civil list was fixed at £9 790 000, of which £7 900 000 was intended for the Queen.

**civil rights** The rights guaranteed by a state to its citizens. It incorporates the notion that governments should not arbitrarily act to infringe these rights, and that individuals and groups, through political action, have a legitimate role in determining and influencing what constitutes them. In common usage, the term is taken to mean the rights of groups, particularly ethnic and racial minorities; in particular, it has become closely asssociated with movements in the USA, especially 1954–68, which aimed to secure the legal enforcement of the guarantees of racial equality contained in the US Constitution.

The US movement began as an attack on specific forms of racial segregation in the Southern states, then broadened into a massive challenge to all forms of racial subordination, and achieved considerable success. The first major event (1955) was a boycott of the bus system of Montgomery, Alabama. It arose from a driver's victimization of a Black passenger after she refused to yield her seat to a White, as the law required. The boycott saw the emergence to leadership of Martin Luther King Jr, who was to be the foremost Black spokesman until his assassination in 1968. He led a campaign aimed at the desegregation of all public facilities, including schools, restaurants, stores, and transport services, and at winning the rights to vote and hold public office. Major instances included the struggle to desegregate the schools of Little Rock, Arkansas (1957), following the outlawing of school segregation in 1954 by the US Supreme Court, and the 'Freedom Rides' of 1961 aimed at ending discrimination in long-distance bus transport. By 1965 the original goals seemed won. Court decisions, major legislation, and the actions of Presidents Eisenhower, Kennedy, and especially Johnson put the power of the federal government on the Black side. The result can be seen in the fact that Southern communities which were once bastions of segregation now have Black mayors and other officials. The powerful candidature of the Rev Jesse Jackson for the Democratic presidential nomination in 1988 demonstrated that a Black American could become a serious figure in national politics. ▷ **activism; Black Consciousness; civil disobedience; constitution**

**class**   A group of people who share the same economic, occupational, or social position in a particular society. The term is used in two main ways. First, it provides a way of organizing people into groups, such as 'manual' and 'non-manual' or 'professional' and 'clerical' occupations. Second, classes are defined in terms of relationships between groups with particular inherent properties, such as the Marxist notions of the 'bourgeoisie' (middle class) and the 'proletariat' (working class) in capitalism. The term is also used as part of an analysis of types of society. For example, a *class society* is a system of social inequality based on the unequal distribution of income and wealth between different classes. A *classless society* is an idealistic goal which has motivated many social reformers and theorists. ▷ **Marxism; sociology**

**classical music**   Music which is part of a long written tradition, which lends itself to advanced study and analysis, and which is heard in concert halls, opera houses, and churches (rather than in dance halls, public houses, and discotheques). In its most general sense, works are 'classical' if they have stood the test of time, and become an established part of musical performance. They are usually thought to display a sophisticated formal structure, and to have a seriousness of conception which is lacking in most popular forms of music. The term (often with a capital *C*) is often reserved for the historical period from about 1770 to 1830, which embraces the mature works of Haydn, Mozart, Beethoven, and Schubert. These days, there is a strong trend not to introduce too sharp a division between classical music, on the one hand, and folk music, light music, jazz, pop, etc, on the other. The distinction is no longer felt to be very illuminating — especially as many 'classical' composers (such as Gershwin) have introduced jazz and popular elements into their works, and many 'popular' composers (such as Duke Ellington and Paul McCartney) have written serious works of considerable breadth and complexity. ▷ **cantata; chamber music; concerto; motet; oratorio; overture; programme music; sonata; symphonic poem; symphony**

**classicism** Any approach which revives or imitates the artistic qualities of ancient Greece and Rome; when found in a later period, often called **neoclassicism**. These qualities are seen in the use of balanced and elegant formal proportions, dignified poses and gestures, and a restrained emotional expression. The archaeologist and art historian Johann Winckelmann (1717–68), in a famous phrase, referred to the 'noble simplicity and calm grandeur' of the approach. A return to classical standards is seen in the Italian Renaissance (15th–16th century), as illustrated in the paintings of Raphael, the sculpture of Michelangelo, and the architecture of Palladio. In Western art the pendulum seems to swing between 'classical' and 'non-classical' approaches (eg Gothic, Mannerist, Baroque, Romantic), although in certain periods a tension between the two is maintained. In music, the greatest period of classicism was in the late 18th century, seen especially in the works of Haydn, Mozart and Handel, and in the way a formal shaping emerged in the new kinds of composition (such as the movements of the symphony and concerto). In literature, classicism is associated especially with Latin poets such as Horace and Virgil, and in later periods can be seen in the tragedies of the French dramatists Racine and Corneille, and in the English poets Dryden and Pope. It implies the skilful imitation and adaptation of permanent forms and themes, rather than new departures and originality. In architecture, buildings usually display a pure geometrical form, restrained decoration, unbroken contours, an overall severe appearance, and sometimes monumental proportions. ▷ **classical music; neoclassicism**

**climatology** The study of long-term prevailing weather conditions in a region or place. There are a number of different schemes for dividing the Earth into climatic regions, the majority of which are based on a combination of indices of mean annual temperature, mean monthly temperature, annual precipitation totals, and seasonality. The climate of a place is influenced by several factors. Latitude determines the amount of solar radiation received, with the greatest in equatorial regions and the least in polar regions. Elevation affects both temperature and precipitation; mountainous areas are generally cooler and wetter. Location close to the sea or large bodies of water moderates temperature; continental areas are generally more arid and affected by greater extremes of temperature. Aspect is of local importance; in the northern hemisphere, south- and west-facing slopes are warmer than north- and east-facing slopes. ▷ **meteorology**

**clock paradox**   A phenomenon resulting from an experiment involving two identical clocks, initially together and showing the same time, one of which is carried off on a round-trip journey. Upon returning, the clock which moved will have lost time relative to the motionless clock by an amount prescribed by the theory of special relativity. Such effects have been observed using a pair of atomic clocks, one of which is flown around the world. However, a principle of relativity which claims that all observers are equivalent appears violated. The apparent paradox is resolved within special relativity by noticing that any clock undergoing a round-trip journey must be accelerated at some stage. The paradox is sometimes expressed in terms of identical twin brothers, one of whom undertakes a journey and finds himself younger than his brother upon returning (the **twin paradox**). ▷ **special relativity**

**coalition**   An arrangement between countries or political parties to pursue a common goal. Coalition governments are quite common in multi-party political systems, or in electoral systems using proportional representation. The nature of a ruling coalition is defined by those parties with seats in the cabinet. Often, it proves impossible to reconcile the differences between the political groups comprising the coalition, and the government falls. Famous examples of coalition governments in recent British history include David Lloyd-George's 1916 ministry, during World War I, and Winston Churchill's 1940 ministry, during World War II. Famous examples of international coalitions are the three coalitions set up to oppose France during the Revolutionary and Napoleonic Wars (1792–1815). ▷ **adversary politics; proportional representation**

**cognitive psychology**   A branch of psychology which studies the higher mental processes, such as memory, attention, language, and reasoning. In contrast to behaviourists, cognitive psychologists are more ready to posit mechanisms and processes that are not directly observable, such as memory stores and switches of attention. Cognitive psychologists may subscribe to the 'computer metaphor', in which the brain and the computer are seen as having the same essential characteristics. ▷ **cognitive science; psychology**

**cognitive science**   The study of the mind, in which models and theories originating in artificial intelligence (AI) and in the human sciences (particularly psychology, linguistics, and philosophy) are developed in an interdisciplinary way. For example, a grammar written by a linguist might be implemented on a computer by an AI scientist, and its predictions tested by a psychologist observing human subjects. The dominant partner in this enterprise is often the AI scientist, since the major criterion for success is usually whether a program can be written and successfully implemented on a computer. ▷ **artificial intelligence; cognitive psychology; linguistics**

**cold war**    A state of tension or hostility between states which is expressed in economic and political terms, and stops short of a 'hot' or shooting war. The policies adopted are those which attempt to strengthen one side and weaken the opposition, particularly those relating to military and weapon superiority. Thus the term is often used to describe the relationship between the USSR and the major Western non-communist powers — especially the USA — between 1945 and the mid-1960s, when the nuclear 'arms race' intensified. The process of detente, begun in the late 1960s, led to a 'thaw' in relations between the major powers. ▷ **arms race; detente; glasnost**

**collage**    A technique of picture-making in which pieces of paper, fabrics, or other materials are glued to the surface of the canvas; pronounced *kuh-lahzh*. It was introduced by the Cubists about 1912, and much used by the Surrealists in the 1920s. The technique is not restricted to professional artists; in everyday contexts, collage techniques are often found in scrapbooks. ▷ **Cubism; montage; Surrealism**

**collateral**    A valuable item used as security for a loan — often land, shares, jewellery, or an insurance policy. It is a safeguard, in case the borrower defaults. If the borrower does fail to repay the debt, the collateral can be sold, and the debt (along with any costs) deducted from the proceeds.

**colonialism**  ▷ **imperialism**.

**colourants**  ▷ **additives**.

**command economy**  ▷ **market economy**.

**Common Agricultural Policy (CAP)**    The most important of the common policies of the European Community, absorbing about 65% of the total Community budget. The basic principles behind the CAP are free trade for agricultural commodities within the Community, Community preference for domestic production, control of imports from the rest of the world, and common prices and subsidization. The objectives of the CAP were stated in the Treaty of Rome to be increased agricultural productivity, a fair standard of living for farmers, reasonable consumer prices, stability of markets, and secure food supplies. Most of these objectives have been met, through the use of high price-support measures, which in turn have generated surpluses in most major commodities (eg the 'butter mountain' and 'wine lake'). An important additional objective for the CAP is now to contain these surpluses and limit the huge cost associated with their disposal, by restructuring agriculture. ▷ **European Economic Community**

**Common Market** ▷ **European Economic Community**.

**Commons, House of** ▷ **House of Commons**.

**Commonwealth** A free association of independent nations formerly subject to British imperial government, and maintaining friendly and practical links with the UK. In 1931 the Statute of Westminster established the British Commonwealth of Nations; the adjective 'British' was deleted after World War II. Most of the states granted independence, beginning with India in 1947, chose to be members of the Commonwealth. There are annual meetings between finance ministers, and meetings between heads of government every two years, to discuss international affairs and areas of cooperation. Ireland resigned from the association in 1948, South Africa in 1961, Pakistan in 1972, and Fiji in 1987. There are now 48 members of the Commonwealth, 17 of which accept the British Queen as their head of state. The Commonwealth has a Secretariat based in London, and is headed by a Secretary General. Commonwealth Day is the second Monday in March. The Commonwealth Games are held every four years. ▷ **imperialism**

**Commonwealth of Independent States** ▷ **CIS**

**communication theory** The application of information theory to human communication in general. Communication is seen to involve an information source encoding a message (a 'sender') which is transmitted via a channel to a decoder (a 'receiver'), where it is interpreted and has an effect. Efficient, error-free transmission is assumed to be the primary goal, especially in engineering contexts. Attempts to apply this model more generally have been criticized for neglecting the importance of other factors, such as social context, the return of information to the sender (*feedback*), and the active role played by human receivers in the production of meaning. ▷ **information theory; semiotics**

**communism** A political ideology which has as its central principle the communal ownership of all property, and thereby the abolition of private property. Modern communism is specifically associated with the approach of the German political theorist Karl Marx (1818–83). Marx saw the emergence of a communist society as the final stage in a historical process that was rooted in human material needs, preceded by feudalism, capitalism, and (a transitional stage) socialism. Communism, according to Marx, would abolish class distinctions and end the exploitation of the masses inherent in the capitalist system. The working class, or proletariat, would be the instrument of a revolution that would overthrow the capitalist system and liberate human potential. A fully developed communist system would operate according to the principle of 'from each according to his ability, to each according to his need', and as there would be no need for the state to regulate society, it would 'wither away'.

Marx's writings have provided a powerful ideological basis for communist and many socialist parties and governments. The Communist Party of the Soviet Union (CPSU), first of all under Lenin's leadership and followed by Stalin, was particularly influential. This reinterpreted Marxist ideology in terms of democratic centralism. Unlike the spontaneous, decentralized organization envisaged by Marx, the CPSU became a highly centralized, monolithic, and secretive organization. Under Stalin it was an instrument in the development of a totalitarian dictatorship, which provided the ideological lead for European communist parties. The compulsory leadership of the CPSU later came to be questioned and challenged, though Hungary, Czechoslovakia, and Poland were prevented by military force from breaking away from the Soviet model. The assumption of leadership by Gorbachev led to radical reforms in the CPSU through the process of perestroika. Other socialist and social democratic parties have increasingly rejected the revolutionary path to socialism, advocating instead a gradual, reformist strategy operating within constitutional frameworks. China is now the only surviving major Marxist state. ▷ **capitalism; ideology; Maoism; Marxism; perestroika; totalitarianism**

**community education** ▷ **adult education**.

**computer science** The whole area of knowledge associated with the use and study of computers and computer-based processes. It includes computer design, programming, and inter-computer communication, and intersects with a number of other established disciplines such as mathematics, information theory, and electronic engineering. ▷ **cybernetics; information theory**

**concerto** A musical work for one or more solo instruments and orchestra. The earliest examples, such as those written in the 1680s by the Italian composer Arcangelo Corelli (1653–1713), contrasted two instrumental groups of unequal size. The early concerto with a single soloist is associated above all with Vivaldi, whose three-movement form (fast–slow–fast) was adopted by J S Bach, and remained standard in the concertos of Mozart, Beethoven, and most later composers. Some composers (such as Bartók and

Kodály) have written 'concertos for orchestra', in which the orchestral instruments are treated as soloists in turn. ▷ **classical music**

**Congregationalism**   A movement which sees the Christian Church as essentially a gathered community of believers, covenanting with God, keeping God's law, and living under the Lordship of Christ. It derived from the Separatists of the 16th-century Reformation in England, of whom Robert Browne (c.1550–1633) was an early leader. Persecution drove the Congregationalists to Holland and the USA (the Pilgrim Fathers, 1620). Church affairs, including calling a minister and appointing deacons to assist, are regulated by members at a 'Church Meeting'. As a world denomination, it has a strong missionary tradition. One denomination formed the International Congregational Council in 1949, which merged with Presbyterians as the World Alliance of Reformed Churches in 1970. With a strong tradition of tolerance and freedom of belief, its major contribution to ecumenism has been its insistence on the importance of the local church in the event of union with other denominations. ▷ **Christianity; ecumenism; Presbyterianism; Reformation**

**Congress**   The national, or federal, legislature of the USA, instituted in 1789, and consisting of two elected chambers: the Senate and the House of Representatives. Unusually powerful for a modern legislature, Congress can initiate legislation, and significantly amend or reject presidential legislative proposals. The consitution endows it with the 'power of the purse', as all revenue bills must originate in the House. For a bill to become law it must be passed in identical form by both chambers and signed by the president. A presidential veto may be overturned by a two-thirds majority in both chambers. Legislation receives detailed consideration in the powerful Congressional committees. The majority party leader of the House occupies the influential position of Speaker. ▷ **bicameral system; House of Representatives; Senate**

**conscientious objection**   A refusal to accept a particular policy, plan, or course of action, because to do so would go against one's conscience. It is often invoked by pacifists or others objecting to military service, though the State may not always recognize conscientious objection as a citizen's 'right'. There were conscientious objectors in both World Wars, who often served in medical and other non-combatant units or engaged in various kinds of civil work. ▷ **activism; pacifism**

**conservation**   The protection and preservation of the Earth's resources (eg plants, animals, land, energy, minerals) or of historical artefacts (eg books, paintings, monuments) for the future. The term is most widely used with reference to the environment, where several reasons are given for conservation. The World Conservation Strategy (1980) concluded that conservation of living resources was needed to preserve genetic diversity, to maintain essential ecological processes, and to ensure the sustainable use of species and ecosystems. This would maintain viable stocks of all animal and plant species, pure air and water, and fertile soil for future use, and allow animals, plants, and land to be there indefinitely. In this way conservation ensures that both present and future generations will be able to make maximum sustainable use of available resources. This definition is essentially economic. Other reasons for conservation include the enjoyment and spiritual nature of wildlife and the land, the continued use of the land for recreation, and the moral responsibility to future generations to conserve the Earth and its resources. ▷ **ecology; environment; recycling; Sites of Special Scientific Interest**

**conservatism**    A set of political ideas, attitudes, and beliefs which stress adherence to what is known and established in the political and social orders, as opposed to the innovative and untested. It is generally associated with right-wing political parties. Conservatives view humanity as inherently imperfect, and emphasize the need for law and order and the value of tradition. Society is often viewed as an organic whole, and as it is only imperfectly understood, change should rarely, or only gradually, be attempted. It implies the acceptance of inequality in society and limited state intervention. ▷ **Conservative Party; New Right; right wing; Thatcherism**

**Conservative Party**    One of the two main political parties in the UK, its full name being the **Conservative and Unionist Party**. It developed from the Tory Party during the 1830s and 1840s, becoming identified with landed interests, the monarchy, the British Empire, and the Church of England, but later that century embarking on a programme of parliamentary and social reform. It has been the most successful party electorally this century. In common with other conservative parties it is on the right of the political spectrum, committed to the promotion of private enterprise. ▷ **conservatism; New Right; right wing; Thatcherism**

**constitution**    The principles which determine the way a country may be governed, usually in the form of a written document. A **constitutional government** is one which acts in accordance with these principles, and whose powers are limited by them. One of the best-known examples of a written constitution is that of the United States, drawn up in 1787. The UK is one of a few exceptions in having an unwritten constitution. Written constitutions normally include several components: a preamble; a description of governmental institutions and their powers, including the processes for amending the constitution and reviewing decisions that are claimed to infringe the constitution; a bill of rights; and articles of amendment, added over a period of time. ▷ **bill of rights**

**consul**  ▷ **ambassador**.

**continental drift**  A theory which proposes that the present positions of the continents and oceans result from the breaking up of a single large land mass or 'supercontinent', termed *Pangaea*, about 200 million years ago. The idea is generally ascribed to German geophysicist Alfred Wegener (1880–1930), but gained little support until the 1960s, when the theory of plate tectonics (explaining movements in the Earth's crust) was established.

**continuing education**  ▷ **adult education**.

**cosmogony**  ▷ **cosmology**.

**cosmology**  The study of the universe on the largest scales of length and time, particularly the propounding of theories concerning the origin, nature, structure, and evolution of the universe. A cosmology is any model said to represent the observed universe — such as the 'big bang' theory. The study of the origin and mode of formation of various celestial objects, particularly the Solar System, is known as **cosmogony**.  ▷ **astronomy; big bang**

**cost of living**  ▷ **retail price index**.

**Cubism**  The most influential of all modern art movements, from which grew most of the early forms of abstraction. About 1907, the Spanish artist Pablo Picasso (1881–1973) and the French artist Georges Braque (1882–1963) rejected Renaissance perspective and Impressionist attention to light and atmosphere. Objects, painted in sombre shades of brown and grey, were analysed into geometrical planes with several views depicted simultaneously (*analytic cubism*). After about 1912 a flatter, more colourful and decorative hard-edged style emerged (*synthetic cubism*), using collage and painted relief constructs.  ▷ **abstract art; collage; Impressionism; modern art**

**cult**  Any set of beliefs and practices associated with a particular god or group of gods, forming a distinctive part of a larger religious body. The focus of the worship or devotion of a cult is usually a god or gods, spirit or spirits, associated with particular objects and places. The focus of devotion may be an animal (eg the whale cult in Eskimo religions), a particular deity (eg the Hindu cult devoted to Shiva), or even a deified human being (eg the emperor cult in ancient Rome).  ▷ **religion; sect**

**Cultural Revolution**  ▷ **Maoism**.

**culture**  The way of life of a group of people, consisting of learned and

**49**

symbolic patterns of behaviour and thought passed on from one generation to the next. The notion includes the group's beliefs, customs, values, language, political organization, and economic activity, as well as its equipment, techniques and art forms (referred to as *material culture*). ▷ **anthropology; sociology**

**customs duty** ▷ **excise tax**.

**cybernetics** The study of control systems that exhibit characteristics similar to those of animal and human behaviour. The term was coined in the 1940s by US mathematician Norbert Wiener (1894–1964), based on a Greek word meaning 'steersman'. Although the term has tended to fall into disuse with the expansion of the computer field, cybernetics is essentially a broad-based discipline which includes information, message, and noise theories, and can reconcile the work of neurophysiologists, psychologists, and computer engineers. ▷ **automation; computer science; psychology**

**Dada** or **Dadaism** A modern art movement founded in Zürich in 1916 which, against the background of disillusionment with World War I, attacked traditional artistic values. The name, which is French for 'rocking horse', was chosen at random from a dictionary. The founders included poets such as Tristan Tzara (1896–1963) as well as artists such as Hans Arp (1887–1966). Important contributors included German painter Max Ernst (1891–1976) and French painter Marcel Duchamp (1887–1968), whose *Fountain*, 1917 — a porcelain urinal — is perhaps the best-known 'work' of the Dada movement. The Dadaists influenced the Surrealists, and their deliberate shock-tactics were revived by some artists in the 1960s. ▷ **modern art; Surrealism**

**Dalai Lama** The name given since the 14th century to the traditional spiritual and political ruler of Tibet. The words are from the Mongolian language, and mean 'ocean-like guru'; the pronunciation is **da**-*lie* **lah**-*ma*. He is head of the leading school of Tibetan Buddhists. There have been 14 Dalai Lamas, each chosen by oracle after the death of the previous leader. A Dalai Lama is thought to be the rebirth (or reincarnation) of the Buddha of compassion, Avalokiteshvara. The 14th Dalai Lama is Tensin Gymatsho (1935–  ), who ruled in Tibet from 1940 to 1959. He was forced to flee from Tibet following the Chinese invasion of his country, but Tibetans still regard him as their spiritual leader. He won the Nobel Peace Prize in 1989. ▷ **Buddhism; reincarnation**

**Darwinism** The theory of evolution proposed by the British naturalist Charles Darwin (1809–82) and independently by the British naturalist Alfred

Wallace (1823–1912). Its most influential statement came from Darwin, in his book *On the Origin of Species by Means of Natural Selection*, published in 1859. The basic observation of the theory is that more offspring are produced, on average, than are needed to replace the parents, but population size remains more or less stable in nature. How does this happen? It is argued that individual members of a species show variation in their physical characteristics and behaviour. Given the large numbers of offspring produced, there must be competition for survival, and it is those individuals best suited to their environment which survive and reproduce. This is called **natural selection**. Evolution occurs by means of the processes of natural selection acting on this individual variation, resulting in the 'survival of the fittest'. When biologists discovered the genetic mechanism causing variation, the theory was re-expressed in an approach known as **neo-Darwinism**. ▷ **evolution**

**decadence**    A period of cultural decline in literature, with writers reacting against the norms of artistic and moral standards. Themes are morbid and perverse; treatment is sensational and self-indulgent. A famous period of decadence was the 1890s; it included such French writers as Charles Baudelaire (1821–67) and Paul Verlaine (1844–96), the British playwright Oscar Wilde (1854–1900), and the American short-story writer Edgar Allen Poe (1809–49). In popular usage, any real or mock tendency towards a degenerate lifestyle is often called 'decadence'. ▷ **literature**

**deconstruction**    An approach to literary criticism which denies that texts can have 'a meaning', in any simple sense. Rather, texts present a wide range of possible interpretations (some of which may even go against the intentions of the author), and the aim of criticism should be to break open (or 'deconstruct') the text in order to expose its various assumptions and meanings. The approach is also known as **post-structuralism**, because it takes the insights of structuralism to their logical conclusion by emphasizing the arbitrariness and instability existing between words and what they stand for. The French philosopher Jaques Derrida (1930–  ) has argued in several books how language must fail in its attempt to relate by reference to a world 'out there' beyond our discourse, and how this discourse must itself be deconstructed in order to expose the fallacies of our word-centred conception of reality. ▷ **hermeneutics; literature; structuralism**

**decorative arts**    The design and ornamentation of objects, usually with some practical use and outside the field of 'fine art' (painting, sculpture, and architecture); nowadays more exactly called the **applied arts**. Metalwork, ceramics, glass, textiles, and woodwork have all been wrought and decorated to a degree which transcends their functional purpose, and gives them an important role in the development of mainstream artistic styles.

The distinction with fine art is often almost non-existent, as in the case of ceramic sculpture and tapestry hangings. ▷ **art; Art Deco**

**deduction**   In logic, any inference whose conclusion follows validly and necessarily from its premises. The premises may or may not be true: 'London and Chicago are planets; therefore London is a planet' is a valid deduction, even though we know that the facts are not true. On the other hand, 'Either London or Mars is a planet; therefore Mars is a planet' is an invalid deduction. Deductive reasoning deals in certainties, and in this respect contrasts with inductive reasoning, which deals only in probabilities. ▷ **induction; logic; premise**

**defamation**   ▷ **libel**.

**deficit**   ▷ **balance of payments**.

**deflation**   A government economic policy designed to reduce inflationary pressures. Steps taken include higher interest and tax rates, and a tighter money supply. ▷ **inflation; reflation**

**deism**   Originally, a belief in the existence of a god or gods; pronounced *day*-izm. In the 17th and 18th centuries, it was the name given to a movement of religious thought, found largely in Britain, which emphasized the importance of basing any belief in God on the study of nature. Today, deists are those who believe in the existence of a supreme being who is the ground and source of reality, but who does not intervene or take an active interest in the nature or affairs of the world. ▷ **God; theist**

**déjà vu**   The mental phenomenon which takes place when people feel they have experienced on a previous occasion the events that are taking place around them; the term is from French, meaning 'already seen'. The illusion may seem very real, but cannot be given any rational explanation.

**democracy**   A widely-used term which comes from the Greek words for 'people' (*demos*) and 'authority' (*kratia*), and means 'rule by the people'. It should be contrasted with 'rule by the few' (*oligarchy*) and 'rule by a single person' (known as *monarchy* or *tyranny*). In modern times, you will also hear it called a **liberal democracy**. Since the Greeks first introduced the approach in many city-states in the fifth century BC, there has been disagreement about the essential elements of democracy. One debate is about who should compose 'the people', particularly in relation to the increasing size of states, which has resulted in a shift from direct democracy to systems of representation. Today it is widely accepted that because the people are too numerous and scattered to come together in assemblies, decision-making has to be handed over to a small group of representatives.

Elections, including the right to choose among different groups of representatives offering different party programmes, have therefore become seen as essential to democracy. Further necessary conditions are the legal equality of citizens, and the free flow of information to ensure that citizens are in an equal and informed position to choose their rulers. Some radicals argue that economic equality is also necessary, but moves towards economic democracy have been limited. ▷ **constitution; political science; proportional representation**

**deoxyribonucleic acid** ▷ **DNA**.

**depression** An economic situation where demand for goods and services is slack, order-books are low, firms dispense with staff, and profits are poor or absent. The Great Depression of the early 1930s (often referred to as the *slump*) saw many firms going bankrupt, and many millions of people out-of-work. A shorter downturn in economic activity is a *recession*. ▷ **recession; trade cycle**

**deregulation** Action taken by a government to reduce or abolish state controls over a business, an industry, or the economy as a whole. In the USA, for example, the airline system was deregulated in the 1970s. In Britain, buses were deregulated in the 1980s. ▷ **privatization**

**desertification** The environmental degradation of arid and semi-arid areas through overcultivation, overgrazing, deforestation, and bad irrigation practices. The land loses its fertility, and is no longer able to support its population. The problem is worsened in many regions by climatic instability (particularly drought), by rapidly-growing populations, and by cash cropping, which reduces the area available for the production of food crops for the local population. In the 1970s and 1980s, desertification occurred at one time or another in most of the area south of the Sahara Desert (the Sahel). ▷ **conservation; habitat loss**

**designer drugs** Synthetic drugs, often narcotics, which are not controlled by law in the USA; they are so called because they are specifically designed by chemists to be slightly different structurally to drugs that are controlled by law (which are 'named', and thus illegal), yet still chemically so close to them that they have similar biological effects. These 'legal' drugs are produced covertly and sold on the streets to illicit drug users. The normal dangers of drug abuse are increased by the possibility of contamination. In the early 1980s, such contamination was found to induce permanent symptoms of Parkinson's disease in young users. ▷ **pharmacology**

**detente** An attempt to lower the tension between states in order to reduce the possibility of war and to achieve peaceful coexistence between different social and political systems; pronounced *day-***tawnt**. It was a prominent feature of relations between the USA and USSR in the 1970s, and led to several agreements over arms, security, and cooperation. In the early 1980s, there was a cooling towards detente on the part of the USA, on the grounds that too many concessions had been made and that the USSR did not adhere to the spirit of such agreements; but there was a considerable improvement in relations in the later part of the decade. ▷ **cold war; glasnost; perestroika**

**devaluation**   A term used when there is a fall in the rate of exchange from one currency to another. For example, if you see a formula such as £1=$2, this means that for every £1 you own you would be given $2, if you went to the USA. But the exchange rate can alter, and when it does the pound falls or rises in value. If it falls to £1=$1.80, this would mean that for every £1 you own you would now be given only $1.80. In such circumstances, economists say that 'the pound has fallen against the dollar'. The pound has thus lost some of its former value. Until the early 1970s, currencies had fixed exchange rates, and devaluations were resisted. Nowadays, currencies 'float', and market forces alter exchange rates all the time — though limits on the movement of certain currencies are imposed in the European Monetary System. Devaluation makes a country's exports cheaper and its imports dearer, thus helping to build up its reserves of currency. ▷ **European Monetary System; exchange rates**

**developing countries**   A label used for most of the countries of Africa, Asia, and Latin America. Many have largely agricultural economies, though Brazil, India, and Pakistan have a well-developed industrial base, and others have rich mineral wealth. In these countries, people have a very low income and low savings, compared with standards in Europe or the USA. Development has often been held back by rapid population growth, crop failure, drought, war, and insufficient demand (at a reasonable price) for their commodities, crops, and goods. Many aid programmes have now been devised by the international agencies, such as the Commonwealth Development Corporation, Alliance for Progress, and USAid. There are also many privately-funded charities with aid programmes. Western banks have lent large sums to the developing nations, but several countries are so poor that they are unable to repay the interest on what they owe. ▷ **International Monetary Fund; Three Worlds theory; World Bank**

**deviationism**   A tendency within communist parties to move away or 'deviate' from the official party position. It can be a move to either the left or the right. Deviation is regarded as a political offence because it undermines the principle of democratic centralism, and it can therefore occur even in cases where those so charged hold to an orthodox Marxist position. It is often used as a term of abuse and denunciation. ▷ **communism; left wing; Marxism; right wing**

**devil's advocate**   Anyone who adopts the less accepted position in an argument, in order to help the argument develop. The term is a translation from Latin, originating in the Roman Catholic Church for an official whose role is to examine the life and miracles of someone who has been put forward for beatification or canonization as a saint. The official is required to find out everything which is unfavourable to the cause, so that it can be taken into account before a decision is reached. In everyday contexts, likewise, it is applied to someone who thinks up objections to a point of view, for the sake of the argument.

**devolution**   The delegation of authority from a country's central government to a subordinate elected institution on a more limited geographical basis. In the UK, this process took place for the first time when the Northern Ireland parliament was established at Stormont in 1921 (direct rule was restored in 1972). Proposals for devolution in Wales and Scotland in the 1970s were unsuccessful. Devolution is distinguished from federalism, where the independent powers of the central government and the federal bodies are set out in the constitution. Under devolution, the subordinate body receives its power from the government, which retains some right of oversight. The idea is to provide more self-government and to bring decision-making closer to the people. Critics argue that to allow for major differences in decision-making within a state poses a threat to the state's unity. ▷ **federalism; home rule**

**dialectic**   The study of the logic involved in conversational argument, emphasizing the techniques involved in putting forth hypotheses, counter-hypotheses, criticisms, refutations, and modifications of one's original views. As used by the German philosopher G W F Hegel (1770–1831), dialectic is an analogous process that occurs in nature. All developments in thought and society proceed by proposing something (the 'thesis'), then contradicting it (the 'antithesis'), then moving to something which contains a greater portion of truth in its new complexity (the 'synthesis'). According to Marx, change in the material conditions of society takes place through a process of contradiction, as one type of social system clashes with another (*dialectical materialism*). ▷ **logic; Marxism**

**dictator**   In strict terms, a single ruler who is not elected but enjoys authority by virtue of some personal characteristic — in other words, an **autocrat**. In practice, a dictatorship often refers to rule by several people, who are nonetheless unelected and authoritarian in character, such as a military dictatorship. Personal dictatorships are now very rare. Not all involve arbitrary rule, and some dictators take account of popular wishes ('benevolent dictatorships'). Dictatorships have been common in several Latin American and Arab countries in recent decades. Examples of modern dictators include Hitler in Germany, Mussolini in Italy, Mao Zedong in

China, Salazar in Portugal, Perón in Argentina, and Stalin in Russia. ▷ **democracy**

**diplomacy**   ▷ **shuttle diplomacy; summit diplomacy**.

**disarmament**   Arms control which seeks to promote international security by a reduction in armed forces and/or weapons. The levels are set by agreement, and then opened up for inspection and enforcement by the other side or an independent inspectorate. Disarmament which is both general (ie applying to all countries) and comprehensive (ie applying to all categories of forces and weapons) was first attempted by the League of Nations in the 1920s, and by the United Nations in the 1950s, but such moves have not been successful. Disarmament is therefore limited to agreements between two or a few countries, and restricted to particular classes of weapons and troop levels. Problems arise in determining equivalences between different types of weapons held by different countries, and in verifying arms reduction treaties, especially in respect of nuclear weapons, largely because weapons can be reassembled. There is also the possibility of nuclear disarmament involving no agreement with other countries, used as a means of encouraging others to follow. Such *unilateral* action may also be taken for moral reasons and as a means of diminishing the chances of being attacked, particularly by nuclear and chemical weapons. ▷ **arms control; cold war; detente; nuclear weapons; pacifism**

**discrimination**   ▷ **racism**.

**dissidents**   People who oppose the particular regime under which they live, often through peaceful means, and who as a result suffer discrimination and harassment from the authorities. Dissidents may, for example, lose their jobs or be banished to certain areas of the country. Famous dissidents in recent decades include the Russian writer Alexander Solzhenitsyn (1918–   ), who was deported in 1974, and the Russian physicist Andrei Sakharov (1921–89), who was placed under restriction in the Soviet Union between 1980 and 1986.

**distance learning**   Teaching people, usually at home or in their place of work, by means of correspondence units, radio, cassettes, telephone, television, or microcomputer, rather than through face-to-face contact. Often, though not always, a tutor may be involved to give advice or mark written work, either at a distance or through occasional meetings. Distance education has been particularly popular in sparsely populated areas, or for people not able to attend courses in schools and colleges. Institutions such as the British Open University and Open College have made extensive use of it. ▷ **adult education**

**Divisionism**   In painting, a technique (sometimes called **Pointillism**) whereby small patches or spots of pure colour are placed close together so that they mix not on the palette or canvas, but in the eye of the beholder. It was developed systematically by some of the French Post-Impressionists, notably Georges Seurat (1859–91), and labelled **Neoimpressionism** by the French critic Félix Fénéon (1861–1944). ▷ **art; Impressionism**

**divorce**   ▷ **annulment**.

**DNA**   The abbreviation for **deoxyribonucleic acid**, the nucleic acid which occurs in combination with protein in the chromosomes, and which contains the genetic instructions for the structure and functioning of cells. The skeleton of the DNA consists of two chains of alternate sugar and phosphate groups twisted round each other in the form of a double spiral, or 'double helix'; to each sugar is attached a base; and the two chains are held together by hydrogen bonding between the bases. The sequence of bases provides in code the genetic information (the 'genetic code'), which is transcribed, edited, and acted on by another nucleic acid, **RNA** (short for **ribonucleic acid**). Each human cell nucleus contains approximately $6 \times 10^9$ base pairs of DNA, totalling in length about 2 m/6.6 ft, but coiled upon itself and coiled again and again, so that it fits inside the cell nucleus of less than 10 mm in diameter. DNA replicates itself accurately during cell growth and duplication, and its structure is stable, so that heritable changes (mutations) are very infrequent. The structure of DNA was discovered in 1953 by geneticists James Watson (1928–   ) and Francis Crick (1916–   ). ▷ **genetics**

**dualism**   In philosophy, any theory which asserts that there are two fundamentally different kinds of thing which underlie the whole of existence. The most famous dualism, held by Plato, Descartes, and many other philosophers, is between mind and matter. Descartes claimed that matter is a substance, whose essence is to extend in space, and that the mind or soul is a non-spatial substance, whose essence is thinking. A person, then, is a dualistic compound of these substances, and mental properties of persons that are in no way reducible to physical properties. A different kind of dualism is involved in regarding morality exclusively in terms of good versus evil. ▷ **philosophy**

**dyslexia**   Reading disability, observed in people with apparently adequate intellectual and perceptual abilities and adequate educational opportunities; sometimes called **alexia**. **Developmental dyslexia** is the term applied to children with special problems in learning to read. **Acquired dyslexia** describes those who could once read, but who have lost this ability as a result of brain damage. There is no single theory which explains

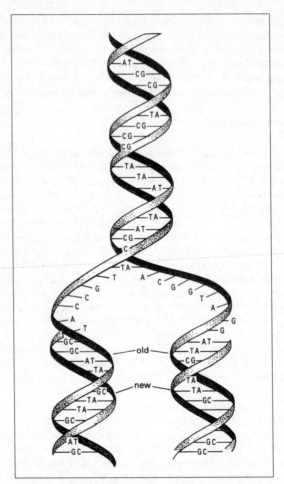

DNA replication, following Watson and Crick. The two
strands of the double helix separate, and a daughter strand
is laid down alongside each with a constitution determined
by the base sequence of its parent strand.

dyslexia, and the nature of the problem has been a source of some dispute.
Nevertheless it is common for several members of a family to exhibit similar
difficulties with reading and writing, and various educational programmes
have been developed for helping sufferers to cope. ▷ **special education**

**earth sciences**   A general term for the study of the Earth and its atmosphere. It includes geology and its subdisciplines, as well as oceanography, glaciology, meteorology, and the origin of the Earth and the Solar System. ▷ **environment; geology; meteorology**

**ecology**   The study of the interaction of living organisms with their physical, biological, and chemical environment. Because of the complexity of ecosystems, ecological studies of individual ecosystems or parts of ecosytems are often made, from which links between different systems can be established. In this way, ecologists attempt to explain the workings of larger ecosystems. Important ecological concepts have had considerable influence in conservation; an example is *carrying capacity*, which relates the available resources of an area to the number of users that can be sustained by these resources. The ecological movement of the 1960s onwards has argued that people must live within the limitations of the Earth's finite supply of resources, and that humanity is very much dependent on its environment. Ecology is therefore seen as a social as well as a scientific subject, providing a link between physical and human environments. ▷ **conservation; ecosystem; environment**

**econometrics**   ▷ **economics**.

**economics**   The study of the allocation of scarce resources among competing ends, the creation and distribution of wealth, and national income. Two main aspects are often recognized. **Microeconomics** is the study of the economic problems of firms and individuals, and the way individual elements in an economy are determined (such as product prices, wages, and labour supply). **Macroeconomics** is the study of the economy as a whole, including such matters as international trade, monetary policy, price levels, national income, exchange rates, economic growth, and forecasting (*econometrics*). Particular concerns are how to manage an economy to achieve high growth, low inflation, and high employment; and, for individual firms, to predict those economic factors which will affect them in the future, thus enabling them to improve their own planning. ▷ **Keynesianism; monetarism; social science**

**ecosystem**   An ecological concept which helps to explain the relationships and interactions between living organisms and their physical, biological, and chemical environment — such as a pond and its associated plants, fish, insects, birds, and mammals. The concept is helpful in describing interactions at any level, from the individual plant in its community to planet Earth. The study of ecosystems is commonly based on transfers of energy along a food chain by examining four elements: *abiotic* or inorganic and dead organic substances (eg inorganic compounds in soil and water);

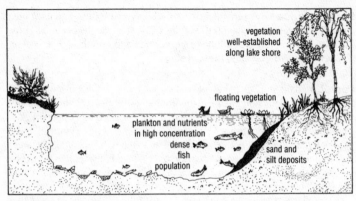

*A freshwater ecosystem*

green plants or *producers*, which fix energy from the Sun by photosynthesis and use inorganic material from the soil or atmosphere to manufacture complex organic substances; *consumers* (eg birds, insects, mammals) which use the energy fixed by plants; and *decomposers* (eg bacteria, fungi), which break down dead organisms, releasing nutrients back to the environment for use by the producers. In most natural ecosystems, several food-chains interact to form complex food or energy webs. ▷ **ecology; environment**

**ecu** or **ECU**　The abbreviation of **European Currency Unit**, the unit of currency introduced into the European Economic Community. It is a value which has been worked out as an average derived from all EC currencies, and this alters as new countries join the Community. For example, in 1989 the composition of the ECU was redefined for the first time since 1984, to allow the inclusion of the currencies of Spain and Portugal. ▷ **European Monetary System**

**ecumenism**　A movement seeking visible unity of divided churches and denominations within Christianity; the term comes from the Greek *oikoumene*, meaning 'the inhabited world', and is pronounced e-**kyoo**-muhn-izm. A dramatic increase of interest in ecumenism and the reuniting of Churches followed the Edinburgh Missionary Conference in 1910, and led to the formation in 1948 of the World Council of Churches. Assemblies are held every seven years, the decisions of which guide but do not bind member Churches. The movement encourages dialogue between Churches of different denominations, unions where possible, joint acts of worship, and joint service in the community. The ecumenical movement received considerable encouragement from Pope John XXIII, who invited observers from other Churches to the Second Vatican Council (1962–5), and a great deal of dialogue has since taken place (eg between Anglicans and Roman Catholics). ▷ **Christianity; World Council of Churches**

**egalitarianism**  A political philosophy which places a high value on equality among members of society, and advocates the removal of barriers to it. It is based on the view that all people are fundamentally equal, and that certain social and political institutions produce inequalities, such as in wealth and income, education, legal rights, and political power. Egalitarianism was one of the tenets of the French Revolution, and is associated with radical and socialist politics. ▷ **radicalism; socialism**

**embargo**  An order obstructing or impeding the movement of ships of a foreign power, which can prevent them from either leaving or entering a port. In the past, embargoes were associated with anticipating the outbreak of war, but their use is limited today. The term is also employed to describe any attempt to suspend trading with another country. An example is the oil embargo placed on Egypt by other Arab countries, following the peace treaty between Egypt and Israel in 1979. ▷ **boycott; sanctions**

**emigration**  ▷ **migration**.

**empiricism**  A term used in philosophy in two main ways. Strictly speaking, an empiricist is one who believes that all knowledge is founded on sense experience, and claims that his/her own knowledge satisfies the test of experience. The other use of the term derives from debates with *rationalism*, where empiricists deny the views that knowledge is either inborn or can be produced by arguing independently of experience. The US linguist Noam Chomsky (1928–   ), for example, claims that to explain the ease with which children acquire language, some innate knowledge must be presumed. Many who have called themselves empiricists deny this to be possible — but since their denial cannot be founded on sense experience they are in a peculiar position. You will find a further context for the term 'empirical' in scientific enquiry, where 'empirical evidence', in the form of objective and quantifiable observations, is used in order to confirm or falsify hypotheses. ▷ **epistemology; scientific method**

**employee relations**  ▷ **industrial relations**.

**emulsifiers**  ▷ **additives**.

**energy**  One of the most important concepts in physics: an abstract quantity associated with all physical processes and objects, whose total value is found always to be conserved. It is sometimes called the capacity for doing work. Energy may be transferred but never destroyed, and so provides a useful book-keeping device for the analysis of processes. Although many terms are used to describe energy (eg thermal energy, kinetic energy), they refer to the same energy, but indicate its different manifestations. For example, a battery driving a propeller immersed in water converts chemical energy to electrical energy, which is converted to mechanical energy in the propeller, and finally to heat energy as the water temperature is increased. The main sources of energy are fossil fuels (petroleum, coal, and natural gas), water power, and nuclear power. Solar power, wind power, oil, and coal provide almost 75% of world energy needs; natural gas about 20%; water power (hydroelectricity) about 2%; and nuclear energy about 1%. The search for new sources of energy is a continuing one, since the energy provided by the fossil fuels will eventually run out. ▷ **fossil fuel; nuclear reactor**

**engraving**   The process of incising marks into a hard surface, especially metal or wood, so that the result can be printed; also the resulting print

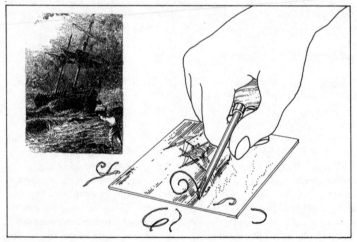

*Engraving*

itself. In the *intaglio* method (the word comes from Italian, to engrave), a design is incised into a metal plate; ink is forced into the cut lines, and wiped off the rest of the surface; damp paper is laid on top; and both plate and paper are rolled through a press. This differs from other types of printing, in which the ink lies on the raised surface of the plate or block. A contrast can also be made with **etching**, where the design on a copper plate is bitten with acid, rather than cut directly with an engraving tool. Before the advent of photography, engravings were often used to reproduce works of art. An original engraving is a work of art in its own right. ▷ **art**

**Enlightenment**   A European philosophical movement of the 18th century, which claimed the superiority of reason as a guide to all knowledge and human concerns. The period of the Enlightenment is also called the 'Age of Reason'. It was rooted in the 17th-century Scientific Revolution and in the ideas of the English philosopher John Locke (1632–1704), the English scientist Isaac Newton (1642–1727), and the French philosopher Voltaire (1694–1778). From this movement flowed the notion of progress and a challenging of traditional Christianity. Several European monarchs introduced reforms based on these ideas (the 'enlightened despots', such as Frederick the Great of Prussia). ▷ **philosophy**

**enterprise zones**   In the UK, parts of the country designated by the government as areas where business start-up schemes will get favourable financial help; for example, no rates might be payable for 10 years. They are usually located in inner-city areas with high unemployment levels. Over 20 such zones exist in the USA, and a similar number in the UK. Schemes of this kind are in operation in many West European countries.

**E-number**   A code number on food labels, used by food manufacturers in member states of the European Economic Community, which identifies all materials added to the food. Among food additives, four categories each have code numbers: preservatives (which prevent deterioration), colourants (which improve colour), anti-oxidants (which slow down the process of oxidation), and emulsifiers (which help liquids to mix with each other). For example, E102 is the colourant tartrazine, E210 the preservative benzoic acid, and E420 is the emulsifier guar gum. ▷ **additives; European Economic Community**

**environment**   The conditions and influences of the place in which an organism lives. The large number of different types of environment (eg urban environment, tropical rain forest environment) makes it impossible to formulate a single definition. In general, the *physical* environment describes the characteristics of a landscape (eg climate, geology) which have not been markedly changed by human impact, whereas the *geographical* environment includes the physical environment together with any human modifications (eg agricultural systems, urbanization). The relationship between living organisms and their environment forms part of the subject of *ecology*. Concern that large parts of the physical environment are suffering from misuse and overexploitation is central to conservation, and the environmental movement which promotes conservation has gained considerable momentum in recent decades as new threats (eg acid rain, soil erosion, ozone depletion) are widely recognized — see the entry on **environmentalism**.   ▷ **conservation; ecology; ecosystem; environmentalism**

**environmentalism**   A term which has several meanings according to the perspective of the user. Its broadest meaning is a concern with all environmental matters — a recognition of increasing environmental degradation brought about by mismanagement of the Earth's resources (eg the excessive burning of fossil fuels), and therefore the need for conservation. More narrowly, its use can be applied to the ideology which rejects the 'technocentric' view of the environment, that all environmental problems can be solved through the use of technology and without a reduction in economic growth. Environmentalism adopts an 'ecocentric' approach. This advocates that environmental problems cannot be solved without a shift away from policies of economic growth at any price. There is the recognition that the Earth's resources are finite, and that higher priority should be given to non-material values. Little confidence is placed in the ability of conventional science to solve environmental problems. ▷ **conservation; ecology; environment; ideology**

**epic**   Traditionally, a heroic poem; a narrative of wars and adventures where larger-than-life characters perform deeds of great public and national significance. The earlier epic poems, in the oral tradition, reached back into myth and legend, where men and gods moved on the same scene; among these are the Sumerian epic *Gilgamesh* (c.3000BC), the Homeric epics *Iliad* and *Odyssey* (c.1000BC), and the Indian *Mahabharata* and *Ramayana* (c.500BC): also the North European epics such as the Old English *Beowulf* (eighth century), the Norse sagas, and the 13th-century German *Nibelungenlied*. The term 'secondary epic' refers to works written in conscious imitation of these primary epic models, such as Virgil's *Aeneid* (30–19BC) and Milton's *Paradise Lost* (1667). The novel has been presented as an 'epic poem in prose', and some works of significant scale such as Melville's *Moby Dick* (1851) and Tolstoy's *War and Peace* (1863–9) may be so described. The German playwright Bertolt Brecht (1898–1956) also proposed an 'epic theatre'. Although some films have achieved truly epic status, the form and the term have generally been handled superficially in the cinema. ▷ **literature**

**epistemology**   The philosophical theory of knowledge: What is it? Can we have any? Are there different kinds? How are they justified? These are often taken to be the central questions of philosophy, and they have motivated several schools of thought. For example, empiricists claim that all non-trivial knowledge is derived from experience. Rationalists disagree, claiming that some if not all significant knowledge is independent of experience and demands argument. Sceptics argue either that we can have no definite knowledge at all, or that what we call knowledge does not really describe things as they are. ▷ **empiricism; philosophy; scepticism**

**Establishment, the**   The institutions and people who control public life, represent authority, and support the existing social order. In Britain they include the monarchy, the government, the Church, the civil service, the law, the BBC, the city financial institutions, the police, the armed forces, the public schools, and the universities (especially Oxford and Cambridge). In a school, the Establishment will be the governors, teachers, and other staff. The definition is never precise. Much depends on who is using the term, and where in the social hierarchy they find themselves. Sometimes, the label is used, pejoratively, to mean simply 'anyone who has more power or money than I have'.

**etching** ▷ **engraving**.

**ethics** Generally, the moral standards by which people live; more specifically, in philosophy, the theoretical study of human values and conduct. Its main branch (*normative ethics*) attempts to address such topics as what sort of life we should live, and what sorts of things have ultimate value. One view claims that there are some ultimate principles of rightness and wrongness which should govern the behaviour of all societies, independent of what societies might happen to believe. Another claims that nothing is absolutely right or wrong, even if all cultures believe the contrary. Several other views are possible. ▷ **abortion; euthanasia; genetic engineering; philosophy**

**ethnicity** A shared cultural identity that has a range of distinctive behavioural and possibly linguistic features, passed on through socialization from one generation to another. There are never clear boundaries, cultural or geographic, that mark the limits of ethnic groups, even though many regard ethnicity as though it were naturally determined. Ethnic differences have been a source of political conflict, often associated with national, religious, or clan membership. **Ethnocentrism** is a limited or parochial perspective which evaluates other societies and their cultures according to one's own cultural expectations. It implies a very restricted understanding of foreign cultures, and a notion that one's own culture is not only different, but 'better'. ▷ **anthropology; Black Consciousness; class; culture**

**ethnocentrism** ▷ **ethnicity**.

**ethology** The study of animal behaviour from the viewpoint of zoology and ecology, the animals being studied in their natural environments. The approach was developed by Austrian zoologist Konrad Lorenz (1903–89) and Dutch zoologist Nikolaas Tinbergen (1907–88). It considers the fine details of the behaviour of individual species in relation to properties of the natural environment to which the species has adapted (its *ecological niche*). Typical behaviours studied include feeding, courtship, and prey–predator

relationships. The data are derived from direct observation and monitoring (eg by radio-tracking) of animals under natural or quasi-natural conditions.
▷ **ecology**

**European Atomic Energy Community** ▷ **European Community**.

**European Coal and Steel Community** ▷ **European Community**.

**European Commission** The administrative bureaucracy of the European Community, conducting both political and administrative tasks. Its functions are to uphold the European ideal, propose new policy initiatives, and ensure that existing policies are implemented. In a narrow sense it comprises 17 commissioners directly nominated by the member states; the UK, France, Germany, Italy, and Spain each nominate two commissioners, the rest one each. They serve a four-year term, are each responsible for a specific area of work, and are supported by a bureaucracy employing about 15000 people. The Commission decides by majority vote, and is collectively responsible to the European Parliament. The Commission was originally intended to be the main source of direction and decision-making within the Community, but in practice this role has fallen to the Council of Ministers.
▷ **European Community**

**European Community (EC)** A community of 12 states in Western Europe created for the purpose of achieving economic and political integration. It is made up of three communities. The first of these was the **European Coal and Steel Community**, established in 1952 under the Treaty of Paris by France, West Germany, Italy, Belgium, the Netherlands, and Luxembourg. It created common institutions for regulating the coal and steel industries under a common framework of law and institutions, thereby producing the first breach in the principle of national sovereignty. In the early 1950s, unsuccessful attempts were made to establish a European Defence Community and a European Political Community. In 1958, under the Treaty of Rome, the six states established the **European Economic Community** and the **European Atomic Energy Community**, which provided for collaboration in the civilian sector of nuclear power. Six members have been added to the original six: Denmark, Ireland, and the UK (1973); Greece (1981); and Portugal and Spain (1986). To develop and oversee the policies of economic and political integration there are a number of supranational community institutions: the Commission, the Council, the European Parliament, and the European Court of Justice. While the Community has grown in the 1970s and 1980s and continues to progress towards economic integration, full political union seems still a distant possibility.
▷ **European Commission; European Council; European Economic Community; European Monetary System; European Parliament**

**European Council**   The body which brings together the heads of state and/or government of the member states of the European Community. Since the mid-1960s, when President de Gaulle demanded the right of veto over any decision taken by the Council, it has tended to take decisions on the basis of unanimity rather than majority voting. The need for agreement among 12 states has resulted in severe difficulties in achieving reform, particularly in the area of agriculture. ▷ **European Community**

**European Currency Unit**  ▷ **ecu**.

**European Economic Community (EEC)**   An association within the European Community, established in 1958 after the Treaties of Rome (1957); often referred to as the **Common Market**. It is essentially a customs union, with a common external tariff and a common market which removes barriers to trade among the members. In addition, it has a number of common policies, the most important of which is the Common Agricultural Policy, providing for external tariffs to protect domestic agriculture and mechanisms for price support. There are also common policies for fisheries, regional development, industrial intervention, and economic and social affairs. There is also a European Monetary System, which regulates exchange rate movements among the member states' currencies in an attempt to achieve monetary stability. In 1986 the Single European Act was passed, allowing for the completion of the process of creating a common market within the Community by the end of 1992. This will generate further competition among the industries of member states. ▷ **Common Agricultural Policy; European Commission; European Community; European Council; European Monetary System; European Parliament; free trade; tariff**

**European Free Trade Association (EFTA)**   An association originally of seven West European states who were not members of the European Economic Community (EEC), intended as a counter to the EEC; it was established in 1959 under the Stockholm Convention. The members (Austria, Denmark, Norway, Portugal, Sweden, Switzerland, and the UK) agreed to eliminate over a period of time trade restrictions between them, without having to bring into line individual tariffs and trade policies with other countries. Agriculture was excluded from the agreement, although individual arrangements were permitted. Both the UK (1973) and Portugal (1986) left to join the EEC, but there has been a free trade agreement between the remaining EFTA countries and the European Community, and considerable trade between the two groupings. Finland joined in 1985. ▷ **European Economic Community; free trade**

**European Monetary System**   A financial system set up in 1979 by some members of the European Community with the aim of stabilizing and harmonizing currencies. Member-states use a special currency — the *European Currency Unit* (ECU). A percentage of members' foreign exchange reserves is deposited with the European Monetary Cooperation Fund, and ECUs are received in exchange. Members join an *exchange rate mechanism* (ERM) which regulates currency exchange fluctuations. The UK joined the ERM, after much controversy, in 1990. ▷ **ecu; European Economic Community; exchange rates**

**European Parliament** The representative assembly of the European Community. Despite its name, it has no legislative powers, but it does have the right to be consulted by the European Council, to dismiss the European Commission (a right never so far used), and to reject or amend the Community budget. The more forceful role played by the Parliament in recent years reflects the fact that it has been directly elected since 1979. Europe-wide elections are held every five years, with seats divided as follows: UK, France, Germany, and Italy (81); Spain (60); the Netherlands (25); Belgium, Greece, and Portugal (24); Denmark (16); Ireland (15); and Luxembourg (6). The administration of the Parliament lies in Luxembourg; its plenary sessions are held in Strasbourg; and its committees are in Brussels, where the Commission is based and the Councils meet. ▷ **European Community; European Council**

**euthanasia** The painless ending of life, usually as an act of mercy to relieve chronic pain or suffering; the term comes from Greek, meaning 'easy death'. It may take the form of a positive step ('active' euthanasia, such as the administration of a drug) or the withholding of treatment ('passive' euthanasia). Euthanasia has been advocated by pressure groups such as *Exit*, and by some physicians as a dignified death for the very poorly elderly who have lost the will or desire to live. However, no country officially sanctions the practice. ▷ **ethics; pressure group**

**evangelicalism** Since the Reformation, a term which has been applied to the Protestant Churches because of their principles of justification through faith alone and the supreme authority accorded to scripture. It is also applied more narrowly to those Protestant Churches which emphasize intense personal conversion ('born-again Christianity') and commitment in their experience of justification and biblical authority. Evangelicals adhere strictly to traditional interpretations of the Bible, to which many witness with considerable fervour. ▷ **charismatic movement; Christianity; fundamentalism; Protestantism**

**evolution** The cumulative changes in the characteristics of populations of organisms from generation to generation. Evolution occurs by the fixation of changes (*mutations*) in the structure of the genetic material, and the passing on of these changes from ancestor to descendant. It is well dem-

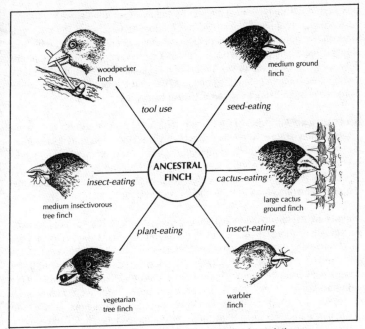

*Evidence advanced for the theory of adaptive radiation in evolution*

onstrated over geological time by the sequence of organisms preserved in the fossil record. There are two opposing schools of thought regarding the pattern and tempo of evolution. One view claims that species change gradually through time by slow directional change within a lineage, producing a long graded series of differing forms. The other view claims that species are relatively stable and long-lived in geological time, and that new species appear during outbursts of rapid formation. ▷ **Darwinism; genetics**

**exchange rates** The price at which one currency may be bought in terms of a unit of another currency — for example, so many dollars for a pound, or so many francs for a dollar. Until the mid-1970s, rates were fixed from time to time. Today, most rates are floating — in other words, determined by the ongoing supply and demand for the currency. An exception is the exchange rate mechanism of the European Monetary System. ▷ **devaluation; European Monetary System**

**excise tax** A tax levied on many goods and services by governments as a way of raising revenues; often called 'duty'. Best-known are the duties on tobacco, alcoholic drinks, and fuel, Value Added Tax in the UK, and Sales Tax in the USA. A distinction is drawn between excise tax, which is charged on goods produced or consumed within a country, and customs duty, which is charged on the import of foreign goods. Taxes in relation to certain kinds of activity are also included under the heading of excise, such as motor vehicle licences. ▷ **free trade; taxation**

**executive**   An individual or group which controls or directs an organization; often distinguished from those who are concerned with formulating the planning or theory behind the organization. An executive officer is one who holds a position of managerial responsibility, and actually carries out decisions. The senior executive officer in an organization is often called the **Chief Executive** — as in British local government.

**existentialism**   A term applied to several different 20th-century schools of thought, variously inspired by the Russian novelist Fyodor Dostoevsky (1821–81), the Danish theologian–philosopher Sören Kierkegaard (1813–55), and the German philosopher Friedrich Nietzsche (1844–1900). Its founders include the German philosophers Martin Heidegger (1889–1976) and Karl Jaspers (1883–1969). Existentialism grew amid dissatisfaction with generally accepted traditions and conventions, and previous attempts to explain life in impersonal terms. It in general considers what 'I' experience or witness of my existence in the world in which I find myself, and the ultimate decisions I am compelled to make as regards my character, my intentions, the world, and my perspectives on it. Heidegger emphasizes dread and awareness of death; Jaspers emphasizes 'boundary' situations in which ultimate decisions and discoveries are made. Sometimes these lead to new awareness of the meaning of old beliefs, as in Christian existentialism. New perspectives on psychology and problems of ethics have arisen, with considerable impact on literature, as seen in the work of the French playwright Albert Camus (1913–60) and of the novelist and philosopher Jean-Paul Sartre (1905–80). ▷ **philosophy**

**Expressionism**   A movement in art, architecture, and literature which aims to communicate the internal emotional realities of a situation, rather than its external 'realistic' aspect. The term was first used in Germany in 1911, but the roots of the movement can be traced to the artists Vincent Van Gogh and Paul Gauguin in the 1880s. Their influence was felt by the Norwegian Edvard Munch (1863–1944), and the Belgian James Ensor (1860–1949), but the full flowering of Expressionism occurred in Germany from about 1905 until suppressed by Hitler. In this approach, traditional ideas of beauty and proportion are disregarded, so that artists can express their feelings more strongly by means of distortion, jarring colours, and exaggerated linear rhythms. The movement was also influential in literature, especially in German theatre after World War 1. The use of dislocation and distortion in fiction and poetry (eg in the writing of Kafka and Joyce) has also been described as Expressionist. ▷ **architecture; literature; modern art; realism**

**extradition**   The removal of a person by a state in which that person is currently located to the territory of another state where the person has been convicted of a crime, or is said to have committed a crime. For example, if a known IRA terrorist were found living in France, the British government could apply for the extradition of the terrorist to the French government. The process is normally conducted through extradition treaties, which specify the cases and the procedures under which extradition will take place. There are many differences between countries. Treaties are normally restricted to more important crimes, but exclude political crimes.

**extraversion**   ▷ **introversion/extraversion**.

**Fabian Society**   A socialist group established in 1884 which took its name from the Roman general Fabius Cunctator, noted for his cautious military tactics. It adopts a gradualist approach to social reform, and sometimes 'Fabian' is applied to people who are not members of the Society but who believe in this kind of approach. The Society has remained a small select group, but has a close association with the British Labour Party, and has been a continual source of socialist ideas and arguments. Famous Fabians include the dramatist George Bernard Shaw (1856–1950) and the social reformer Sidney Webb (1859–1947). ▷ **socialism**

**factor VIII**   An enzyme (a protein molecule which causes a particular biochemical reaction) present in the blood, which controls the clotting process. Sufferers from haemophilia lack this factor, and their blood therefore lacks the capacity to clot. They are treated by intravenous administration of factor VIII that has been separated from fresh blood. This process carries the risk of transferring infections from the blood donor, such as AIDS. In the future, factor VIII may be produced using genetic engineering which will eliminate this risk. ▷ **AIDS; genetic engineering**

**factory farming**   An intensive form of livestock production, usually carried out indoors with strict control over the environment and over feeding regimes; also known as **battery farming**. The animals are kept for most of their lives in pens which severely restrict their movement. It is currently the predominant production technique for eggs, poultry meat, and pig meat. It is opposed by many people concerned about animal welfare, on the grounds that it is inhumane. ▷ **environmentalism**

**faith healing**   The curing or relieving of physical or mental ailments by the prayer of a healer relying on a higher source (usually, the power of God) working in response to faith. Known in several religions, the practice is now a major feature of Christian pentecostal and charismatic movements, often accompanied by the laying on of the healer's hands, usually during a service of worship. Critics argue that, even when apparently effective, it is difficult to ascribe healing to the action of the higher source, because so little is currently understood by medical science about the effects of psychological attitudes upon the body's biochemistry. ▷ **charismatic movement; Pentecostalism; placebo**

**fallacy**   In logic, a mistake made in a chain of reasoning. 'All cats are mammals, Fido is a mammal; therefore Fido is a cat' is a fallacy, easily confused with the valid 'All cats are mammals, Fido is a cat; therefore Fido is a mammal'. Fallacies and correct reasoning can be more difficult to demonstrate, when arguments become more complex and abstract. For example, 'Everything the Bible says is so; the Bible says that God exists; therefore God exists' is an example of a valid inference, but it commits the fallacy of *begging the question* if we accept the first premise only because we accept the conclusion. A list of classical fallacies has been produced in traditional logic, but faulty reasoning is so various and complex that there is no easy way of detecting them. ▷ **deduction; logic; premise**

**fascism**   A term applied to a variety of vehemently nationalistic and authoritarian movements that reached the peak of their influence in 1930–45. The name comes from the *fasces*, the bundles of rods which symbolized the authority of magistrates in ancient Rome; it is pronounced **fash**-*izm*. The original fascist movement was founded by the Italian dictator Benito Mussolini in 1919, and during the 1930s several such movements grew up in Europe, the most important being the German Nazi Party. In the UK, the British Union of Fascists was formed by Oswald Mosley in the 1930s. The central ideas of fascism are a belief in the supremacy of the chosen national group over other races, and the need to subordinate society to the leadership of a dictator who can increase national power without taking account of different interests. Fascism advocates the abolition of all institutions of democracy, and the suppression of sources of opposition such as trade unions. It is also strongly associated with militaristic and belligerent foreign policy stances. Since World War II its appeal has declined, although it survived in Spain under General Franco until the 1970s, and in some Latin American countries fascist-type governments have held office. The label 'fascist' is now often used as a term of abuse for anyone with extreme right-wing views. ▷ **authoritarianism; democracy**

**fast reactor**   ▷ **nuclear reactor**.

**fatalism**  A philosophical doctrine which maintains that the future is as unalterable as the past. It claims that what will be will be, no matter what a person may do to avert its happening. ▷ **philosophy**

**federalism**  A form of territorial political organization which aims to maintain national unity while allowing for regional diversity. This is achieved by distributing different constitutional powers to national and regional governments, giving a substantial role to each. Power is not distributed in a single hierarchy, but allocated among independent yet interacting centres; the national government is thus not in a position to dictate to regional governments, as could happen under a system of local government. The key features of federalism usually are: (at least) two tiers of government enjoying their own right of existence under the constitution; separate legislative and executive powers; separate sources of revenue; an umpire (normally the supreme court) to decide upon disputes between the different levels; and a two-chamber parliament which provides for representation in regional or state government. However, federalism can and does take a wide variety of forms: examples include the USA, Canada, Australia, and Germany. ▷ **devolution; executive; legislature**

**feedback**  ▷ **communication theory**.

**feminism**  A socio-political movement whose objective is equality of rights, status, and power for women and men. It has its roots in early 20th-century struggles for women's political emancipation (the suffragettes), but in its political scope it was broadened in the 1960s by the influence of radical left-wing beliefs, especially Marxism. This has led feminists to challenge both sexism and the capitalist system which is said to encourage patriarchy. Feminists are not necessarily 'anti-men', but against any social system which produces female subordination. ▷ **Marxism; sexism; women's liberation movement**

**field sports**  ▷ **blood sports**.

**figurative art**  Any form of visual art in which recognizable aspects of the world, especially the human figure, are represented, in however simplified, stylized, or distorted a form. A contrast is intended with abstract or *non-figurative art*. ▷ **abstract art; art**

**filibuster**  To hold up the passage of a bill in the US Senate, by organizing a continuous succession of long speeches in opposition. The term originally referred to 16th-century pirate adventurers, and developed a political sense only in the 19th century. If more than a third of the senators in a vote on the issue are opposed to closure of the debate, the filibuster cannot be prevented, and the bill is 'talked out'. The term is also more generally applied to any attempt to delay a decision or vote by exercising the right to talk on an issue. In the Senate, there is no limit on the time which may be devoted to debating a bill, and in 1957 one senator talked for over 24 hours in an attempt to obstruct a piece of civil-rights legislation. Many legislatures have procedures for curtailing this kind of obstructionism. ▷ **Senate**

**Financial Times–Stock Exchange Index** ▷ **FT–SE Index**.

**First World** ▷ **Three Worlds theory**.

**fiscal drag**  The effect of inflation on tax revenues. If tax allowances are not kept in line with inflation, individuals pay relatively higher amounts of tax, thus dragging down post-tax incomes. Consequently the demand for goods and services falls. ▷ **fiscal policy; inflation; taxation**

**fiscal policy**  The use by government of tax and its own spending to influence demand in the economy. When a government decides to lower taxes or raise public expenditure, the effect is to stimulate economic activity by increasing the demand for goods and services. There is a risk that this may lead to increasing inflation, or an increase in imports, resulting in a trade deficit. In contrast, a tightening of fiscal policy is where taxes are raised or public expenditure is reduced, in order to reduce overall demand. ▷ **balance of payments; inflation; supply and demand; taxation**

**flavouring agents** ▷ **additives**.

**flexitime**  An employment system used in the UK in which employees work an agreed number of hours per week, but can choose their starting and finishing times from within a limited range. For example, employees might arrive any time between 8 and 10am and leave any time between 4 and 6pm — as long as they achieve their agreed target in a given week. The system has proved especially popular in parts of the country where it enables people to avoid peaks of rush hour travel.

**fluoridation of water**  Water containing small amounts of fluorine (one part per million), whose regular consumption greatly reduces the incidence of caries of the teeth. Water supplies in many regions contain fluorine naturally in sufficient concentrations to increase the resistance of teeth to attack. This has led the authorities to recommend the addition of fluorine to reservoirs deficient in the element. While this is done in many instances, a vociferous minority of the population who object to adding 'chemicals' to water have succeeded in preventing it from becoming universal. ▷ **preventive medicine**

**fluorocarbons** ▷ **CFCs**.

**flying pickets**  ▷ **picketing**.

**forensic medicine**   The discipline which relates the practice of medicine to the law. There are several relevant laws authorized in the UK by Acts of Parliament: these include the provision of medicines, the supply of drugs of addiction, the supply of human tissues for surgical transplantation, the control of experiments on living animals, the mental health acts, and abortion. Forensic medicine concerns itself with the interpretation of these laws, and with their application by individual doctors. In addition, **forensic pathology** is concerned with the study of wounds, self-inflicted or caused by others, and with death in which other factors than natural causes might have played a part. It involves the identification of individuals (such as following a mass disaster), the detection of death from poisoning, and analysing sequences of DNA in body cells in possible criminal cases. ▷ **ballistics**

**fossil fuels**  ▷ **alternative energy**.

**Fourth World**  ▷ **Three Worlds theory**.

**fractals**   Geometrical entities characterized by basic patterns that are repeated at ever decreasing sizes. For example, trees describe an approximate fractal pattern, as the trunk divides into branches which further subdivide into smaller branches which ultimately subdivide into twigs; at each stage of division the pattern is a smaller version of the original. Fractals are not able to fill spaces, and hence are described as having fractional dimensions. They were devised in 1967 by French mathematician Benoît Mandelbrot (1924–  ), during a study of the length of the coastline of Britain. They are relevant to any system involving self-similarity repeated on diminishing scales, such as in the study of chaos, fork lightning, or the movement of oil through porous rock. They are also used in computer graphics. ▷ **chaos**

**franchise**   (economics) A licence to carry out some business activity, using the name, products, and know-how of the company giving the licence (the *franchisor*). The person or company receiving the licence (the *franchisee*) pays a licence fee and a percentage of the business done to the franchisor, and undertakes to conform to pre-set standards. This kind of working relationship is commonly found in fast-food restaurants.

**free trade**   An economic doctrine that trade between countries should not be controlled in any way; there should be no tariffs (special charges) or other barriers. The problems which result from tariffs were identified in 1776 by the Scottish economist and philosopher Adam Smith (1723–90), and the cause of free trade, taken up by Sir Robert Peel (1788–1850), led to the repeal of the Corn Laws in 1846. Since the 19th century, tariff barriers have become universal, but groups of countries may agree to lower or remove them, forming a *free-trade area*, as in the case of the European Economic Community. Under the General Agreement on Tariffs and Trade (GATT), concluded in 1947, many tariffs in the world have been reduced. ▷ **import quotas; laissez-faire**

**Freons** ▷ **CFCs**.

**fresco** An ancient technique for painting on walls, perfected in the 14th–16th centuries in Italy. It is difficult, and is nowadays uncommon. The wall is prepared with layers of plaster, sometimes as many as four, the penultimate being marked out with the artist's design (the underdrawing or *sinopia*). The final layer of lime-plaster (*intonaco*) is then laid, and, while it is still wet (*fresco* means 'fresh' in Italian), the artist works on this with a water-based paint. Just enough intonaco is laid for one day's work. The colours bond into the plaster by chemical action and are therefore very permanent, but they dry lighter, a factor the artist must bear in mind. Masters of fresco include the Italian artists Michelangelo (1475–1564) and Raphael (1483–1520) ▷ **art**

**Friends, Religious Society of** A Christian sect founded by George Fox (1624–91) and others in mid-17th-century England, and formally organized in 1667; members are popularly known as **Quakers**, possibly because of Fox's injunction 'to quake at the word of the Lord'. Persecution led William Penn to establish a Quaker colony (Pennsylvania) in 1682. Belief in the 'inner light', a living contact with the divine Spirit, is the basis of its meetings for worship, where Friends gather in silence until moved by the Spirit to speak. They emphasize simplicity in all things, and are active reformers promoting tolerance, justice, and peace. Today most meetings have programmed orders of worship, though meetings based on silence (unprogrammed) still prevail in the UK and parts of the USA. ▷ **Christianity**

**FT–SE Index** A UK share index which records changes in the prices of shares of 100 leading British companies; it is an abbreviation of **Financial Times–Stock Exchange Index**, and is popularly known as 'Footsie'. It has been in operation since 1984, when it started with a notional value of 1000. The level of this index at the close of a day's trading is routinely reported in the media. ▷ **shares**

**functionalism** (art and architecture) The theory, rooted in Greek philosophy, that beauty should be identified with functional efficiency. Occasionally discussed in the 18th and 19th centuries, it became fashionable in the 1920s and 1930s, especially under the influence of the German artistic movement known as the Bauhaus. In architecture, the form of a building was to be determined by the function it was meant to fulfil — as in the famous definition of a house as a machine for living in. ▷ **aesthetics; architecture**

**functionalism**   (sociology) A theory widely accepted in social anthropology and sociology in the mid-20th century, which states that particular social institutions, customs, and beliefs all have a part to play in maintaining a social system. The central notion is that a community or society has an enduring structure, its parts fitting together to form a single integrated system. In social theory, the approach was dominated by American  sociologists, such as Talcott Parsons (1902–79) and Robert Merton (1910–   ). It is now generally thought that functionalism offers too static a view of social organization, and understates the conflicts which are likely to be present in the life of any community. The strength of functionalist theory was that it directed attention to the relationships between the institutions in a society. ▷ **anthropology; sociology; structuralism**

**fundamentalism**   A theological tendency seeking to preserve what are thought to be the essential doctrines ('fundamentals') of the Christian faith. The term was originally used of the conservative US Protestant movement in the 1920s, characterized by a literal interpretation of the Bible. Examples of fundamentalist beliefs include the second coming of Christ and the existence of an eternal hell. It was revived as part of conservative Christian movements in the late 20th century. Generally, it is any theological position opposed to liberalism, or to scientific thought which seems to be in conflict with the Bible (eg evolutionary theory). ▷ **conservatism; evangelicalism; Moral Majority**

**further education**   A level of educational provision offered in many countries, often distinguished from **higher education**. Further education is post-school education leading, usually, to qualifications at sub-degree level, though it may not lead to any award at all but simply be taken for its own sake. A great deal is of a vocational nature, and involves study and practical work related to someone's job; but it can also be non-vocational, and take place in informal settings like the home. Higher education, by contrast, takes place in institutions where most or all of the work is at degree level or above. ▷ **tertiary education; vocational education**

**game theory**   The branch of mathematics that analyses a range of problems involving decision-making. Although often illustrated by games of chance, there are important applications to military strategy, economics, and other applied sciences. Game theory was developed in this century, principally by French mathematician Emile Borel (1871–1956) and US mathematician Johann von Neumann (1903–57). Games involving one, two, or more players are distinguished, as in patience, chess, and roulette respectively. Game theory analyses the strategies each player uses to max-imize the chance of winning, and attempts to predict outcomes.

**gas-cooled reactor** ▷ **nuclear reactor**.

**Gaullists** Members of the French political party, the *Rassemblement pour la République* ('Rally for the Republic') or RPR, formed in 1976 by Jacques Chirac (1932– ). Its programmes are based on the doctrine developed by President de Gaulle in 1958–69. Nationalistic in character, Gaullists emphasize the need for strong government, especially in relations with the European Economic Community and foreign powers such as the USA. ▷ **nationalism**

**Gaza Strip** A strip of land in the Middle East, some 50 km/30 ml long, about 200 sq km/78 sq ml in area, bounded north-west by the Mediterranean

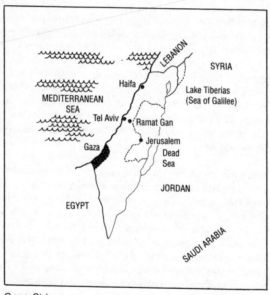

Gaza Strip

Sea. Its chief town is Gaza. It was the only part of Palestine held by the Egyptians after the Arab–Israeli War of 1948–9. Since 1967 it has been an Israeli-occupied district under military administration, and a continual source of political tension, as it contains many Palestinian refugee camps. ▷ **West Bank**

**gender** The social expression of physiological differences between men and women. It refers to social behaviour which is deemed to be appropriate to 'masculine' or 'feminine' roles, and which is learned through the process of becoming a part of society. Sex is a biological matter, but gender is socially and culturally constructed. ▷ **sexism**

**general relativity**   A theory of gravity deriving almost entirely from the work of the physicist Albert Einstein (1879–1955), presented in 1916. It supersedes Newton's theory of gravitation, replacing the Newtonian concept of instantaneous action at a distance via the gravitational field (as suggested by the fall of an apple from a tree) with a distortion of space-time due to the presence of mass. For example, the Earth moves round the Sun because of the distortion of space-time by the Sun's greater mass. An analogy represents space-time as a rubber sheet distorted by a heavy ball representing the Sun; a smaller ball rolling by, representing a planet, will tend to fall into this depression, apparently attracted. General relativity is supported by experiments which measure the bending of star light due to the presence of the Sun's mass, and also by the nature of Mercury's orbit. Other predictions include black holes and the expansion of the universe.
▷ **cosmology; special relativity**

**genetic engineering**   The formation of new combinations of heritable material. Nucleic acid molecules, produced artificially or biologically outside the cell, are inserted into a carrier (such as a virus) so as to allow their incorporation into a host organism in which they do not naturally occur, but in which they are capable of continued propagation. Genetic engineering has many uses. Particular DNA sequences from an organism can be produced in large amounts, and with very great purity, so that the structure of specific DNA regions can be analysed. Biological compounds can be produced industrially (eg human insulin, vaccines). Ultimately it will be possible to identify genes responsible for hereditary disease and replace them with normal DNA sequences.

The implications of genetic engineering have led to considerable public debate, and in most countries there is government control over work using these techniques. There is also some public fear that the presence of foreign genetic elements may adversely affect the normal functions of cells. To counter this, physical and biological safety measures are used to minimize the risk of spread of a host organism with foreign genetic elements inserted.
▷ **DNA; ethics; genetics**

**genetics**   The modern science of heredity. It originated with the discovery by Austrian biologist Gregor Mendel (1822–84) that observable hereditary characteristics are determined by factors transmitted without change and in predictable fashion from one generation to the next. Initially slow to develop, its pace increased rapidly during this century, and today it is one of the most vigorous areas of science. Genetics occupies a unique

| Eon | Era | Period | Epoch | Million years before present | Geological events | Sea life | Land life |
|-----|-----|--------|-------|------------------------------|-------------------|----------|-----------|
| Phanerozoic | Cenozoic | Quaternary | Holocene | | Glaciers recede. Sea level rises. Climate becomes more equable. | As now. | Forests flourish again. Humans acquire agriculture and technology. |
| | | | Pleistocene | 0.01 | Widespread glaciers melt periodically causing seas to rise and fall. | As now. | Many plant forms perish. Small mammals abundant. Primitive humans established. |
| | | Tertiary | Pliocene | 2.0 / 5.1 | Continents and oceans adopting their present form. Present climatic distribution established. Ice caps develop. | Giant sharks extinct. Many fish varieties. | Some plants and mammals die out. Primates flourish. |
| | | | Miocene | 24.6 | Seas recede further. European and Asian land masses join. Heavy rain causes massive erosion. Red Sea opens. | Bony fish common. Giant sharks. | Grasses widespread. Grazing mammals become common. |
| | | | Oligocene | 38.0 | Seas recede. Extensive movements of earth's crust produce new mountains (eg Alpine-Himalayan chain). | Crabs, mussels, and snails evolve. | Forests diminish. Grasses appear. Pachyderms, canines and felines develop. |
| | | | Eocene | 54.9 | Mountain formation continues. Glaciers common in high mountain ranges. Greenland separates. Australia separates. | Whales adapt to sea. | Large tropical jungles. Primitive forms of modern mammals established. |
| | | | Paleocene | 65 | Widespread subsidence of land. Seas advance again. Considerable volcanic activity. Europe emerges. | Many reptiles become extinct. | Flowering plants widespread. First primates. Giant reptiles extinct. |
| | Mesozoic | Cretaceous | Late / Early | 97.5 | Swamps widespread. Massive alluvial deposition. Continuing limestone formation. S America separates from Africa. India, Africa and Antarctica separate. | Turtles, rays, and now-common fish appear. | Flowering plants established. Dinosaurs become extinct. |
| | | Jurassic | Malm / Dogger / Lias | 144 / 163 / 188 | Seas advance. Much river formation. High mountains eroded. Limestone formation. N America separates from Africa. Central Atlantic begins to open. | Reptiles dominant. | Early flowers. Dinosaurs dominant. Mammals still primitive. First birds. |
| | | Triassic | Late / Middle / Early | 213 / 231 / 243 / 248 | Desert conditions widespread. Hot climate gradually becomes warm and wet. Break up of Gondwanaland into continents. | Icthyosaurs, flying fish, and crustaceans appear. | Ferns and conifers thrive. First mammals, dinosaurs, and flies. |

| | | Epoch/Stage | Age | Geology | Animal life | Plant/insect life |
|---|---|---|---|---|---|---|
| | | Early | | movements form mountains. Glaciation in southern hemisphere. | | insect varieties. |
| Paleozoic | Carboniferous | Pennsylvanian | 286 | Sea-beds rise to form new land areas. Enormous swamps. Partly-rotted vegetation forms coal. | Amphibians and sharks abundant. | Extensive evergreen forests. Reptiles breed on land. Some insects develop wings. |
| | | Mississippian | 320 | | | |
| | Devonian | Late | 360 | Collision of continents causing mountain formation (Appalachians, Caledonides and Urals). Sea deeper but narrower. Climatic zones forming. Iapetus ocean closed. | Fish abundant. Primitive sharks. First amphibians. | Leafy plants. Some invertebrates adapt to land. First insects. |
| | | Middle | 374 | | | |
| | | Early | 387 | | | |
| | Silurian | Pridoli | 408 | New mountain ranges form. Sea level varies periodically. Extensive shallow sea over the Sahara. | Large vertebrates. | First leafless land plants. |
| | | Ludlow | 414 | | | |
| | | Wenlock | 421 | | | |
| | | Llandovery | 428 | | | |
| | Ordovician | Ashgill | 438 | Shore lines still quite variable. Increasing sedimentation. Europe and N America moving together. | First vertebrates. Coral reefs develop. | None. |
| | | Caradoc | 448 | | | |
| | | Llandeilo | 458 | | | |
| | | Llanvirn | 468 | | | |
| | | Arenig | 478 | | | |
| | | Tremadoc | 488 | | | |
| | Cambrian | Merioneth | 505 | Much volcanic activity, and long periods of marine sedimentation. | Shelled invertebrates. Trilobites. | None. |
| | | St David's | 525 | | | |
| | | Caerfai | 540 | | | |
| Precambrian / Proterozoic | Vendian | | 590 | Shallow seas advance and retreat over land areas. Atmosphere uniformly warm. | Seaweed. Algae and invertebrates. | None. |
| | Riphean | Late | 650 | Intense deformation and metamorphism. | Earliest marine life and fossils. | None. |
| | | Middle | 900 | | | |
| | | Early | 1300 | | | |
| | Early Proterozoic | | 1600 | Shallow shelf seas. Formation of carbonate sediments and 'red beds'. | First appearance of stromatolites. | None. |
| Archaean | Archaean (Azoic) | | 2500 | Banded iron formations. Formation of the earth's crust and oceans. | None. | None. |
| | | | 4600 | | | |

*Geological time scale*

position, for its principles and mechanisms extend throughout almost all biology. It ties together all branches that deal with individual and population variation, and gives a unifying core at all levels — the molecular structure of cells and tissues, the development of individuals, and the evolution of populations. Today the mechanisms of genetics are being applied to make, in the laboratory, substances formerly obtainable only from organisms (eg vaccines, hormones), and genetic errors responsible for disease may eventually be correctable by such procedures. ▷ **DNA; genetic engineering; molecular biology**

**genre painting**   Realistic scenes from everyday life, typically on a small scale, as produced by such Dutch 17th-century masters as Jan Vermeer (1632–75) — an example is his *Young woman reading a letter* (painted in about 1662). The term may be applied to any period, however, and in fact this kind of painting flourished in 19th-century Britain, largely due to the popularity of scenes of Scottish village life produced by David Wilkie (1785–1841). ▷ **art**

**geochemistry**   A branch of geology concerned with the abundances of elements and their isotopes in the Earth, and the processes that affect their distribution. It also subsumes the study of chemical processes in the evolution of the Earth and the Solar System. Commercial applications include geochemical prospecting, in which the chemical analysis of soils, sediments, and stream waters is used to detect concealed ore deposits. ▷ **geology; isotopes**

**geology**   The science of the Earth as a whole: its origin, structure, composition, processes, and history. It includes several distinct subdisciplines, such as mineralogy (the study of the properties and distribution of minearals) and stratigraphy (the study of sequences of layers of rock). It also deals with the study of the structure of the Earth's crust and the movements which take place there (*tectonics*) and the study of the geological time scale — the major periods of time in the Earth's history, classified into eons, eras, periods, and epochs. ▷ **earth sciences; geochemistry**

**glasnost**   (Russ 'speaking aloud') A term describing the changes in attitude on the part of leaders of the Soviet Union since 1985 under Mikhail Gorbachev (1931–   ). The result has been a greater degree of openness both within Soviet society and in its relations with foreign powers. It is now possible to engage in public debate on matters which previously would have been considered too sensitive, including criticism of the authorities and the publication of controversial ideas in literature, the media, and the arts. A recent example is the criticism within the Soviet Union which followed the nuclear accident at Chernobyl in 1986. ▷ **communism; detente; perestroika**

**global warming**  ▷ **greenhouse effect**.

**God**  A supernatural being or power, the object of worship. In some world religions (eg Christianity, Judaism, Islam) there is one God only, who is transcendent, all-powerful, and related to the cosmos as creator: this is **monotheism** (from the Greek for 'one god'). In other religions (eg Hinduism, Classical Greek and Roman religions, and primitive religions) many gods may be recognized, with individual gods having particular properties and powers: this is **polytheism** (from the Greek for 'many gods'). In the Judaeo-Christian tradition, God is believed to have revealed himself in history through the life and response of the people of Israel; and, in the Christian tradition, supremely and finally in the life, death, and resurrection of Jesus of Nazareth, all as testified to in the scriptures of the Old and New Testaments. The conviction that Jesus stood in a unique relation to God led to the development in Christian thought of the Trinitarian understanding, whereby the one God is seen in terms of three persons (Father, Son, and Holy Spirit) of one substance.

In the mainstream Western tradition, influenced by Classical Greek philosophy as well as Christianity, God is conceived as 'being itself' or 'pure actuality' (St Thomas Aquinas). He is said to be absolute, infinite, eternal, immutable (incapable of change), incomprehensible (that is, unable to be comprehended by human thought), all-powerful (omnipotent), all-wise (omniscient), all-good (omni-benevolent), and everywhere present (omnipresent). From the time of the ancient Greeks, philosophers have tried to prove the existence of God by reason alone. While the general view seems now to be that none of these arguments is totally compelling, discusssion in the 20th century about the merits of individual arguments has continued unabated. Attempts to disprove the existence of God or to show concepts of God to be incoherent have likewise been generally unpersuasive. ▷ **agnosticism; atheist; Christianity; deism; Hinduism; Islam; Judaism; religion; theology; Trinity**

**Gothic**  A term first used by Renaissance artists to mean 'barbaric', referring to the non-classical styles of the Middle Ages. (The allusion is to the Goths, who invaded the Roman Empire.) Since the 19th century, it has been in standard use with reference to European art roughly of the 12th to the 15th century — as seen, for example, in the work of the Italian artist Gentile da Fabriano (c.1370–c.1427). Gothic architecture is a style from the same period, characterized by such features as lofty interiors, large window areas with stained glass, pointed arches, rib vaults, and flying buttresses, as seen in the Cathedrals of Notre Dame in Paris and at Chartres. In the late 18th and early 19th century, there was a revival of this style, seen especially in churches, but also in hotels, town halls, railway stations, and other prominent buildings. The parliament buildings in London provide a well-known example. In literature, the 'Gothic novel' refers to a type of

*Salisbury Cathedral*

narrative fiction, popular in the late 18th century, which relies on mystery and terror, and licenses extreme emotions. Examples include *The Mysteries of Udolpho* (1794) by Ann Radcliffe and *The Monk* (1796) by Matthew Gregory Lewis. It influenced such later writers as Edgar Allen Poe (1809–49), and of course Bram Stoker's *Dracula* (1897). ▷ **architecture; art; literature; Renaissance**

**greenhouse effect**   A process of planetary warming of the atmosphere, which results from the absorption of infrared radiation. Radiant energy arrives at the planetary surface mainly as visible light from the Sun, which is then re-emitted by the surface at infrared wavelengths as heat. Carbon dioxide and water vapour in the atmosphere absorb this infrared radiation and behave as a blanket — somewhat like a greenhouse — with the net effect that atmospheric temperatures rise. On Earth, the burning of fossil fuels and large-scale deforestation enhance the effect, so that there is likely to be a gradual increase in mean air temperature of several degrees, with the consequent melting of polar ice and a rise in mean sea level. Experimental models predict global temperature increases of between 1°C and 5°C by 2050, but there are many uncertainties about possible effects. It is also likely that global rainfall patterns will shift away from the sub-tropical areas towards higher latitudes, so disrupting present agricultural patterns.

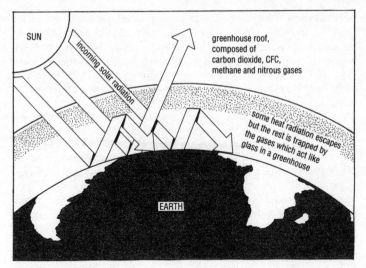

*Greenhouse effect*

(The term 'greenhouse' could be misleading, since the mechanism by which glasshouses provide warming is mainly due to slowing the process of convection.) ▷ **acid rain; CFCs; fossil fuels**

**Greens**   A label applied to members of political parties or movements which oppose many of the ecological and environmental effects resulting from modern technological and economic policies, and base their demands on a set of post-materialist values. The movement as a whole contains such groups as Friends of the Earth and Greenpeace. Political parties emerged in the West in the 1970s, when they had only limited electoral success. However, they made considerable political gains in the 1989 European elections. ▷ **conservation; ecology; environment; materialism**

**gross domestic product (GDP)**   A measure of the income or output of a nation, calculated in any of three ways. The *output method* is the total of selling prices less the cost of inputs. The *income method* is the total of wages, rents, dividends, interest, and profits. The *expenditure method* is the national expenditure on goods and services (known as 'GDP at factor cost'), less indirect taxes and subsidies. The **gross national product (GNP)** is similarly calculated, but includes residents' income from economic activity overseas. ▷ **balance of payments**

**gross national product (GNP)**   ▷ **gross domestic product**.

*h*  **habitat loss**  The loss of distinctive areas which provide breeding and range territories for plants and wildlife. Destruction and disturbance by human activity is a major threat to wild species. Many areas of wilderness have been modified into artificial landscapes of settlement, agriculture, and industry. There is increased intrusion into remote areas for exploitation of timber, oil, and mineral resources. ▷ **conservation; desertification**

**hacker**  A computer user who communicates with other remote computers usually via the telephone network. In recent years, the term has acquired a pejorative sense, referring to those who access remote computers without permission, often obtaining access to confidential information of a personal or business nature. The position of the hacker in law is unclear.

**half-life**  The average time taken for a group of atoms in a radioactive isotope to decay to half their original number. It varies from seconds to thousands of years. The half-life of plutonium-239 is 24000 years; for helium-6 it is 0.8 seconds. The term has now taken on an extended meaning, referring to the average time it takes for any general process to happen — such as the time it takes to sell half a certain number of goods. ▷ **isotopes**

**happening**  A modern art 'event', or performance; often planned but sometimes 'spontaneous'. Happenings (so-called since about 1960) need not take place in a gallery but may occur in the street, or anywhere, and usually involve spectator participation. The event itself, rather than any finished, saleable product, is what is thought to be important. A group of mime artists, for example, might stand frozen on a street corner, along with a notice which asks passers-by to move their head and limbs into any positions. ▷ **art; Body art**

**Hare Krishna movement**  A religious movement founded in the USA in 1965 by His Divine Grace Swami Prabhupada as The International Society for Krishna Consciousness; it is pronounced *ha-ree krish-nah*, the words being Sanskrit for 'Hail Krishna'. Krishna, according to Hindu tradition, is the eighth incarnation, in human form, of the deity Vishnu. A great hero and ruler, his story is told in the Hindu epic, the Mahabharata. The movement promotes human well-being by promoting God consciousness based on the ancient Vedic texts of India. It is one of the best known of the new religious movements coming from the East, largely as a result of saffron-robed young people gathered in town centres chanting a mantra, from which their popular name is derived. In their pursuit of spiritual advancement devotees practise vegetarianism, do not use intoxicants, do not gamble, and are celibate apart from procreation within marriage. ▷ **Hinduism; religion**

**hazardous substances**  Generally human-made substances, potentially damaging to health, which result in contamination and pollution of the environment if they are disposed of incorrectly. They include poisonous substances (such as might be produced in a factory's waste matter), heavy metal pollutants (such as lead and mercury), and radioactive waste produced in the generation of nuclear power. The disposal of hazardous substances is a source of environmental concern in many countries. ▷ **pollution; radioactive waste; waste disposal**

**health service** ▷ **National Health Service**.

**Heisenberg uncertainty principle** ▷ **uncertainty principle**.

**heresy** Originally, any false doctrine, or the formal denial of doctrine, which is defined as part of the Catholic or universal faith. For example, the Monophysites of the fourth and fifth centuries denied that Christ had both a divine and a human nature — a view which was condemned by Pope Leo in 449. If consciously adhered to, a heretic will be formally expelled from the Church (*excommunicated*), and in certain countries heresy has been punishable as a crime. Total heresy or the rejection of all faith is termed **apostasy**. In more recent times, the term has been applied to any opinion which runs contrary to generally accepted belief. ▷ **Christianity**

**hermeneutics** The theory of the interpretation and understanding of texts; pronounced *her-muh-***nyoo***-tiks*. Though its origins lie in ancient Greek philosophy, hermeneutics received fresh impetus in 18th-century discussions of the problems of biblical interpretation. How is it possible to understand the written discourse of different cultures and ages? The discussion has since expanded to embrace all aspects of the understanding of texts and entered many fields, including literary theory, the social sciences, social philosophy, and aesthetics. ▷ **allegory; deconstruction; rhetoric**

**heuristic** Any set of rules whose application to a complex problem will tend to yield satisfactory if not optimal results (in contrast to an algorithm). 'Control the centre of the board' is a heuristic for playing chess. Some heuristics can be made precise enough to be programmed into computers. ▷ **algorithm**

**hidden curriculum** A term developed by sociologists of education to describe the unwritten, informal code of conduct to which children are expected to conform in the classroom. Children are said to be rewarded not only for learning their subject curriculum but appearing to do so with enthusiasm, alertness, and deference to and respect for authority. In this way education imparts not only formal knowledge but an understanding of how to act 'properly' in wider society. More broadly, the term has been used to refer to any of the skills and intuitions which teachers expect children to pick up, without being formally taught, as learning takes place — such as how to organize time for revision. ▷ **sociology**

**higher education** ▷ **further education**.

**Hillsborough disaster**    The worst disaster in English sporting history, which took place at the Hillsborough football stadium in Sheffield, England on 15 April 1989: 95 Liverpool fans died and 400 people were injured at the FA Cup semi-final match between Liverpool and Nottingham Forest. The tragedy occurred when police opened a main gate into the terraced area to relieve pressures caused by a build-up of people at the entrance allocated to Liverpool fans. This caused a flood into the packed terraces, and people were crushed at the perimeter fences.

**Hinduism**    The Western term for a religious tradition developed over several thousand years and intertwined with the history and social system of India. Hinduism does not trace its origins to a particular founder, has no prophets, no set creed, and no particular institutional structure. It empha-sizes the right way of living (*dharma*) rather than a set of doctrines, and thus embraces diverse religious beliefs and practices. There are significant variations between different regions of India, and even from village to village. There are differences in the deities worshipped, the scriptures used, and the festivals observed. Hindus may be theists or non-theists, revere one or more gods or goddesses, or no god at all, and represent the ultimate in personal (eg Brahma) or impersonal (eg Brahman) terms.

   Common to most forms of Hinduism is the idea of reincarnation or transmigration. The term *samsara* refers to the process of birth and rebirth continuing for life after life. The particular form and condition (pleasant or unpleasant) of rebirth are the result of *karma*, the law by which the consequences of actions within one life are carried over into the next and influence its character. The ultimate spiritual goal of Hindus is *mohsha*, or release from the cycle of samsara.

   There is a rich and varied religious literature, and no specific text is regarded as uniquely authoritative. The earliest extant writings come from the Vedic period (about 1200–500BC), and are known collectively as the Veda. Later (about 500BC–AD500) came the religious law books, which were the bases of the Indian caste system. To this was added the great epics, the Ramayana and the Mahabharata. The latter includes one of the most influential Hindu scriptures, the Bhagavadgita.

   Brahma, Vishnu, and Shiva are the chief gods of Hinduism, and together form a triad (the *Trimurti*). There are numerous lesser deities, including the goddesses Maya and Lakshmi. Hinduism is concerned with the realization of religious values in every part of life, yet there is a great emphasis upon the performance of complex and demanding rituals under the supervision of Brahman priests and teachers. Pilgrimage to local and regional sites is common, and there is an annual cycle of local, regional and all-Indian festivals. In 1990 there were over 700 million Hindus worldwide. ▷ **reincarnation; religion**

**holistic medicine**   An approach to medical treatment based on the theory that living creatures and the non-living environment function together as a single integrated whole (*holism*). The approach is based on the notion that, when individual components of a system are put together to produce a larger functional unit, qualities develop which are not predictable from the behaviour of the individual components. The holistic approach to medicine insists not only on the study of individual disease but also on the study of the response of people to their disease physically, psychologically, and socially. All aspects of an illness are taken into account, such as the effect of the illness on personal relations, the family, work, and the patient's emotional well-being. ▷ **alternative medicine**

**Holocaust**   The attempt by Nazi Germany to systematically destroy European Jews. From the inception of the Nazi regime in 1933 Jews were deprived of civil rights, persecuted, physically attacked, imprisoned, and murdered. With the gradual conquest of Europe by Germany, the death toll increased, and a meeting at Wannsee in January 1942 made plans for the so-called 'final solution'. Jews were herded into concentration camps, slave labour camps, and extermination camps. By the end of the war in 1945, more than six million Jews had been murdered out of a total Jewish population of eight million in those countries occupied by the Nazis. Of these the largest number, three million, were from Poland. Other minorities (gypsies, various religious sects, homosexuals) were also subject to Nazi atrocities, but the major genocide was against the Jewish people. ▷ **Judaism**

**home rule**   The handing down of certain legislative powers and administrative functions, previously exercised by a higher authority, to an elected body within a particular geographical area; usually put forward as an alternative to separatism. It was illustrated by the government of Northern Ireland until 1972 when Stormont, the Northern Ireland Parliament, was abolished. Since the early 1970s in the UK, for political movements such as the Scottish National Party and Irish republicans, home rule has tended to mean the same as separatism. ▷ **devolution; separatism**

**homeopathy**   A practice of medicine devised in the early 19th century by German physician Christian Hahnemann (1755–1843), based on the notions that 'like cures like' and that drug activity can be enhanced by dilution. A drug which in large doses would induce particular symptoms in a healthy individual is used after a series of dilutions to treat a sick individual suffering such symptoms. There is no scientific evidence that the theory of homeopathy is correct. ▷ **alternative medicine**

**House of Commons**   The lower, and effectively the ruling, chamber of the UK parliament. It contains 650 elected members, each representing a single constituency. The Commons is elected for a maximum period of five years, though the prime minister may call an election at any time within that period. The government is drawn from the party that wins the majority of seats. The ascendancy of the House of Commons over the House of Lords was established by the late 16th century, and was completed with the passage of the Parliament Acts of 1911 and 1949. The Commons is dominated by a disciplined party system, which means that governments are generally assured of a majority when votes are taken. ▷ **bicameral system; House of Lords**

**House of Lords**   The non-elected house of the UK legislature. Its membership includes hereditary peers and life peers (including judicial members — the *Lords of Appeal in Ordinary*); also the two archbishops and certain bishops of the Church of England. Its total membership is over 1 000, and its Speaker is the Lord Chancellor. The House can no longer veto bills passed by the House of Commons, with the exception of a bill to prolong the duration of a parliament — though its influence in altering legislation was notable during the 1980s. Its functions are mainly deliberative, its authority being based on the expertise of its membership. The House of Lords also constitutes the most senior court in the UK. Appeals heard by the House are confined to matters of law. ▷ **bicameral system; House of Commons; legislature; parliament**

**House of Representatives**   In the USA, one of the two chambers of the legislature, in which, under the constitution, all legislative power is vested. The 435 members of the House are elected from single member constituencies, and serve two-year terms. Their distribution among the states is based on population figures, with each state having at least one representative. All revenue bills originate in the House. ▷ **Congress; Senate**

**humanism**   Historically, a movement that arose with the Italian Renaissance, emphasizing the liberation of humanity from subservience to the medieval church and state. Humanists looked back to the achievements of classical Greece and Rome, and to the contemporary achievements in arts and science. It can be seen in the writing of such thinkers as the Dutch scholar Desiderius Erasmus (c.1466–1536) and the English statesman and scholar Thomas More (1478–1535). More generally, humanism refers to any position which stresses the importance of persons, typically in contrast with something else, such as God, inanimate nature, or totalitarian societies. In the 20th century — in notable contrast with its earlier meaning — humanism commonly implies atheism and the rejection of (especially

Christian) religious values. ▷ **atheism; classicism; Renaissance**

**humanities**  The cultural branches of learning — notably literature, languages, philosophy, history, theology, and the arts. The term came into use during the Renaissance, and enables a useful distinction to be drawn with the natural and social sciences. ▷ **Renaissance; social science**

**human rights**  A concept deriving from the doctrine of natural rights, which holds that individuals, by virtue of their humanity, possess fundamental rights beyond those prescribed in law. Examples include the right to life, liberty, and the security of the person, the right to own property, freedom from slavery and torture, freedom of movement and residence, and freedom of thought and religion. First formally incorporated into the US Declaration of Independence (1776), a Declaration of the Rights of Man and the Citizen was adopted by the French National Assembly (1789). Most written constitutions contain a bill of rights. Although having no legal standing, the United Nation's General Assembly adopted a Universal Declaration of Human Rights in 1948, detailing individual and social rights and freedoms, followed in 1953 by the European Convention on Human Rights. The European Court of Human Rights was established within this framework.
▷ **Amnesty International; civil rights; constitution**

**hydroelectric power (HEP)**  Electricity generated using the potential energy of water. It is a renewable energy source with considerable potential worldwide, although it accounts for only a small proportion of the world's energy needs. It is especially important in countries with scarce oil, coal, or gas reserves. A major source of energy in countries such as Norway, Switzerland, and Sweden, it is also important in developing countries. The

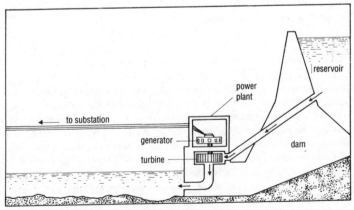

*The generation of electricity by hydroelectric power*

world's largest HEP scheme, at Itaipu on the Parana River, will supply 20% of Brazil's electricity needs and a large proportion of those of Paraguay. ▷ **alternative energy; renewable resources**

*i* **ideology**   A term first coined by the philosopher Destutt de Tracy (1754–1836) to refer to the study of ideas — a study which would reveal the underlying prejudices and biases in people's thought. The word is now typically used to describe any set of beliefs and attitudes that support particular interests. For example, an ideology of revenge can motivate a sectarian terrorist group; an ideology of profit can motivate a business organization. The prevailing ideologies in society are likely to reflect and justify interests of the dominant groups — such as in politics or religion. Ideological beliefs are usually felt to be in some way exaggerations or distortions of reality. To continue the example, 'They're only interested in profits' would not usually be an adequate account of the motives of a business. ▷ **class; Marxism; racism; sociology**

**imagery**   Figurative language; the illustration and emphasis of an idea by analogies and parallels of different kinds, to make it more concrete and objective. Images may be explicit in the form of a simile ('As cold as any stone') or implicit in the form of a metaphor ('You blocks, you stones, you worse than senseless things'). They may be incidental, or form part of a system of imagery running through a work. Imagery is often thought of as mainly visual, but this is far from being the case: images often invoke the other senses (smell, taste, touch, hearing) individually or combined. Imagery is a recognized grace of poetry, but also plays an important part in much prose writing. ▷ **allegory; literature; Symbolism**

**immigration**   ▷ **migration**.

**imperialism**   The extension of the power of a state through the acquisition, normally by force, of other territories, which are then subject to rule by the imperial power. Many suggest that the motivation behind imperialism is economic, through the exploitation of cheap labour and resources, and the opening up of new markets. Others suggest that non-economic factors are involved, including nationalism, racism, and the pursuit of international power. The main era of imperialism was the 1880s to 1914, when many European powers sought to gain territories in Africa and Asia. Imperialism of the form associated with the establishment of European empires has in large measure disappeared, but the term is now often applied to any attempts by developed countries to interfere in underdeveloped countries. There is also increasing interest in the idea of **neo-colonialism**, where certain countries are subjugated by the economic power of developed countries, rather than through direct rule. ▷ **associated state; indirect rule**

**import quotas**   A means of restricting imports of a commodity or product by limiting the quantity that can be imported in a particular period. The aim is to protect domestic industry and preserve foreign currency reserves. They were extensively imposed in the UK in the late 1940s and 1950s, but have now been eliminated for many goods. ▷ **free trade**

**Impressionism**   A modern art movement which started in France in the 1860s; the name, coined by a hostile critic, was taken from Claude Monet's picture, *Impression: sunrise* (1872). The Impressionists, who included the French artists Camille Pissarro (1830–1903) and Pierre Renoir (1841–1919), rejected the dark tones of 19th-century studio painting, set up their easels out-of-doors, and tried to capture the brilliant effects of sunlight on water, trees and fields, and pretty girls. Impressionist pictures are typically bright and cheerful, and have been enormously popular with 20th-century art-lovers and collectors. ▷ **modern art**

**income tax**   A major means for governments to raise revenue, consisting of a levy on wages and salaries, often set as a fixed percentage of income. Low incomes are usually not taxable, and higher levels of income often attract very high tax rates. The rates of income tax can vary from time to time, and are fixed by a government in its budgetary statement. Employers are usually obliged to collect the tax directly before paying wages to their staff. ▷ **budget; taxation**

**incomes policy**   ▷ **prices and incomes policy**.

**index-linking**   Adjusting the price of goods, the interest on investments, or the level of salaries and wages, upwards or downwards in proportion to rises or falls in the retail price index. The strategy is popular in times of high inflation. ▷ **inflation; retail price index**

**indirect rule**   A form of colonial rule especially characteristic of British rule in Africa during the years between the two World Wars. In general terms it involved the use of existing political structures, leaders, and local organs of authority. Local political elites enjoyed considerable autonomy, although they still had to keep in accord with the interests of the colonial power. Indirect rule was adopted on grounds of its cheapness, and to allow for independent cultural development, but it was increasingly criticized for its failure to modernize colonial administration, and was gradually given up after 1945. ▷ **imperialism**

**induction**   The notion that we arrive at general conclusions by way of a series of observations. The observations will make the generalization more likely to be true. There is no guarantee of generality, because a counter-instance is always possible, and scientific generalizations are never certain.

Putting this in the terms of logic: it is always possible for the conclusion of an induction to be false even if the premisses are true. 'The Sun has always risen in the past; therefore it will rise tomorrow' illustrates the point. ▷ **deduction; empiricism; scientific method**

**industrial action**　The activities of a trade union, or other group of employees in a company or industry, where ordinary negotiating to improve pay or conditions has proved unsuccessful. The aim is to disrupt normal output, by introducing 'work-to-rule' and 'go-slow' tactics, as well as strike action. Sit-ins and other forms of occupation of a company's premises have also been popular forms of industrial action since the 1970s. ▷ **ACAS; trade union**

**industrial relations**　The dealings and relationships which exist between the workforce and management of a business, particularly one where trade unions are present and collective bargaining is normal; also known as **labour** or **employee relations**. The aims are to preserve the best possible relationship, to ensure that output is maintained, and to ensure that employees are properly rewarded for their work. ▷ **industrial action; trade union**

**inflation**　An economic situation where the general level of prices is rising, as popularly measured by the retail price index. Inflation causes the real value of money to fall, and savings to lose their value. It is also believed to slow down economic growth. If inflation is too high ('galloping inflation') or very severe ('hyperinflation'), a country's currency becomes unacceptable. The most serious examples of inflation running out of control took place in Germany in the early 1920s, and in many South American countries in the 1970s and 1980s. The control of inflation is a major aim of government economic policy in many countries; but its causes and cures are subjects of much debate by economists and politicians. The major fear is that action to reduce inflation causes an increase in unemployment. ▷ **deflation; fiscal drag; retail price index**

**information technology**　A term commonly used to cover the range of technologies relevant to the transfer of information, in particular to computers, digital electronics, and telecommunications. Technological developments during the 1970s and 1980s, such as satellite and optical-based communication methods, have been responsible for enormous scientific and commercial growth in this area. ▷ **telecommunications**

**information theory**　The mathematical theory of information, deriving from the work of the US mathematicians Claude E Shannon and Warren Weaver, in particular *The Mathematical Theory of Communication* (1949), and from the theory of probability. It is concerned with defining and measuring the amount of information in a message, with the encoding and decoding of information, and with the transmission capacity of a channel of communication. The basic notion is that the less predictable something is, the more information it contains. For example, the letter $z$ carries a lot more information than $e$ (in English), when it occurs in a message. In contrast, the $u$ after $q$ carries little or no information, since in most cases it is wholly predictable, and thus redundant. The theory also deals with the problem of *noise* (random interference) in the channel, which can impair the reception and decoding of a signal. Information theory has been influential in generating models for understanding communication processes and in the design of codes for the transmission of information, especially by computers. It is not, however, concerned with the content, meaning, or importance of that information or any other communication. ▷ **communication theory; computer science**

**injunction**   A court order instructing a defendant to refrain from committing some act; the term **interdict** is used in Scottish law. It is a remedy — for example, an injunction might be granted to stop the demolition of a building or to prevent someone disclosing confidential information.   ▷ **writ**

**insider dealing**   (UK) or **insider trading** (US) A business situation where an individual takes advantage of information about a company before it is made public, in order to make a profit (or avoid a loss) by dealing in the company's stocks or shares. It is illegal in most countries. In the UK it has been so since 1980, but there were few prosecutions until the Financial Services Act (1986) was passed, which gave the Department of Trade and Industry power to investigate and prosecute. However, it is not always easy to prove that such activities have taken place. ▷ **shares; stocks**

**insurance**   A system of guarding an individual or institution against the possibility of an event occurring which will cause some harm — usually financial. The insured pays a fee (the *premium*) to an insurance company. The size of the premium (calculated by specialists called *actuaries*) depends on the size of the risk at stake, the number of premiums to be received, and the risk (or chance) of the event occurring. It is possible to obtain cover against most events. There are four main classes of insurance: marine, fire, life, and accident. An **insurance broker** is an agent for anyone who wishes to be insured, by finding others who are willing to underwrite the risk. Their commission is termed *brokerage*. ▷ **National Insurance**

**intelligence**   The ability to respond adaptively to novel situations. Psychologists attempt to measure this ability by constructing tests which appear related to intelligence, and extensively using these tests on a target population, so enabling them to assess the mental age of any individual. (For a given score on a particular test, the 'mental age' is the average age of those members of the tested population having this score.) Your **IQ** (**Intelligence Quotient**) equals your Mental Age divided by your actual (Chronological) Age. It is usual to distinguish *fluid intelligence* (your mental flexibility) from *crystallized intelligence* (your knowledge). Various subcategories of ability have also been recognized, such as the distinction between *verbal intelligence*, which is measured by tasks that depend on a knowledge of language (such as grouping similar concepts together) and *non-verbal intelligence*, where the tasks do not involve language at all (such as copying a drawing). ▷ **cognitive psychology**

**interdict** ▷ **injunction**.

**interest** The amount of money charged by a person or institution that lends a sum to a borrower. The sum lent, on which interest is calculated, is known as the *principal*. The lender will be paid a percentage of the principal as interest on the loan, the rate of interest depending on the amount of the principal, the length of time the loan is outstanding, and the risk involved. Interest rates in general vary according to the state of the economy. Economists regard interest as the price of money, the rate rising and falling as the demand for money rises and falls. The **interest rate** is the percentage payable; for example, an 8% interest rate on £100 gives the lender £8 interest at the end of a year. The **annual percentage rate** (APR) shows the actual rate of interest payable on borrowings, especially hire-purchase agreements, where interest has to be paid more often than once a year.

**interest group** ▷ **pressure group**.

**International Bank for Reconstruction and Development** ▷ **World Bank**.

**International Monetary Fund (IMF)** A financial agency affiliated to the United Nations, formed in 1945 to promote international monetary cooperation, the expansion of international trade, exchange rate stability, and to give financial assistance to states in need. Each member country contributes to the fund; the more a country pays, the more voting rights it has in decision-making. The IMF's headquarters is in Washington DC. ▷ **World Bank**

**introversion/extraversion** Psychological terms formerly used as two distinct categories of personality ('introvert', 'extravert'), but now considered to be a dimension with high levels of extraversion and introversion at the extremes. Strongly extraverted individuals are sociable, excitement-seeking, and carefree. They are often aggressive, may lose their temper quickly, and be unreliable. Strongly introverted individuals are quiet, reserved, and have few friends. They dislike excitement, are reliable, serious-minded, and like a well-ordered life. ▷ **psychiatry; psychology**

**invisibles** The export and import of services, as distinct from goods, which are known as **visibles**. Invisible exports and imports include tourism, shipping, air freight, banking, insurance, and other financial services. They are a major contributor to Britain's balance of payments. ▷ **balance of payments**

**IQ** ▷ **intelligence**.

**Irangate** The popular nickname for a political scandal in 1986 that grew out of the Reagan administration's efforts to obtain the release of US captives held in the Middle East by the covert supply of arms to the hostile government of Iran. In an additional complication, officials (notably, Colonel Oliver North) tried to use the proceeds of arms sales to Iran as a means of financing support for the anti-government *Contra* rebels in Nicaragua, despite official prohibition by Congress, and without the knowledge of the President. In addition to questions surrounding violations of the law, the affair raised issues concerning executive incompetence, which a Congressional Committee reported on in 1988. ▷ **Watergate**

**Iron Curtain** A term used to describe the separation of certain East European countries from the rest of Europe by the political and military domination of the Soviet Union. It was first used by Nazi propaganda minister Joseph Goebbels in 1943, and became widely known after Winston Churchill used it in a speech in 1946. ▷ **Warsaw Pact**

**Islam** The Arabic word for 'submission' to the will of God (Allah), the name of the religion originating in Arabia during the seventh century AD through the Prophet Mohammed. Followers of Islam are known as Muslims, or Moslems, and their religion embraces every aspect of life. They believe that individuals, societies, and governments should all be obedient to the will of God as it is set forth in the Koran, which they regard as the Word of God revealed to his Messenger, Mohammed. The Koran teaches that God is one and has no partners. He is the Creator of all things, and holds absolute power over them. All persons should commit themselves to lives of grateful and praise-giving obedience to God, for on the Day of Resurrection they will be judged. Those who have obeyed God's commandments will dwell for ever in paradise, but those who have sinned against God and not repented will be condemned eternally to the fires of hell. Since the beginning of creation God has sent prophets, including Moses and Jesus, to provide the guidance necessary for the attainment of eternal reward, a succession culminating in the revelation to Mohammed of the perfect word of God.

There are five essential religious duties known as the 'Pillars of Islam'. (1) The *shahada* (profession of faith) is the sincere recitation of the two-fold creed: 'There is no god but God' and 'Mohammed is the Messenger of God'. (2) The *salat* (formal prayer) must be performed at fixed hours five times a day while facing towards the holy city of Mecca. (3) Alms-giving through the payment of *zakat* ('purification') is regarded primarily as an act of worship, and is the duty of sharing one's wealth out of gratitude for God's favour, according to the uses laid down in the Koran. (4) There is a duty to fast (*saum*) during the month of Ramadan. (5) The *Hajj* or pilgrimage to Mecca is to be performed if at all possible at least once during one's lifetime.

*Shari'a* is the sacred law of Islam, and applies to all aspects of life, not just religious practices. It describes the Islamic way of life, and prescribes the way for a Muslim to fulfil the commands of God and reach heaven. There is an annual cycle of festivals, including Hijra, the beginning of the Islamic year, and Ramadan, the month during which Muslims fast during the hours of daylight. There is no organized priesthood, but great respect is accorded the Hashim family, descendants of Mohammed, and other publicly acknowledged holy men, scholars, and teachers, such as mullahs and ayatollahs. There are two basic groups within Islam. Sunni Muslims are in the majority, and they recognize the first four caliphs as Mohammed's legitimate successors. The Shiites comprise the largest minority group, and regard the imam as the principal religious authority. In 1990, there were 935 million Muslims throughout the world. ▷ **jihad; religion**

**isolationism**   A foreign policy strategy of withdrawing from international affairs as long as the country's interests are not affected. It is a means of avoiding involvement in international conflicts, and implies neutrality in most cases. It was practised most notably by the USA, which kept out of the League of Nations and World War II until attacked by the Japanese.

**isotopes**   Species of the same element that are chemically identical, having the same proton number, but of different atomic masses due to a differing number of neutrons in the nucleus. An isotope is identified by its chemical symbol along with a nucleon number (a nucleon is a combined term for proton and neutron): for example, 14C (carbon 14), used in radiocarbon dating. All elements have isotopes. Radioactive isotopes (or *radioisotopes*) are important in the creation of nuclear reactors and nuclear weapons. ▷ **half-life; radiocarbon dating**

**Jainism**   A religion which developed in India, which regards Vardhamana Mahavira (599–527 BC) as its founder; it is pronounced **jiyn**-*izm*. Mahavira is seen as the last *Tirthankara* — one of the 24 great heroes of their tradition who, by their teaching and example, taught them the way to cross the stream from the bondage of physical existence to freedom from rebirth (Tirthankara is Sanskrit for 'ford-maker'). They are also called *Jina* ('conqueror'), from which Jains take their name. Jains believe that salvation

consists in conquering material existence through adherence to a strict ascetic discipline, thus freeing the 'soul' for eternal all-knowing bliss. Liberation requires detachment from worldly existence, an essential part of which is the practice of *Ahimsa*, non-injury to living beings. The ascetic ideal is central to both monastic and lay Jainism, although final renunciation is possible only within the former. In 1990 they numbered over 3.5 million.
▷ **reincarnation; religion**

**Jehovah's Witnesses**    A millenarian movement organized in the USA in 1884 under Charles Taze Russell (1852–1916). They adopted the name Jehovah's Witnesses in 1931; previously they were called 'Millennial Dawnists' and 'International Bible Students'. They have their own translation of the Bible, which they interpret literally. They believe in the imminent second coming of Christ, avoid worldly involvement, and refuse to obey any law which they see as a contradiction of the law of God — refusing, for example, to take oaths, enter military service, or receive blood transfusions. They publish *The Watchtower*, meet in Kingdom Halls, and all 'witness' through regular house-to-house preaching. They number about one million. ▷ **millenarianism**

**jihad**    The term used in Islam for 'holy war'; it is Arabic for 'struggle', and pronounced *jee-had*. According to the Koran, Muslims have a duty to oppose those who reject Islam, by armed struggle if necessary, and jihad has been invoked to justify both the expansion and defence of Islam. Islamic states pledged a jihad against Israel in the Mecca declaration of 1981, though not necessarily by military attack. ▷ **Islam**

**Judaism**    The religion of the Jews, central to which is the belief in one God, the transcendent creator of the world who delivered the Israelites out of their bondage in Egypt, revealed his law (*Torah*) to them, and chose them to be a light to all humankind. The Hebrew Bible is the primary source of Judaism. Next in importance is the *Talmud*, which consists of the *Mishnah* (the codification of the oral Torah) and a collection of extensive early rabbinical commentary. Various later commentaries and the standard code of Jewish law and ritual (*halakhah*) produced in the late Middle Ages have been important in shaping Jewish practice and thought.

However varied their communities, all Jews see themselves as members of a community whose origins lie in the patriarchal period. This past lives on in its rituals, and there is a marked preference for expressing beliefs and attitudes more through ritual than through abstract doctrine. The family is the basic unit of Jewish ritual, though the synagogue has come to play an increasingly important role. The Sabbath, which begins at sunset on Friday and ends at sunset on Saturday, is the central religious observance. The synagogue is the centre for community worship and study. Its main feature is the 'ark' (a cupboard) containing the hand-written scrolls of the Pentateuch. The rabbi is primarily a teacher and spiritual guide. There is an annual cycle of religious festivals and days of fasting. The first of these is Rosh Hashanah, New Year's Day; the holiest day in the Jewish year is Yom Kippur, the Day of Atonement. Other annual festivals include Hanukkah and Pesach, the family festival of Passover.

Anti-Semitic prejudice and periods of persecution have been a feature of the Christian culture of Europe, and increased with the rise of European nationalism, culminating in the Nazi Holocaust. Its effect has been incalculable, giving urgency to the Zionist movement for the creation of a Jewish homeland, and is pivotal in all relations between Jews and non-Jews today. In 1990 there were over 17 million Jews. ▷ **Holocaust; religion; Zionism**

**jurisdiction**    The factors which govern the competence of a judicial body to decide issues. A civil court, for example, is not allowed to deal with criminal matters, such as a murder trial — this matter would be 'outside of the court's jurisdiction'. The term may also refer to the geographical area covered by a particular legal system — which is not necessarily the same area as that of the national political unit. For example, in the UK, the jurisdiction of courts in England and Wales does not apply to Scotland, which has its own system; and in the USA, the individual states constitute separate jurisdictions. ▷ **legislature**

**justice of the peace (JP)**    A judicial appointment in England and Wales, also known as a **magistrate**. JPs are appointed, and may be removed, by the Lord Chancellor. Their principal function is to sit in the magistrates' courts, administering immediate (or 'summary') justice in the majority of cases, and committing the most serious cases for further trial elsewhere. JPs are not necessarily legally qualified — most are not — though the absence of a legal qualification is not quite as surprising as it seems, as most cases involve disputes about the facts and not the law. A legally qualified clerk advises on the law. Magistrates now receive basic training, but no salary.

**Keynesianism**    The economic concepts and policies derived from the writings of British economist John Maynard Keynes (1883–1946) since the late 1930s; his name is pronounced *kaynz*. The 'Keynesian revolution' is so-called because it radically changed the view of how economies should be managed, particularly in relation to the notion of full employment. Prior to Keynes, the classical school of economics believed that economies would tend towards full employment equilibrium. Keynesian thinking challenged this, with a view based on the experience of Western economies, after World War 1, that economies could be in equilibrium at less than full employment. Unless demand in the economy is stimulated, growth and therefore full employment are not possible. Keynesian theories were subject to critical appraisal in the 1960s and 1970s by Monetarists. Many argue that the fundamental theory holds good, but does not fully address current economic problems, such as inflation. ▷ **economics; inflation; monetarism**

**KGB** An acronym of **Komitet Gosudarstvennoy Bezopasnosti** ('Committee for State Security'), introduced in 1953 as one of the Soviet Union's two secret police organizations with joint responsibility for internal and external order and security. Its tasks included the surveillance of key members of the Communist Party, the administration, and the military; the monitoring and regulation of dissidents; and espionage and subversion abroad. It is now undergoing radical reform, following the changes in the USSR which took place in 1991. ▷ **perestroika**

**kinetic art** A term applied to certain types of modern art, especially sculptures, which move. Examples include the hanging mobiles of the US sculptor Alexander Calder (1898–1976), all the parts of which revolve separately to create changing patterns in space. Kinetic works usually rely on air currents, but some are connected to a motor. ▷ **modern art**

**Kremlin** The medieval citadel of a Russian town, generally used with reference to the Kremlin at Moscow, which occupies a wedge-shaped 36 ha/90 acre site by the Moscow River. The Moscow Kremlin, which was built in the 12th century, was subsequently altered and embellished so that its palaces and cathedrals reflect a variety of architectural styles. It was the residence of the Czars until 1712, and in 1918 became the political and administrative headquarters of the USSR.

**Labour Party** A British political party, originally formed in 1900 as the Labour Representation Committee to represent trade unions and socialist societies as a distinct group in Parliament. Twenty-six MPs were elected in 1906, and the name changed to the Labour Party. In 1922 it overtook the Liberals as the main opposition party. The first majority Labour government (1945–51) established the welfare state and carried out a significant nationalization programme. Since then Labour have been in office 1964–70 and 1974–9. The breakaway social democratic movement of the 1980s reduced the Party's electoral chances throughout that decade. Outside Parliament, the annual conference and the National Executive Committee share policy-making, though their influence is greater in opposition. The leader and deputy leader are elected annually when in opposition by an electoral college composed of trade unions, constituency parties, and the Parliamentary Labour Party. The British Labour Party has been little influenced by Marxism, unlike the corresponding parties in Europe. ▷ **Marxism; Militant Tendency; Social Democratic Party; socialism; welfare state**

**labour relations** ▷ **industrial relations**.

**laissez-faire** An economic doctrine advocating that commerce and trade should be permitted to operate free of controls of any kind. The government is involved as little as possible. It is of French origin, first used in the 18th century, meaning literally 'leave alone to do', and is pronounced *lay-say* **fair**. The phrase was used by British statesman Benjamin Disraeli (1804–81), relating to the work of the free trade reformers Richard Cobden (1804–65) and John Bright (1811–89). It was a popular view in the mid-19th century. ▷ **free trade**

**Lambeth Conference** ▷ **Anglican Communion**.

**lateral thinking** A term coined by British psychologist Edward de Bono (1933– ) for a method of thinking which aims to solve problems by reformulating them in different terms; contrasted with **vertical thinking**. When getting to grips with a problem, a vertical approach is the one which stays within conventionally perceived boundaries. A lateral approach aims to avoid these difficulties by conceiving the problem in a radically different way. For example, how might people be persuaded to make more use of a library? A vertical approach might suggest the purchase of more books, or the provision of a better cataloguing system. A lateral approach might suggest providing more car-parking space or adding a coffee-bar. ▷ **brainstorming**

**left wing** A place on the political continuum, ranging from left to right, occupied by those with radical and reforming attitudes towards social change and the political order. The term, often abbreviated as 'the left', encompasses many shades of opinion, but generally includes a commitment to greater liberty and economic equality, and a belief in social progress through political action. ▷ **centre, the; radicalism; right wing**

**Legal Aid** A British scheme which provides the public with advice and assistance from solicitors, and aid with representation at civil and criminal trials. The money comes from public funds. Civil legal aid is administered by the Law Society under general guidance from the Lord Chancellor; help is means-tested, and a contribution may be required. A person seeking criminal legal aid applies to the court (in Scotland, to the Legal Aid Board), which may grant such aid if it is both needed and in the interests of justice to grant it.

**legislature** The institution in a country which is recognized as having the power to pass laws. In the UK the legislature is the Queen-in-Parliament, comprising the monarch, the House of Lords, and the House of Commons. The role of the monarch in this respect is now purely formal. In the USA, the President has a qualified power of veto over bills from Congress. ▷ **jurisdiction; parliament; Privy Council**

**libel**   A statement which harms someone's name or reputation, published in permanent form. By statute this is extended to include broadcast by wireless telegraphy (radio, television), and words spoken during the public performance of a play. The libel need not involve words — a sculpture or painting may be libellous. **Slander**, by contrast, is a harmful statement about a person made in some transient form — everyday speech or gestures. However, the distinction between libel and slander is not always recognized; in Scotland, for example, both are considered to be types of **defamation**.

**liberal democracy**   ▷ **democracy**.

**Liberal Party**   A British political party, originating in the 1860s, whose electoral appeal was to the new middle classes and working-class elite of skilled artisans. The Liberals and Conservatives were the two major parties until 1922, when the Labour Party overtook the Liberals in popular support. Since then their status has declined to a centrist minority party. Espousing the values of individual and economic freedom combined with social justice, the Liberal Party played a significant part in the development of the welfare state. After the formation of the Social Democratic Party (SDP) in 1980, it entered into an electoral 'Alliance', and in 1987 voted to merge with the SDP, subsequently forming the **Social and Liberal Democratic Party**. ▷ **Social Democratic Party**

**liberalism**   A political philosophy, developed largely in the 18th and 19th centuries and associated with the rise of the new middle classes, which challenged the traditional monarchical, aristocratic, or religious views of the state. Liberals sought political power to match economic power, and argued for secular, constitutional, and parliamentary governments. Classical liberalism argues for limited government, the values traditionally espoused being those of freedom — of the individual, religion, trade and economics (expressed in terms of *laissez faire*), and politics. In the 20th century, liberalism in most countries has been overtaken by socialism as the major challenge to conservative parties, and has come to occupy a position in the centre ground, finding it difficult to establish a firm electoral base. In some countries (such as the UK), liberals have combined traditional values with a belief in the need for governmental intervention to overcome social injustice. ▷ **centre, the; laissez-faire; Liberal Party**

**linguistics**   The scientific study of language. The discipline is concerned with such matters as providing systematic descriptions of languages, investigating the properties of language structures as communicative systems, exploring the possibility that there are universals of language structure, and accounting for the historical development of linguistic systems. *Applied linguistics* is the application of linguistics to the study of such language-based fields as foreign language teaching and learning, speech disorders, translation, and dictionary writing. ▷ **anthropology; communication theory; semantics; semiotics**

**liquidation** ▷ **bankruptcy**.

**liquid crystals** Many organic materials, crystalline in the solid state, which form a partially ordered state (the *liquid crystal state*) upon melting, and become true liquids only after the temperature is raised further. The optical transparency of liquid crystals can be reduced by applying electric fields, a property extensively exploited in displays for watches, calculators, and other electronic devices.

**liquidity** In business and banking, actual money, or assets that are easily convertible into money. Firms need to be sufficiently liquid to be able to pay off debts, to be able to buy assets when required, and to be covered in case of emergencies. *Liquid assets* are cash, short-term investments, and debtors (that is, any amounts due from customers).

**literature** The collective writings proper to any language or nation. World literature includes all these in translation. The term is a site of ideological conflict; it may be taken to refer exclusively to those canonical works in the established genres which 'have pleased many and pleased long' (Dr Johnson), or inclusively to the sum total of writings which are read, even the most ephemeral, such as comics and newspapers. Essays, letters, memoirs, historical, biographical and travel writings, occasional verse, and other forms will all be considered 'literature' depending on the point of view. Fundamental questions are addressed by the French philosopher Jean-Paul Sartre in *What is Literature?* (1948). The term is also used to refer to the body of secondary writings on a given subject, as in 'medical literature' and 'ornithological literature'. ▷ **allegory; black comedy; classicism; decadence; deconstruction; epic; Gothic; imagery; poetic licence; rhetoric; Romanticism; sonnet; structuralism**

**lobbying** A political process, prominent in 19th-century USA, in which organized groups try to influence elected representatives through personal contacts in the 'lobbies' of legislative buildings. Contemporary usage has broadened the term to incorporate making demands upon civil servants, state institutions, and influencing public opinion. Significant in all liberal democracies, many groups now employ paid, professional lobbyists. ▷ **democracy; pressure group**

**local government** A set of political institutions which are subordinate to the national government, with delegated authority to perform certain functions within territorially-defined parts of the state. For example, the 1972 Local Government Act in the UK divided England and Wales into 54 counties, and at a lower level into 300 districts; parish or (in Wales) community councils operate at a still more local level. In a 1973 Act, Scotland was organized into 12 regions, subdivided into 53 districts. Northern Ireland has a single system of 26 district councils. Sovereign authority remains with the higher levels of government, which may create, dissolve, or change local structures and add to or take away their powers and functions. Some of the services most commonly provided by local government include education, public transport, police, roads, social services, housing, leisure and recreation, and public health. The rationale for local government includes the need for local participation, achieved through direct or indirect elections, and in local authorities' revenue-raising powers. Although considerable discretion may be granted to local authorities in some political systems, conflict with central government can occur. This usually relates to the extent of legitimate democratic authority possessed by local government derived from the electoral process, as different views exist about whether local government should be an agent or partner of central government. ▷ **democracy; parliament**

**Lockerbie disaster**  The scene of Britain's worst air disaster, on 21 December 1988, when a Pan Am Boeing 747 flying from Frankfurt to New York via London crashed onto the Scottish Borders town of Lockerbie. There were no survivors. The total death toll was 270, including townspeople killed by plane debris which demolished houses. The explosive device which led to the disaster was incorporated into a radio-cassette player placed in the baggage hold, thought to have been taken on board at Frankfurt. It remains unclear which terrorist group was responsible for the disaster. ▷ **terrorism**

**logic**  The systematic study of reasoned argument, or inference. Logicians seek to determine the principles and forms of sound reasoning, and to diagnose patterns of incorrect reasoning (*fallacies*). The first systematic treatises were written by Aristotle, their soundness and thoroughness ensuring that the Arristotelean (or 'traditional') logic was central for over 2000 years. Logic as a study fell away with the Renaissance and new discoveries in science, but was revived in the 19th century, when a variety of different approaches evolved. Apart from the revival of Aristotle, these included algebraic and symbolic logic, pioneered by George Boole (1815–64) and later developed by Gottlob Frege (1848–1925), which, combined with mathematics, provided procedures important in science and in the later development of computers.

A major branch of logic is known as **deductive logic** — the study of *validity* in argument. 'Leeds and York are in the same county; Leeds is in

Yorkshire; therefore York is in Yorkshire' is a true and valid inference — the first two statements (the *premises*) lead to a valid conclusion. Valid but not true would be to replace 'Yorkshire' with 'Fife'. The structure or form of the argument is still valid, irrespective of its content. Symbolic logic, by proceeding from 'A & B; therefore A', constructed very complex formal procedures for testing arguments. The other main branch of logic does not presume the truth of premises. This includes the **logic of coherence**, which claims that no truth is certain, but that we have a warrant of truth from a consideration of the other propositions a premise implies. It also includes the **logic of induction**, which merely claims that a premise gives good reason to believe its conclusion to be true: 'all observed As are Bs; therefore all As whatsoever are Bs'. This is deductively invalid — it does not follow that because something is observed some of the time, it will happen all of the time — but it nonetheless has value as an argument. The development of inductive reasoning, involving complex statistics, has resulted in probability theory. ▷ **deduction; fallacy; induction; premise; tautology**

**Lord Chancellor** ▷ **Chancellor of the Exchequer**.

**Lords, House of** ▷ **House of Lords**.

**Lutheranism** Churches derived from the beliefs of the German reformer Martin Luther (1483–1546), and the doctrines which they share. Lutheran Churches originally flourished in Germany and Scandinavia, then in other parts of Europe; later, through immigration from Europe, in the USA, and through missionary activity in Africa and Asia. Their beliefs are based on the Augsburg Confession, a statement of faith drawn up by Luther and others in 1530, Luther's two Catechisms, and certain other formulations. Lutheranism emphasizes justification by faith alone, the importance of scripture, and the priesthood of all believers. Three sacraments are recognized: baptism, Eucharist, and penance. The Lutheran World Federation, a free association of Lutheran Churches, was founded in 1947, and is the largest of the Protestant confessional families, numbering around 59 million in 1990. ▷ **Protestantism**

*m* **macroeconomics** ▷ **economics**.

**mad cow disease** ▷ **BSE**.

**magistrate** ▷ **justice of the peace**.

**mainstreaming** The introduction of children with special educational needs, many of whom were formerly known as 'handicapped', into ordinary schools — a term primarily used in the USA. In both the USA and UK, it was decided in the late 1970s and early 1980s to reduce the number of such children who attended special schools. The argument in favour was that many children in special schools were set targets which were too low, and also that they would gain from being educated alongside so- called 'normal' children. Reservations were expressed about most schools' ability, without substantial training for staff and extra resources, to offer skilled specialist help to children with different needs. ▷ **special education**

**maladministration** ▷ **ombudsman**.

**Maoism** Specifically, the thought of Mao Zedong (Mao Tse-tung) (1893–1976), and more broadly a revolutionary ideology based on Marxism-Leninism adapted to Chinese conditions. Maoism shifted the focus of revolutionary struggle from the urban workers or proletariat to the countryside and the peasantry. There were three main elements: strict Leninist principles of organization, Chinese tradition, and armed struggle as a form of revolutionary activity. Mao gained political power in 1949 through a peasant army, his slogan being 'Political power grows through the barrel of a gun'. While there were attempts to take account of the views of the masses, the Chinese Communist Party was organized along strict centralist, hierarchical lines, and increasingly became a vehicle for a personal dictatorship. In domestic terms Mao pursued a radical and far-reaching attempt to transform traditional Chinese society and its economy, using thought reform, indoctrination, and the psychological transformation of the masses. Maoism was regarded in the 1960s, at the height of the reforms known as the 'Cultural Revolution', as a highly radical form of Marxism-Leninism that was distinct from the bureaucratic repression of the Soviet Union, and had a strong appeal among the New Left. Since Mao's death, his use of the masses for political purposes, his economic reforms, and his conception of political power have been increasingly criticized inside and outside China as too rigid. ▷ **communism; Marxism**

**market economy** An economic system where prices, wages, and what is made and sold are determined by market forces of supply and demand, with no state interference. The contrast is with a **command economy**, where the state takes all economic decisions. Most Western economies these days are mixed, with varying degrees of state control. ▷ **free trade; laissez-faire**

**market forces** or **market mechanism** The network of interactions between buyers and sellers which determines the price and quantity of products and goods. Prices are set by the forces of supply and demand. The process assumes that there is no interference by, for example, government. ▷ **market economy; supply and demand**

**market research** A technique to find out more about the market in which a business is operating, or may operate in the future. Survey techniques are often used, seeking the opinions of individuals who might be buyers, and providing information about the potential size and characteristics of a particular market segment. Market research also enables advertising agencies to target their campaigns more accurately.

**martial law**   The imposition of military rule on the civilian population, either by the leader of an occupying army, or by a territory's own government. In the latter case, it most commonly occurs after there has been a military coup or during a period of colonial rule. Many countries' constitutions have provision for the introduction of martial law in times of foreign threats and emergencies, although in many liberal democracies there are severe restrictions on its implementation which render it largely impractical. The military in such countries can, however, be more readily mobilized in support of the civil authorities.

**Marxism**   The body of social and political thought informed by the writings of Karl Marx (1818–83). It is essentially a critical analysis of capitalist society arguing that such societies are subject to crises which create the conditions for proletarian revolutions and the transformation to socialism. Much of Marx's writing, especially *Das Kapital*, was concerned with the economic dynamics of capitalist societies, seeing the state as an instrument of class rule supporting private capital and suppressing the masses. Because of private capital's need to earn profits or extract surplus value, wages have to be kept to a subsistence minimum. This produces economic contradictions, because it restricts the purchasing power of workers to consume the goods produced. Capitalism is, therefore, inherently unstable, being subject to crises of booms and slumps. Marx's view was that these crises would become increasingly worse, and eventually lead to revolution, whereby the working class would seize the state and establish a dictatorship of the proletariat, productive power would be in public hands, and class differences would disappear (socialism). This classless society would eventually lead to the withering away of the state, producing a communist society.

   Marxism has sought to popularize and extend this method of analysis to contemporary conditions. In particular, Western Marxism has examined the impact of state intervention in smoothing out the crises of capitalism and establishing a legitimacy for the existing capitalist order through its control over education and the media. In non-industrialized societies Marxism has been adapted to account for revolution in countries where there is no extensive development of capitalism, in contrast to Marx's view of history. It is generally recognized that Marx's writings regarding the transformation to socialism and the nature of socialism lacked detail. In consequence, Marxism has adopted a wide range of interpretations. ▷ **capitalism; class; communism; Maoism; Marxism; socialism**

**mass media**  ▷ **media**.

**materialism**  In one sense, a preoccupation with worldly rather than with spiritual or intellectual matters; or, more generally, the view that material well-being is the highest good. In another sense, the philosophical view that everything is composed exclusively of physical constituents located in space and time. Philosophers who are materialists may deny the existence of such abstract entities as numbers and sets, and/or claim that mental phenomena can be accounted for without positing the existence of anything non-physical. 'Mind', for example, is said to be reducible to various neural processes within the brain.  ▷ **philosophy**

**materials science**  The study of the engineering properties of materials, as dictated by their microscopic structure. It draws on standard mechanical testing techniques from engineering, and methods of structural study derived from physics and chemistry (eg electron microscopy), to understand how bonds are formed between different components of material. It has been responsible for the development of several new materials, such as conducting rubber, metallic glasses, ceramics for use in car engines, special metals for aircraft, and the fibreglass and carbon fibre composites used in sports equipment.

**mechanics**  The study of the motion of objects as a result of the forces acting on them. *Quantum mechanics* is specifically concerned with objects the size of atoms ($10^{-10}$m) or less. *Classical mechanics* is concerned with all other aspects of mechanics, where large masses are involved, and includes the motion of stars and planets (*celestial mechanics*), fluids (*fluid mechanics*), objects moving at high velocity (*relativistic mechanics*), and general relativity.  ▷ **ballistics; general relativity; quantum mechanics**

**media**  A collective term for television, radio, cinema, and the press; also known as the **mass media**. Although each medium of mass communication has always had its own distinctive output, technology, and industrial structure, the media are nowadays often discussed as a single entity. Among the reasons for this are their combined importance as providers of entertainment and information, their presumed power to mould public opinion and set moral and aesthetic standards, the growth of cross-ownership among the various sectors, and their frequent interest in each others' personalities and problems.  ▷ **censorship**

**meltdown**  A catastrophic event in a nuclear reactor. If control of the release of thermal energy is lost, the temperature of the reacting core rises to a point at which the fuel rods melt, and radioactive material may be released into the environment. This happened at Chernobyl in the Ukraine, USSR, in 1986.  ▷ **nuclear reactor**

**Mennonites** ▷ **Anabaptists**.

**mentalism** The view that mental states and processes can explain behaviour, and have an existence independent of behaviour. It is opposed to behaviourism, which denies the existence or relevance of mental realities. A modern mentalist is the US linguist Noam Chomsky (1928– ), who argues that language competence is fundamentally a matter of the mind, and that child language learning takes place in the way it does because the mind is innately predisposed to it. ▷ **behaviourism; psychology**

**merger** A business arrangement in which two companies bring together their operations and form a single company. The share capital of the two companies is replaced by an issue of shares in the new company, share-holders of the old companies receiving new shares on a formula basis. The extent to which operations are merged depends on the nature of the companies, ranging from total merging (as when two building firms merge) to the merging of head office activities only (where the two firms are in different business sectors). Countries often monitor proposed mergers carefully: in the UK, for example, this is done by means of the Monopolies Commission. ▷ **monopoly**

**metaphysics** A branch of philosophy which deals with questions about what exists (*ontology*), the nature of things, and how things are related to each other. The term was used by early philosophers to name the group of Aristotle's texts which followed the text named *Physics*, in the collection of his works. It means 'after' or 'beyond' physics. ▷ **materialism; philosophy**

**meteorology** The scientific study of global atmospheric processes — solar radiation, evaporation, precipitation, and changes in atmospheric pressure (and, therefore, wind). Meteorology is generally concerned with the short-term processes (ie hours and days rather than months and seasons) operating in the troposphere and mesosphere, which are the atmospheric layers of the Earth's weather systems. Satellites are now the main source of meteorological data, used for weather forecasting and in research. ▷ **climatology**

**Methodism** A Christian denomination founded in 1739 by John Wesley (1703–91) as an evangelical movement within the Church of England, becoming a separate body in 1795. The movement spread rapidly as he travelled the country on horseback and sent other evangelical leaders to the American colonies, where the movement flourished. In the 19th century, doctrinal disputes caused divisions both in Britain and the USA. These were healed in Britain in 1932, and partially so in the USA, with the uniting of the three main bodies of Methodists. The principal doctrines of the Church are laid down in Wesley's sermons, his notes on the New Testament, and his Articles of Religion. Authority is vested in annual Conferences. Individual churches are grouped into 'circuits'. Hymn singing plays a central role in services, and spontaneous prayer is common. There are around 25 million Methodists worldwide. ▷ **Anglican Communion; evangelicalism; Protestantism**

**microeconomics** ▷ **economics**.

**migration** A movement of population within or between countries. Migration within countries has been mainly from poor to rich regions, or from rural to urban centres, which migrants see as attractive alternatives to rural overpopulation and its associated deprivation. Movement between countries, or international migration (**emigration**), may be a response to other factors, such as warfare or political threats against minority groups. Migrants may not always be given the right to settle in those regions to which they travel, and may be treated as temporary refugees or stateless migrant labourers. In advanced, prosperous societies there has been a considerable out-migration of people from the cities to the surrounding countryside, a phenomenon known as 'population turnaround'. Major migrations in history include the departure of the Pilgrim Fathers for America, and the massive population movements to the USA in the 19th century, and the 20th-century movement of Jewish people to Israel. Immigration into the UK since the 1950s has brought numbers of Commonwealth citizens, especially from Asia and the Caribbean. Controls began to be introduced in 1962. ▷ **sociology; urbanization**

**militant** ▷ **activism**.

**Militant Tendency** A British political group which came to prominence in the 1980s. Ostensibly, *Militant* is a newspaper published by Labour Party members espousing Marxist positions. In practice, critics have argued, the newspaper is a front for a 'party within a party', a separate organization of revolutionary Trotskyists who have entered the Labour Party to use its organizational base for its own political ends. In the 1980s, its supporters infiltrated a number of local Labour Parties and the Young Socialists (its youth wing). Fearing the adverse electoral publicity resulting from Militant activities, the Labour Party moved to expel members of Militant on the grounds that they were members of a separate political party, which is against the Party's constitution. Many of those expelled took the Party to court, but their cases were not upheld. Since then, Militant's influence appears to have declined. ▷ **Labour Party; Marxism; socialism; Trotskyism**

**militia** A military force raised (usually in times of emergency) for national defence, separate from the regular army. These national forces are raised by government decree, and can thus be distinguished from guerrilla forces.

**millenarianism**   The belief held by some Christians that there will be a 1000-year (millennium) reign of the saints, either before or immediately after the return of Christ. The belief is usually based on an interpretation of *Revelation* 20.1–7. The main body of Christians has not endorsed millenarianism, but it had its advocates from the earliest years of Christianity, and in the 19th century several groups renewed these ideas, such as the Plymouth Brethren and the Adventists. In recent decades, the term has been used more broadly by social scientists, referring to any religious group looking forward to a sudden and early transformation of the world. Such movements tend to arise in periods of great social change or during social crises, and usually aim to advance a suppressed social group. ▷ **Adventists; Anabaptists; Christadelphians; Jehovah's Witnesses**

**Minimal Art**   A modern art movement that has flourished since the 1950s, mainly in the USA. It aims to keep the personal, self-expressive element in art to a minimum — contrasting especially with the highly expressive creations of action painting. Typical products are the blank or monochrome canvases of US painter Ad Reinhardt (1913–67), and the prefabricated firebricks of US sculptor Carl André (1935– ). In all cases the art content may be described as 'minimal'. ▷ **abstract art; action painting; modern art**

**minister**   ▷ **secretary of state**.

**mobile communications**   A system which provides a simple, convenient means of communication for people who wish to keep in touch when travelling. The first mobile communication system was ship-borne radio, and there have since been widespread developments in the field of military communications. In modern times the term also refers to personal communication systems such as CB radio, radio paging, and car and pocket phones which use cellular radio. Cellular radio employs local radio transmitters, covering small areas (*cells*), which receive and transmit calls in association with the telecommunications network. Direct-dial calls using special handsets can be made on foot, from cars and trains, and now from aircraft. ▷ **telecommunications**

**modern art**   A term used widely but imprecisely to refer to all the 'progressive' movements in 19th–20th-century art. Accounts vary: some consider Goya the first modern artist; others prefer Manet. What is agreed is that towards the end of the 19th century a number of artists, including Cézanne, Gauguin, van Gogh, Ensor, and Munch, challenged in various ways the traditional approach to painting based on such notions as naturalistic figure-drawing and Renaissance perspective. Their innovations inspired the younger generation, which led to Picasso and Braque developing Cubism (1906–8), the most widely influential of all modern movements. The Blaue Reiter group in Munich pushed further away from imitation (1912–14), and a purely abstract art soon emerged in the hands of Kandinsky and Klee. In Moscow in 1917 Malevich developed a totally abstract art which he called 'Suprematism'. By 1916 a nihilist reaction known as 'Dadaism' was already emerging in Zürich; it attacked all artistic values, but itself contributed to the ideas of the early Surrealists, who launched their first manifesto in Paris in 1924. ▷ **abstract art; art; Body Art; Cubism; Dada; Expressionism; kinetic art; nihilism; Op Art; Pop Art; Surrealism**

**Modernism** Experimental methods in different art forms which took place in the earlier part of the 20th century. These experiments were stimulated by a sharpened sense of the arbitrariness of existing artistic conventions, and doubts about the human place and purpose in the world. Dada, Surrealism, and various other 'anti-genres' are all manifestations of Modernism. Notable works include Joyce's *Ulysses* (1922) and T S Eliot's *Waste Land* (1922); the Cubist paintings of Picasso and Braque; and the 12-tone music of Webern and Schoenberg. ▷ **Cubism; Dada; serialism; Surrealism**

**molecular biology** The study of the structure and function of the large organic molecules associated with living organisms. Particular attention is paid to the nucleic acids (DNA and RNA) and proteins. The field has grown along with such technological developments as the electron microscope. ▷ **DNA; genetics**

**monetarism** An economic policy based on the control of a country's money supply. It assumes that the quantity of money in an economy determines its economic activity, and particularly its rate of inflation. If the money supply is allowed to rise too quickly, prices will rise, resulting in inflation. To curb inflationary pressures, governments therefore need to reduce the supply of money and raise interest rates. This view was a major influence on British and US economic policy in the 1980s. Its best-known supporter has been US economist Milton Friedman (1912– ). ▷ **economics; inflation; Keynesianism; Thatcherism**

**money market** In economic terms, the supply of and demand for money. In a free market, the increasing demand for money leads to pressure to raise interest rates. If governments then raise these rates (in the UK through the Bank of England; in the USA, through the Federal Reserve System), the demand falls. The term also refers to the place where money is traded, such as banks and foreign exchange institutions. ▷ **interest; supply and demand**

**monopoly**  A business situation where there is only one supplier of a commodity or product. The situation is rare in reality, apart from cases of state-owned monopolies, and where there is only one source of supply (a 'natural' monopoly), as in the case of diamonds. In the UK, the Monopolies Commission (set up in 1948) has wide powers to investigate activities which may be against the public interest, such as mergers and takeovers. Antitrust legislation from 1890 likewise intended to control the development of monopoly capitalism. ▷ **capitalism; merger**

**monotheism**  ▷ **God**.

**montage**  In art, a technique whereby illustrations or photographs are cut from papers or magazines, arranged in new ways, and mounted. A development of collage, it was used by the Dadaists and Surrealists, and persists in modern advertising. The notion influenced the cinema, where in film editing it refers to a sequence containing a series of rapidly changing images, often dissolving together or superimposed to convey a visually dramatic effect. ▷ **collage; Dada; Surrealism**

**Moral Majority**  A US pressure group founded in 1979 which has played a leading part in the revival of the New Right. It campaigns for the election of morally conservative politicians and for changes to public policy in such areas as abortion, homosexuality, and school prayers. It is associated with Christian fundamentalists who in the 1980s came to play a prominent role in US politics. ▷ **fundamentalism; New Right; pressure group**

**Mormons**  A religious movement based on the visionary experiences of Joseph Smith (1805–44), who organized it as the 'Church of Jesus Christ of Latter-Day Saints' in 1830 at Fayette, New York. Smith claimed to have been led to the Book of Mormon, inscribed on golden plates and buried 1000 years before in a hill near Palmyra, New York. This book gives an account of an ancient American people to whom Christ appeared after his ascension, and teaches Christ's future establishment of the New Jerusalem in America. It is regarded as equal with the Bible. Subjected to persecution, the Mormons moved west, and Brigham Young finally led most of them to the valley of the Great Salt Lake (1847). Mormons actively engage in missionary work and give two years' voluntary service to the Church. In 1990 there were over 7.5 million members worldwide. ▷ **Christianity**

**motet**  A sacred musical work, originating in the 13th century and cultivated during the Renaissance as an unaccompanied piece in several vocal parts. After 1600, motets often included instrumental accompaniment, but the term continued to distinguish sacred works in Latin from others (cantatas and anthems) in the vernacular. Some German composers (notably Bach and Brahms), however, used the term *Motette* for pieces in the vernacular without independent instrumental support. ▷ **cantata; classical music; Renaissance**

**multilateralism**   In economics, support for an economic trading system where many countries are encouraged to trade with each other (*multilateral trade*). The notion is usually contrasted with **bilateralism**, where there is an agreement between two countries to trade with each other on special terms, usually in the form of reduced tariffs, or on favourable financial terms. It was a common form of trading agreement in the 1930s, and is nowadays used mainly in relation to foreign aid. A *bilateral monopoly* exists where there is only one buyer and one seller of a particular commodity, product, or service. ▷ **monopoly; tariff**

**mysticism**   The spiritual quest in any religion for the most direct experience of God. Characteristically, mysticism concentrates on prayer, meditation, contemplation, and fasting, so as to produce the attitude necessary for what is believed to be a direct encounter with God. Christian mysticism tends to focus on the person and sufferings of Christ, attempting to move beyond image and word to the immediate presence of God. In contrast with other forms of mysticism, Christian mystics reject the idea, common in some other religions, of the absorption of the individual into the divine, and retain the distinction between the individual believer and God. Notable Christian mystics include such diverse figures as St Augustine of Hippo (354–430), St Francis of Assisi (c.1181–1226), and St Teresa of Avila (1515–82). ▷ **God; religion**

**NASA**   An independent agency of the US Government responsible for the civil space programme; it is an abbreviation of **National Aeronautics and Space Administration**. It was established in 1958 by President Eisenhower based on the old National Advisory Committee for Aeronautics (NACA). Its headquarters is in Washington DC, where programme plans originate. Individual projects are implemented at different Field Centers: *Ames Research Center* (Mountain View, California) for aeronautics; *Goddard Space Flight Center* (Greenbelt, Maryland) for astronomy and Earth sciences; *Jet Propulsion Laboratory* (Pasadena, California) for Solar System exploration; *Johnson Space Center* (Houston, Texas) for manned missions; *Kennedy Space Center* (Cape Canaveral, Florida) for launch operations; *Langley Research Center* (Norfolk, Virginia) for aeronautics; *Lewis Research Center* (Cleveland, Ohio) for space technologies; and *Marshall Space Flight Center* (Huntsville, Alabama) for launch vehicles and space science.

*n*

**national accounts**   A set of accounts showing how a nation's income

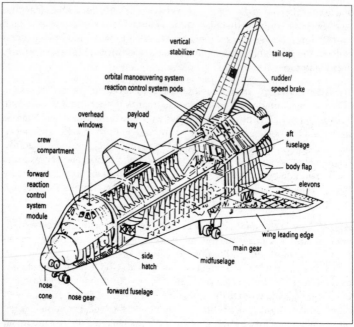

*Space shuttle (see NASA)*

has been generated and used. The amount of income generated by a nation in a year in the form of wages, rents, interest, and profits is known as the **national income**. The **national debt** is the amount of money borrowed by a government over the years. ▷ **gross domestic product**

**National Aeronautics and Space Administration**  ▷ **NASA**.

**national debt**  ▷ **national accounts**.

**National Health Service (NHS)**  A system of health care established in the UK in 1948. World War 2 revealed the need for reform of the health and hospital services which had served up to that time. The new service was to be, and largely remains, a free service available to the whole population, without income limit, and funded out of general taxation. Existing municipal and voluntary hospitals were nationalized and came under the control of regional Health Boards (subsequently called Area Health Committees). Hospital consultants and specialists were salaried (full-time and part-time). General practitioners (GPs) remained self-employed, but were organized by local general medical practice committees, and received fees based on the number of individuals who registered with them as patients. GP services are now largely based on a growing number of Health Centres which accommodate small groups of doctors sharing supportive services. The NHS is supported by nurses, technical and scientific staff, and ancillary workers, and is the largest single employer of labour in the UK. ▷ **welfare state**

**national income**   ▷ **national accounts**.

**National Insurance**   The sum levied on all working people in the UK by the state to finance social benefits, such as sickness and unemployment benefits. Employers, employees, and the self-employed all contribute a percentage of pay. Receipts are collected by the employer and passed on to the government. The individual receives benefit in the form of state medical treatment, sick pay, unemployment benefit, and retirement pensions. ▷ **insurance; National Health Service**

**nationalism**   A political doctrine which views the nation as the principal unit of political organization. It is particularly associated with attempts by national groupings to secure independence from dominance by other nation-states and to maintain that position against threats to it. It is often associated with the struggle against colonialism. More broadly, nationalism can be seen as a general political stance which holds that the principal aim of political activity should be to serve the national interest as opposed to that of a particular class or grouping. In practice, the national interest is, except in extreme cases such as war, open to different interpretations; and nationalism is often no more than an attempt to give legitimacy to a particular political standpoint. Nationalism, with the exception of anti-colonial movements, is based around a conservative, and sometimes romantic political philosophy that emphasizes the nation's past. Examples of nationalist movements include the Scottish National Party in Scotland and Plaid Cymru in Wales, and the movements within the Soviet Union which led to independence for several states in 1991. ▷ **home rule; imperialism; separatism**

**National Security Adviser**   A member of staff who is responsible for advising the US President on security matters. He is regarded as a senior figure in the White House. His views sometimes serve to balance or compete with those of the secretary of state. ▷ **National Security Council; secretary of state**

**National Security Council**   A body created by the US Congress in 1947 to advise the President on the integration of domestic, foreign, and military policies relating to national security. It was designed to achieve effective coordination between the military services and other government agencies and departments, and is composed of the President, Vice-President, Secretary of State, Secretary of Defense, and Director of the Office of Emergency Planning. ▷ **Congress**

**nationalization**  Taking into public ownership an entire industry, normally a public utility, such as water, gas, railways, or electricity. Nationalization takes place with social as well as commercial objectives. The main reasons are that an industry (a) is crucial to the economy and in need of government direction, (b) is a natural monopoly, (c) has suffered a period of decline which needs to be reversed, (d) produces a good or service which would not be available to all areas if commercial profit were the only criterion for supply, and (e) is important to national defence. There is also the view, based on a socialist ideology, that public ownership is desirable to prevent the earning of private profit extracted from labour and the concentration of economic power in private hands. Nationalized industries in the UK are normally set up as public corporations accountable to a government minister. ▷ **privatization; socialism**

**NATO**  The abbreviation for the **North Atlantic Treaty Organization**; pronounced **nay**-toh. The organization was established by a treaty signed in 1949 by Belgium, Canada, Denmark, France, Iceland, Italy, Luxembourg, the Netherlands, Norway, Portugal, the UK, and the USA; Greece and Turkey joined in 1952, West Germany in 1955, and Spain in 1982. NATO is a permanent military alliance established to defend Western Europe against Soviet aggression. The treaty commits the members to treat an armed attack on one of them as an attack on all of them, and for all to assist the country attacked by such actions as are deemed necessary. The alliance forces are based on contributions from the member countries' armed services, and operate under a multi-national command. The remit includes the deployment of nuclear, as well as conventional, weapons. Its institutions include a Council, an International Secretariat, the Supreme Headquarters Allied Powers, Europe (SHAPE), and various committees to formulate common policies. In the 1970s and 1980s  NATO policy of a first-strike nuclear attack to fend off a Soviet conventional attack became controversial in Western Europe, where many thought it increased the possibility of nuclear war. In 1966, France under de Gaulle withdrew all its forces from NATO command, but it remains a member. After the 1989 changes in Eastern Europe, a NATO summit in London in July 1990 began the process of redefining NATO's political and military goals. ▷ **Warsaw Pact**

**Naturalism**  A term used in art criticism for the faithful copying of nature, with no attempt to 'improve' or idealize the subject. It was used in this sense in 1672 by Giovanni Pietro Bellori (1615–96) to characterize the work of Caravaggio and his followers. It later became used to describe the incorporation of scientific method into art, especially literature. This was advocated in the late 19th century by the French novelist Emile Zola (1840–1902), at a time when confidence in science ran high. Zola claimed the writer should be a dispassionate observer of phenomena, his imagination a laboratory. The Naturalist movement provided a philosophical framework for the earlier Realist initiative, but was soon undermined by Symbolist ideas. ▷ **Realism; Symbolism**

**natural selection**   ▷ **Darwinism**.

**neoclassicism**   A classical revival affecting all the visual arts, including architecture and the decorative arts, which flourished from around 1750 onwards, lasting well into the 19th century; often spelled with a capital N. It was a reaction against the decorous excesses of Baroque and the 'frivolity' of Rococo, beginning in Rome, and spreading throughout Western Europe and North America. Its chief characteristics are outlined in the entry on **classicism**. ▷ **Baroque; classicism; Rococo**

**neo-colonialism**   ▷ **imperialism**.

**neo-Darwinism**   ▷ **Darwinism**.

**Neoimpressionism**   ▷ **Divisionism**.

**neurosis**   A mental illness, often associated with high levels of anxiety, in which people retain their sense of reality. Examples include people who have a phobia (eg a fear of spiders) or who are obsessive in their behaviour (eg always having to place an object in a certain position on a table, becoming extremely upset if this is not done). The symptoms are distressing to the individual, who finds them unacceptable. Throughout, people recognize the nature of their problem — for example, they will acknowledge that spiders 'can't harm you' — but still be unable to do anything about it. ▷ **phobia; psychology; psychosis**

**neutralism**   ▷ **neutrality**.

**neutrality**   In foreign policy, a situation where a state will not provide military and sometimes diplomatic support to another state. When the term refers simply to a state's policy, it means the same as **neutralism**; but it also has a more precise legal meaning. Under international laws of neutrality, a non-belligerent enjoys certain rights and obligations in times of war. It may not permit the use of its territory as a base for military operations nor furnish military assistance to the belligerents. A neutralized state enjoys the right of passage on the open seas for its non-military goods. It may, however, show sympathy with one belligerent as long as this is not reflected in its actions.

A member of an alliance may remain neutral in a conflict between another member of the alliance and a third state, if the alliance is not established for the purposes of conflict with that third state. For example, members of NATO stayed neutral during the UK's conflict with Argentina over the Falkland Is. ▷ **NATO; non-aligned movement**

**New Right** A wide-ranging ideological movement associated with the revival of conservatism in the 1970s and 1980s, particularly in the UK and USA. It is strongly in favour of state withdrawal from ownership, and intervention in the economy in favour of a free-enterprise system. There is also a strong moral conservatism — an emphasis on respect for authority, combined with a strong expression of patriotism and support for the idea of the family. Politically, the New Right adopts an aggressive style which places weight on pursuing convictions rather than on generating a consensus. In the USA in the 1980s it has been associated with the emergence of Christian fundamentalism (eg the Moral Majority). ▷ **conservatism; fundamentalism; Moral Majority; Thatcherism**

**nihilism** A term made popular by the Russian author, Ivan Turgenev (1818–83), who used it to describe the beliefs of a character (Basarov) in his novel *Fathers and Sons* (1862), referring to any outlook that denies the possibility of justifying moral values; the word comes from Latin, meaning 'nothing'. All traditional values and institutions are rejected. Nihilism came to characterize several members of the Russian radical intelligentsia, who advocated the total annihilation of all existing institutions in the name of unrestricted individual freedom. The revolutionary activities of these Nihilists culminated in the assassination of the Tsar in 1881. The German philosopher Friedrich Nietzsche (1844–1900) also inspired numerous thinkers whose nihilism was of a quite different character, the emphasis lying on a supposed sole virtue of 'intellectual honesty', allied with a respect for others, a rooting-out of traditional beliefs, and an aloofness in which the nihilist finds satisfaction in intellectual analysis or in art. ▷ **philosophy**

**Nobel Prizes** Prizes awarded each year from the income of a trust fund established by the will of Swedish scientist and industrialist Alfred Nobel (1833-96) to those who, in the opinion of the judges, have contributed most in the fields of physics, chemistry, physiology or medicine, literature, and peace. A sixth prize, for economics, is now awarded by the Swiss National Bank. Each prizewinner receives a gold medal, and a sum of money.

**non-aligned movement** A movement of states which positively hold the position of not taking sides in the major division within world politics between the USA and USSR. Non-alignment differs from neutralism in that it is associated with moves to mediate between the superpowers, and aims to make a direct contribution to the achievement of peace. The neutrality of non-aligned states is supposed to afford them increased diplomatic influence. Attempts in the early 1960s to give impetus to the movement by Mediterranean, African, and Asian countries were badly shaken by superpower hostility. However, a number of recently decolonized countries have favoured non-alignment as a mark of their independence. ▷ **cold war; neutralism**

**Nonconformists**   Originally, those Protestants in England and Wales in the 17th century who dissented from the principles of the Church of England. The name has subsequently been applied to such denominations as Baptists, Congregationalists, and Methodists, and generally refers to Christians who refuse to conform to the doctrine and practice of an established or national Church. ▷ **Christianity; Protestantism**

**non-figurative art**   ▷ **figurative art**.

**non-renewable resources**   Resources (ie objects of material or economic use to society, such as minerals, timber, and fish) which have evolved or formed over such long time periods that their exploitation is not sustainable. They cannot be used without danger of exhaustion because of the timescale needed for new stocks to form. Examples include fossil fuel deposits (coal, oil, gas) and mineral deposits (iron, gold). Some non-renewable resources can be recycled (eg metallic ores). ▷ **fossil fuels; recycling; renewable resources**

**nouvelle cuisine**   A movement away from the elaborate food of classical cuisine to a simpler, more natural presentation; pronounced *noo-vel kwi-zeen*. The approach began in the 1970s, and was given emphasis by the French chef Michel Guérard (1933– ). The first consideration is the quality of the fresh produce, with the aim of achieving lightness by using less fat and no flour in sauces. The movement has also been influenced by the Japanese style of food presentation.

**nuclear disarmament**   ▷ **nuclear weapons**.

**nuclear fission**   The splitting of a heavy atomic nucleus into two approximately equal portions, with the emission of free neutrons and large amounts of energy; *fission* means 'splitting into parts'. The process was discovered in 1934 by Italian physicist Enrico Fermi (1901–54). Fission in uranium and plutonium forms the basic mechanism of nuclear power and atomic bombs. ▷ **nuclear reactor**

**nuclear fusion**   The fusing together of two light-weight atomic nuclei, typically isotopes of hydrogen or lithium, which releases vast amounts of energy. To initiate fusion, the reacting species must be brought close enough

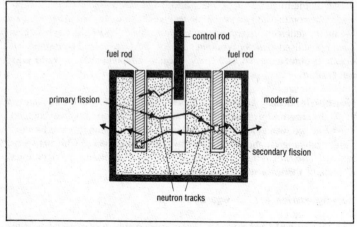

*Diagram showing the principle of nuclear fission*

together so that short-range nuclear forces come into play, as is possible in the high-temperature environments of the Sun and nuclear explosions. Fusion reactors attempt to reproduce such conditions in a controlled way. The chief experimental fusion reactors are the Joint European Torus in the UK, the Tokamak Fusion Test Reactor at Princeton, USA, and JT60 near Tokyo, Japan. ▷ **nuclear fission**

**nuclear pacifism** ▷ **pacifism**.

**nuclear power** ▷ **nuclear reactor**.

**nuclear reactor** A device for producing a continuous supply of heat energy from controlled radioactivity. Certain radioactive atomic nuclei, on being struck by neutrons, generate additional neutrons. This is self-sustaining if the speed of the neutrons is not too great. A nuclear reactor therefore has (i) a 'fuel', which may be uranium 235 or 233, or plutonium 239; (ii) a *moderator*, to control the speed and number of neutrons; and (iii) a heat exchange system, to utilize the heat generated (generally by operating the steam-driven turbines of a conventional electric power station). A **boiling water reactor** uses the cooling water itself as the source of steam for the turbines. In a **pressurized water reactor**, the coolant is water under such pressure that it reaches a high temperature without evaporation, and is used to heat boiler water via a heat exchanger. A **gas-cooled reactor** uses carbon dioxide or some other gas as a coolant, heating turbine water via a heat exchanger. A **fast reactor** has no moderator and generally uses liquid sodium as a coolant. A **breeder reactor** uses uranium 238 enriched with plutonium 239; it produces more Pu 239, and is the type of reactor used to generate material for atomic weapons. Some nuclear reactors are built and used solely for research purposes. ▷ **energy; meltdown; radioactive waste**

**nuclear weapons**   Weapons of mass destruction employing the energy-liberating nuclear phenomena of fission or fusion for their effects. According to their size and the means of delivery, they may be classified as *tactical* short-range weapons for use against enemy battlefield forces; *theatre* medium-range weapons for use against deep military targets; and *strategic* long-range weapons for use against enemy cities and command centres. Soon after their invention, a political movement developed demanding the control of nuclear weapons, the limitation of their spread to other countries, and their eventual abolition. In Britain it took the form of the Campaign for Nuclear Disarmament (CND), founded in 1958. Nuclear disarmament has had some success, such as the Non-Proliferation Treaty signed by the USA, Soviet Union, UK, and over 100 other countries in 1968, seeking to limit the spread of weapons and to pursue only peaceful uses of nuclear energy. However, concern about the proliferation of nuclear weapons continues. ▷ **arms control; disarmament; nuclear fission; nuclear fusion**

**ombudsman**   An official who investigates complaints regarding administrative action by governments — so-called 'mal-administration'. The complaint may not necessarily be confined to illegal action, but can cover broader injustices in administrative decisions. Most ombudsmen's powers are of necessity widely defined, but they normally do not investigate issues that can be considered by the courts or tribunals. Their findings do not have the force of law, and are put in the form of reports from which it is hoped remedial action will result. The first such institution was created in Sweden at the beginning of the 19th century, and today many countries have followed the lead. In Britain, an ombudsman (known as the Parliamentary Commissioner for Administration) was appointed in 1967.

**Op Art**   An abbreviation for **Optical Art**, a modern art movement which exploits the illusionistic effects of abstract spiral or wavy patterns, stripes, spots, etc. Hungarian-born French painter Victor Vasarely (1908–   ) and British painter Bridget Riley (1931–   ) are leading exponents. ▷ **abstract art; modern art**

**OPEC (Organization of Petroleum Exporting Countries)**   An international economic organization set up in 1960 with its headquarters in Vienna; pronounced **oh**-pek. It consists of 13 oil-producing countries:

the founder members were Iran, Iraq, Kuwait, Saudi Arabia, and Venezuela; and they have since been joined by Algeria, Ecuador, Gabon, Indonesia, Libya, Nigeria, Qatar, and the United Arab Emirates (formerly Abu Dhabi). Its purpose is to coordinate the petroleum policy of members to protect their interests, especially in relation to the fixing of prices for crude oil and the quantities to be produced. ▷ **cartel**

**opposition**   The right of parties and political movements not holding government office to criticize the government and seek to replace it by offering alternative policies. In democratic systems **the Opposition** normally consists of those parties which oppose the government through parliamentary channels, their activities being regarded as a necessary activity, and recognized in parliamentary and electoral procedures. Opposition can also occur from parties or movements outside parliament, either because they are too weak or not inclined to gain parliamentary representation. Interest groups may oppose governments on specific issues. In non-democratic systems, oppositions are often outlawed and sometimes repressed, although covert opposition continues. ▷ **adversary politics; democracy; parliament; pressure group**

**Optical Art**   ▷ **Op Art**.

**oratorio**   A non-liturgical, semi-dramatic sacred work, usually for solo voices, chorus, and orchestra. It takes its name from the Italian 'prayer-hall' in which the earliest oratorios were performed in the early 17th century, but until about 1750 it existed also in secular settings. Handel's oratorios, originally performed in the London theatres, represent this type at its finest, but by the time they influenced Haydn's *The Creation* (1798) the oratorio had come to be regarded as a religious rather than a dramatic work, and since then cathedral festivals have frequently provided the occasion for an oratorio performance. ▷ **cantata; classical music; motet**

**orders of architecture**   The arrangement of the parts of a column in classical architecture according to one of five accepted principles (*orders*): Tuscan, Doric, Ionic, Corinthian, Composite. Originally developed by the ancient Greeks, the earliest surviving codification is by the Roman, Vitruvius, writing in the 1st century AD.

**Orthodox Church**   or **Eastern Orthodox Church** A communion of self-governing Churches recognizing the honorary primacy of the Patriarch of Constantinople and confessing the doctrine of the seven Ecumenical Councils (from Nicaea I in 327, to Nicaea II in 787). It includes the patriarchates of Alexandria, Antioch, Constantinople, and Jerusalem, and the Churches of Russia, Bulgaria, Cyprus, Serbia, Georgia, Romania, Greece, Poland, Albania, and Czechoslovakia. It developed historically from the

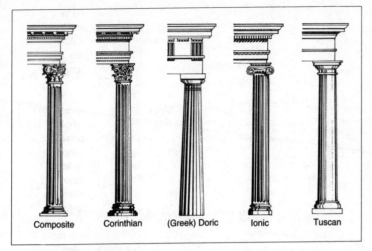

Composite    Corinthian    (Greek) Doric    Ionic    Tuscan

*The five orders of architecture*

Eastern Roman or Byzantine Empire. In doctrine it is strongly trinitarian, and in practice stresses the mystery and importance of the sacraments, of which it recognizes seven. Its highest authority is the Ecumenical Council.
▷ **Christianity; ecumenism; Trinity**

**overture**   An orchestral prelude to an opera or other work, or (since the early 19th century) an independent, usually descriptive, concert piece of similar length. The 'French overture' of the 17th–18th centuries consisted of a slow section followed by a quick one, often ending with a partial return of the opening material; the contemporary 'Italian overture' was on the pattern fast-slow-fast. ▷ **classical music; programme music**

**ovo-lacto-vegetarian**   ▷ **vegetarianism**.

**ozone layer**   The part of the stratosphere at a height of about 22 km/14 ml in which the gas ozone ($O_3$) is most concentrated. It is produced by the action of ultraviolet light from the Sun on oxygen ($O_2$) in the air. The ozone layer shields the Earth from the harmful effects of solar ultraviolet radiation, but can be decomposed by complex chemical reactions. The chief risk here comes from the use of chlorofluorocarbons (CFCs), found as the pressurized propellant in some aerosol sprays, in refrigerating systems, and in the production of foam packaging. International concern over the appearance of a 'hole' in the ozone layer over the Antarctic reached a peak in the mid-1980s, and led to a movement for the withdrawal of CFC-producing devices.

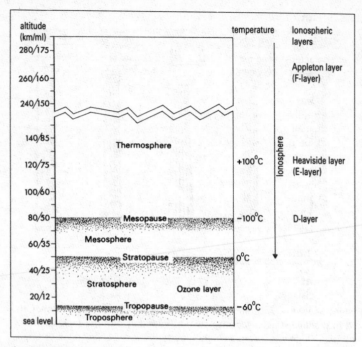

*Layers of the atmosphere*

In 1987 the Montreal Protocol was signed by around 40 countries to limit their use, with the intention that by 1999 worldwide consumption of CFCs should be 50% of 1986 levels. In 1989, the European Community meeting in Brussels agreed to cut CFC consumption by 85% as soon as possible and altogether by the end of the century. ▷ **CFCs; greenhouse effect**

**pacifism**   The doctrine of opposition to all wars, including civil wars. Its most obvious feature is the personal commitment to non-participation in wars, except possibly in a non-combatant role. Pacifists also advocate efforts to maintain peace and support disarmament, especially through the strengthening of international organizations and law. They have long been associated with Christian sects, but in the 20th century they include many who oppose war based on secular moral principles. Pacifism is often associated with support for non-violent political action. A more limited form is **nuclear pacifism**, which is opposed to nuclear, but not conventional, war.
▷ **conscientious objection; disarmament**

**pantheism**   The belief that God and the universe are ultimately identical. It may equate the world with God or deny the reality of the world, maintaining that only the divine is real and that sense experience is an illusion. It is a characteristic feature of Hinduism and certain schools of Buddhism.
▷ **Buddhism; God; Hinduism**

**paranormal**   Beyond the bounds of what can be explained in terms of currently-held scientific knowledge. To describe an event as paranormal requires that all other possible explanations for the event, based on known principles, be ruled out. However, this does not imply that the eventual explanation, as science discovers more about allegedly paranormal events, will be non-physical. It allows for the possibility that new discoveries in physics may account for events which are now classified as paranormal. This is in contrast with the term *supernatural*, which implies a non-physical explanation for events that lie forever beyond natural laws. The scientific study of the paranormal is carried on by **parapsychology**.

**parapsychology**   ▷ **paranormal**.

**parliament**   The general term in most English-speaking countries for the national legislative body, normally elected by popular vote. Its role is to pass legislation and keep a check on the activities of the government or executive. In a parliamentary governmental system it is also responsible for choosing and sustaining a government, though the individual members of the government will be chosen by the prime minister. In some presidential systems (eg France) parliament can also play an essential role in supporting the government, but not the president, who is elected separately and who can be a member of a party which does not hold a parliamentary majority. In other systems, the executive may exist independently of the parliament, as is the case with the US president. In the UK, parliament is constituted by the Crown, the House of Lords, and the elected House of Commons. Proposed laws must go through a defined procedure in both Houses and receive the royal assent, before becoming statutes. ▷ **bicameral system; Congress; executive; House of Commons; House of Lords; legislature; local government; unicameral system**

**Parliamentary Commissioner for Administration**   ▷ **ombudsman**.

**patent**   A document which gives an exclusive right to someone to make, use or sell an invention for a limited period (20 years, in Europe). The basic purpose is to stop someone else stealing your invention. Ideas cannot be patented. There is a central patent office in Munich which coordinates patent applications for many European countries, as well as designs and trade marks. It contains millions of patents, so checking to see whether someone has already invented something is an arduous business. If you do invent something, and wish to patent it, you need to apply to the Patent Office in London, giving full written details.

**Pentecostalism**   A modern Christian renewal movement inspired by the descent of the Holy Spirit experienced by the Apostles at the first Christian Pentecost. The name derives from the Greek words for the period of time when this event took place — some '50 days' after the death and resurrection of Jesus. It is marked by the reappearance of speaking in tongues, prophecy, and healing. The movement began in 1901 at Topeka, Kansas, USA, and became organized in 1905 at Los Angeles. Rejected by their own churches, new churches were established, commonly called 'Pentecostal', and since then their missionary zeal has reached every part of the world. Pentecostal churches are characterized by a literal interpret-ation of the Bible, informal worship during which there is enthusiastic singing and spontaneous exclamations of praise and thanksgiving, and the exercise of the gifts of the Holy Spirit. There are over 22 million Pentecostals worldwide. Since the 1960s, Pentecostal influence (usually referred to as 'charismatic renewal') has appeared within the established Protestant Roman Catholic  and Greek Orthodox Churches. ▷ **charismatic move-ment; Christianity**

**perestroika**   The process of 'reconstructing' Soviet society through a programme of reforms initiated since 1985 by General Secretary Mikhail Gorbachev (1931–  ); pronounced *pe-re-stroy-ka*. Such reforms, meant to be consistent with the ideals of the 1917 revolution, are directed at relaxing state controls over the economy, eliminating corruption from the state bureaucracy, and democratizing the Soviet communist party and the work-place to strengthen workers' control. They became a dominant force in Soviet politics in 1991. ▷ **communism; glasnost**

**pharmacology**   A branch of medical science which studies the actions, uses, and undesirable side-effects of drugs. The subject became a scientific discipline in the 19th century, when pioneers began to study the physio-logical actions of purified drugs. Pharmacological research is now carried out in drug companies, universities, and research institutes, and has led to the development of over 200 essential drugs, as defined by the World Health Organization. ▷ **designer drugs**

**philosophy**   Literally the love of wisdom, a subject which deals with some of the most general questions about the universe and our place in it. Is the world entirely physical in its composition and processes? Is there any purpose to it? Can we know anything for certain? Are we free? Are there any absolute values? Philosophy differs from science, in that its questions cannot be answered empirically or by experiment; and from religion, in that its purpose is entirely intellectual, and allows no role for faith or revelation. Philosophy tends to proceed by an informal but rigorous process of conceptual analysis and argument.

The major branches of philosophy are *metaphysics*, the inquiry into the most general features, relations, and processes of reality; *epistemology*, the investigation of the possibility, types, and sources of knowledge; *ethics*, the study of the types, sources, and justification of moral values and principles; and *logic*, the analysis of correct and incorrect reasoning. Philosophical issues can also arise concerning other areas of inquiry — for example in art education, law, religion, and science. The first philosophers from ancient Greece, notably Plato and Aristotle (fourth century BC), probed virtually every area of knowledge. ▷ **epistemology; ethics; logic; metaphysics**

**phobia** A situation which gives rise to anxiety in a person, but which is not specifically dangerous. Avoidance behaviour invariably occurs. The major forms of phobia are *simple* phobia (in which people are afraid of a specific object or situation) and *social* phobia (in which they are concerned about their behaviour in front of others). Phobias have often been given impressive Greek or Latin names, as the panel on p 130–1 shows. ▷ **neurosis**

**physiology** An experimental science concerned with the study of the functions of living things. Its scope is wide: some studies are concerned with processes that go on in cells (such as photosynthesis in plants); others with how tissues or organs work, and how they are controlled and integrated within the whole organism; yet others deal with how living things respond to their environments. ▷ **biological rhythm**

**picketing** The action by a trade union in an industrial dispute to try to persuade fellow-workers and others not to go to work, or do business with the company involved in the dispute. Pickets stand outside the gates of the factory or offices, and lobby all who would go in. Trade union legislation in the UK now limits picketing to the place where the picket actually works (**primary picketing**), and requires that it be carried out peacefully. Employers may be able to take legal action to stop other forms of action, such as the picketing of locations where the company in dispute is not directly involved (**secondary picketing**), or the use of **flying pickets**, workers not employed by the company in dispute, who are nonetheless ready to travel to the scene of the industrial action to help in the picketing. ▷ **industrial action; trade union**

**Piper Alpha disaster** A disaster on the Piper Alpha oil-drilling platform in the North Sea, off the coast of Scotland, which was destroyed by an explosion in July 1988. The disaster killed 167, and resulted in insurance claims approaching $1.5 thousand million.

## AN A TO Z OF PHOBIAS

| Technical term | Everyday term | Technical term | Everyday term | Technical term | Everyday term |
|---|---|---|---|---|---|
| acero- | sourness | entomo- | insects | nepho- | clouds |
| achluo- | darkness | eoso- | dawn | noso- (patho-) | disease |
| acro- | heights | eremo- | solitude | ocho- | vehicles |
| aero- | air | erete- | pins | odonto- | teeth |
| agora- | open spaces | ereutho- | blushing | oiko- | home |
| aichuro- | points | ergasio- | work | olfacto- | smell |
| ailuro- | cats | geno- | sex | ommato- | eyes |
| akoustico- | sound | geuma- | taste | oneiro- | dreams |
| algo- | pain | grapho- | writing | ophidio- | snakes |
| amaka- | carriages | gymno- | nudity | ornitho- | birds |
| amatho- | dust | gyno- | women | ourano- | heaven |
| andro- | men | hamartio- | sin | pan- (panto-) | everything |
| anemo- | wind | haphe- | touch | partheno- | girls |
| angino- | narrowness | harpaxo- | robbers | patroio- | heredity |
| antropo- | man | hedono- | pleasure | penia- | poverty |
| antlo- | flood | haemato- | blood | phasmo- | ghosts |
| apeiro- | infinity | helmintho- | worms | phobo- | fears |
| arachno- | spiders | hodo- | travel | photo- | light |
| astheno- | weakness | homichlo- | fog | pnigero- | smothering |
| astra- | lightning | horme- | shock | poine- | punishment |
| ate- | ruin | hydro- | water | poly- | many things |
| aulo- | flute | hypegia- | responsibility | poto- | drink |
| aurora- | Northern Lights | hypno- | sleep | pterono- | feathers |
| bacilli- | microbes | ideo- | ideas | pyro- | fire |
| baro- | gravity | kakorraphia- | failure | rypo- | soiling |
| baso- | walking | katagelo- | ridicule | Santano- | Satan |
| batracho- | reptiles | keno- | void | sela- | flash |
| belone- | needles | kineso- | motion | sidero- | stars |
| bronto- (tonitro-) | thunder | klepto- | stealing | sito- | food |
| cheima- | cold | kopo- | fatigue | sperma- (spermato-) | germs |
| chiono- | snow | kristallo- | ice | stasi- | standing |
| chrometo- | money | lalio- | stuttering | stygio- (hade-) | hell |
| chrono- | duration | linono- | string | syphilo- | syphilis |
| chrystallo- | crystals | logo- | words | thaaso- | sitting |
| claustro- | closed spaces | lysso- (mania-) | insanity | thalasso- | sea |
| cnido- | strings | mastigo- | flogging | thanato- | death |
| cometo- | comets | mechano- | machinery | theo- | God |
| cromo- | colour | metallo- | metals | thermo- | heat |
| cyno- | dogs | meteoro- | meteors | toxi- | poison |
| demo- | crowds | miso- | contamination | tremo- | trembling |
| demono- | demons | mono- | one thing | triskaideka- | thirteen |
| dermato- | skin | musico- | music | zelo- | jealousy |
| dike- | injustice | muso- | mice | zoo- | animals |
| dora- | fur | necro- | corpses | xeno- | strangers |
| eisoptro- | mirrors | nelo- | glass | | |
| electro- | electricity | neo- | newness | | |

| Everyday term | Technical term | Everyday term | Technical term | Everyday term | Technical term |
|---|---|---|---|---|---|
| air | aero- | gravity | baro- | ruin | ate- |
| animals | zoo- | heat | thermo- | Satan | Satano- |
| birds | ornitho- | heaven | ourano- | sea | thalasso |
| blood | haemato- | heights | acro- | sex | geno- |
| blushing | ereutho- | hell | stygio- (hade-) | shock | horme- |
| carriages | amaka- | heredity | patroio- | sin | hamartio- |
| cats | ailuro- | home | oiko- | sitting | thaaso- |
| closed spaces | claustro- | ice | kristallo- | skin | dermato- |
| clouds | nepho- | ideas | ideo- | sleep | hypno- |
| cold | cheima- | infinity | apeiro- | smell | olfacto- |
| colour | cromo- | injustice | dike- | smothering | pnigero- |
| comets | cometo- | insanity | lysso- (mania-) | snakes | ophidio- |
| contamination | miso- | insects | entomo- | snow | chiono- |
| corpses | necro- | jealousy | zelo- | soiling | rypo- |
| crowds | demo- | light | photo- | solitude | eremo- |
| crystals | chrystallo- | lightning | astra- | sound | akoustico- |
| darkness | achluo- | machinery | mechano- | sourness | acero- |
| dawn | eoso- | man | anthropo- | spiders | arachno- |
| death | thanato- | many things | poly- | standing | stasi- |
| demons | demono- | men | andro- | stars | sidero- |
| disease | noso- (patho-) | metals | metallo- | stealing | klepto- |
| dogs | cyno- | meteors | meteoro- | stings | cnido- |
| dreams | oneiro- | mice | muso- | strangers | xeno- |
| drink | poto- | microbes | bacilli- | string | linono- |
| duration | chrono- | mirrors | eisoptro- | stuttering | lalio- |
| dust | amatho- | money | chrometo- | syphilis | syphilo- |
| electricity | electro- | motion | kineso- | taste | geuma- |
| everything | pan- (panto-) | music | musico- | teeth | odonto- |
| eyes | ommato- | narrowness | angino- | thirteen | triskaideka- |
| failure | kakorraphia- | needles | belone- | thunder | bronto- (tonitro-) |
| fatigue | kopo- | newness | neo- | touch | haphe- |
| fears | phobo- | Northern Lights | aurora- | travel | hodo- |
| feathers | pterono- | nudity | gymno- | trembling | tremo- |
| fire | pyro- | one thing | mono- | vehicles | ocho- |
| flash | sela- | open spaces | agora- | void | keno- |
| flogging | mastigo- | pain | algo- | walking | baso- |
| flood | antlo- | pins | erete- | water | hydro- |
| flute | aulo- | pleasure | hedono- | weakness | astheno- |
| fog | homichlo- | points | aichuro- | wind | anemo- |
| food | sito- | poison | toxi- | women | gyno- |
| fur | dora- | poverty | penia- | words | logo- |
| germs | sperma- (spermato-) | punishment | poine- | work | ergasio- |
| ghosts | phasmo- | reptiles | batracho- | worms | helmintho- |
| girls | partheno- | responsibility | hypegia- | writing | grapho- |
| glass | nelo- | ridicule | katagelo- | | |
| God | theo- | robbers | harpaxo- | | |

**placebo**   An inactive substance given as a drug to a patient, who may benefit from the belief that the drug is active; pronounced *pla-see-boh*. Because patients can improve under this illusion, in most countries new drugs are tested for clinical efficacy in trials where a placebo is given to one group. The active drug must prove itself to work better than the placebo.

**plebiscite**   ▷ **referendum**.

**poetic licence**   The poet's practice of taking liberty with known facts in the interests of telling a more interesting or more effective story. For example, the historical Hotspur was 20 years older than Prince Henry; but in *Henry IV*, for dramatic purposes, Shakespeare makes them the same age. The term can also refer to licence taken, for poetic effect, with the rules of grammar. ▷ **imagery; literature**

**Pointillism**   ▷ **Divisionism**.

**policy unit**   A small group of officials in a government department, or other public agency, whose role is to supply information, advice, and analysis to policy makers, normally politicians. The main idea behind the unit is to have officials concentrating on strategic issues free from other responsibilities. ▷ **think tank**

**political asylum**   The protection which a state can give to a citizen of another state. Individuals who feel threatened by their own government may apply for asylum in any country which they feel will be sympathetic to their cause. For example, in the days of the Cold War between Western and Eastern Europe, several famous visitors to the West decided to stay, and asked for political asylum — such as the ballet dancer Rudolf Nureyev, who obtained political asylum in Paris while touring with the Kirov Ballet in 1961. In practice, only certain categories of people are likely to succeed in their application — in particular, those accused of certain political offences (such as treason and espionage), and those suffering unacceptable restrictions on their publications, research, or skills. The receiving country often grants asylum as much for selfish reasons as humanitarian ones — the visitor may well have skills of value to offer. ▷ **extradition**

**political science**   The academic discipline which describes and analyses the operations of government, the state, and other political organizations, and any other factors which influence their behaviour, such as economics. A major concern is to establish how power is exercised, and by whom, in resolving conflict within society. The subject draws conclusions by observing and generating data about state organizations and wider societal groupings and their interrelationships. **Political theory** (of which **political philosophy** is a sub-branch) has two principal concerns: the clarification of values in order to demonstrate logically the purpose of political activity, and thereby the way in which society 'ought' to proceed (eg in allocating resources); and the rigorous derivation and testing of theories drawn from empirical research. ▷ **social science**

**pollution**   The direct or indirect introduction of a harmful substance into the environment. The degree of pollution depends on the nature and amount of the pollutant, and the location into which it is introduced; fertilizers become pollutants when used to excess, and when they become concentrated in run-off water entering streams. Different categories of pollution include: air pollution (eg acid rain), freshwater pollution (eg discharge of chemical effluent from industry into rivers), marine pollution (eg oil spills from tankers), noise pollution (eg from aircraft), land pollution (eg the burial of toxic waste), and visual pollution (eg the intrusion of industry into an area of scenic beauty). ▷ **acid rain; hazardous substances; radioactive waste; waste disposal**

**polymerization**   The forming of a large molecule, a **polymer**, by the combination of smaller ones (*monomers*). Combinations of two molecules are called *dimers*; of three, *trimers*. Small polymers (usually of 3–10 monomers) are known as *oligomers*. The monomers may be all of the same type, as in polyethylene, or they may be two complementary molecules, as in polyester or polyamide formation. Polymers may contain anything from 100 to over 10000 monomer residues.

**polytheism**   ▷ **God**.

**Pop Art**   A modern art form based on the commonplace and ephemeral aspects of 20th-century urban life, such as soup cans, comics, movies, and advertising. Pioneer British Pop artists included Eduardo Paolozzi (1924–   ) and Richard Hamilton (1922–   ) in the mid-1950s, and leading US contributors in the 1960s include Jasper Johns (1930–   ), Andy Warhol (1926–87), and Roy Lichtenstein (1923–   ). American Pop is tougher and more deliberately shocking than British, with strong reminiscences of Dada. Humour is an important element, though art critics have been inclined to take it all very solemnly. ▷ **art; Dada; Surrealism**

**post-structuralism**   ▷ **deconstruction**.

**poverty trap**   A situation in a social welfare and taxation system which occurs when individuals, previously unemployed and claiming various social benefits, obtain work, and find that they are taxed, so ending up with less net income than before. The same situation may also apply to low-paid workers who obtain a small rise and find they have lost the right to certain benefits. ▷ **standard of living; taxation; welfare state**

**power** ▷ **alternative energy; nuclear reactor**.

**precedent**   An earlier occurrence of something, especially of an action or statement which can serve as an example justifying similar later actions. The term is particularly used in law, where a previous legal decision is cited in order to justify making the same decision on another occasion. The legal systems of England and America rely greatly on the body of precedent established over centuries.

**predestination**   In Christian theology, the doctrine that the ultimate salvation or damnation of each human individual has been ordained beforehand. A source of endless dispute, the doctrine has been interpreted in many ways. The Protestant Reformers Luther and Calvin defended it, though in varying degrees. ▷ **Calvinism; Lutheranism**

**premise** or **premiss**   A sentence which is explicitly assumed in a chain of reasoning. In the argument 'Paris is larger than London; therefore London is smaller than Paris', the first of these two sentences is the premise, the second is the conclusion. Complex arguments make use of many premises. ▷ **logic**

**Presbyterianism**   The form of Church government developed by the Reformed Churches, deriving from the 16th-century Reformation led by John Calvin (1509–64) in Geneva and John Knox (c.1513–72) in Scotland. Government is by courts at local congregational (eg kirk session), regional (presbytery), and national (General Assembly) levels. *Elders* (ordained laymen) as well as ministers play a leading part in all courts. Through emigration and missionary activity from Scotland, Ireland, and England, Presbyterianism has spread worldwide. The World Presbyterian Alliance was formed in 1878, to be succeeded in 1970 by the World Alliance of Reformed Churches. ▷ **Christianity; Reformation**

**preservatives** ▷ **additives**.

**pressure group**   A voluntary organization formed in active support of a particular political interest or cause; sometimes called an **interest group**. It can directly represent its members (a *sectional* group) or act on behalf of others (a *promotional* group). It tries to influence government and legislature, and also public opinion, by campaigns, lobbying, and demonstrations. It differs from a political party in that it does not seek political office. An example of a pressure group is ASH — Action on Smoking and Health. The broader notion of 'interest group' would include organizations such as the British Medical Association (BMA). ▷ **activism; lobbying; Moral Majority; political science**

**pressurized water reactor**  ▷ **nuclear reactor**.

**preventive medicine**  A branch of medical practice that is concerned with the prevention of disease; also called **preventative medicine**. This is achieved by measures that control the environment, such as clean air legislation; ensure a clean and suitable food and water supply; promote mass medication (eg schemes of immunization); organize programmes for the eradication of disease (eg smallpox, diphtheria); and promote safer life-styles largely by education (eg the reduction in smoking to prevent cancer of the lung, and the promotion of condoms to reduce the possibility of AIDS). ▷ **fluoridation of water; quarantine**

**prices and incomes policy**  A government policy for managing the economy, used in the late 1960s and early 1970s by certain countries, such as Britain, the USA, and The Netherlands. It arises out of a concern that if incomes are allowed to rise too quickly, inflationary pressures will appear, with rising prices. The policy tries to hold down both prices and incomes. Supporters of this policy believe that control of the two elements is necessary for the successful management of the economy. The opposite view is that inflation can be successfully controlled only by control of the money supply, and that regulating prices and incomes interferes with market mechanisms. Full legal backing is necessary if the policy is to be effective, and this step is opposed by some economists and trade unionists, as emerged when such a policy was used in Britain in the 1970s. ▷ **inflation**

**primary picketing**  ▷ **picketing**.

**prisoner of conscience**  ▷ **Amnesty International**.

**private enterprise**  An economic system where individuals, singly or in a group (as in a privately owned firm), may engage in a business venture using their own resources and without needing state approval or control, as long as the venture does not go against existing laws and rules. It contrasts with **public enterprise**, where the activity is carried out by a state-owned or state-controlled organization. ▷ **economics**

**private sector**  Those aspects of an economy which are not controlled by the state, but which are in the hands of individuals or companies, and therefore answerable to the owners. The notion contrasts with the *public sector*, where activities are under state control. ▷ **economics**

**privatization**  The return to private ownership of organizations which are owned at present by the state. The government issues shares in the company to be privatized, and offers them for sale to the public. The company therefore becomes answerable to the shareholders and not to the government. Several cases of privatization took place in Britain in the 1980s, including British Telecom and British Gas. The government was able to raise considerable sums of money by this means, thus helping to reduce its borrowing requirements and cut tax rates, and the managers were left free to manage. ▷ **deregulation; nationalization; shares**

**Privy Council**   A body which advises the British monarch, appointed by the Crown. In previous times, particularly the Tudor period, it was a highly influential group, and might be regarded as the precursor of the cabinet. Today its role is largely formal, enacting subordinate legislation (proclamations and Orders in Council). Its membership is over 300, and includes all cabinet ministers, the Speaker of the House of Commons, the Archbishops of Canterbury and York, and senior British and Commonwealth statesmen. ▷ **cabinet; legislature**

**productivity**   The ratio of output to input in an industrial context. It usually refers to the quantity of goods or services produced in relation to the number of employees engaged in the operation (*labour productivity*). Low productivity is the major cause of a company's decline, since it results in high costs per unit, and therefore high prices that are not competitive. The notion is important in wage negotiations: *productivity bargaining* balances a proposed increase in wages with an anticipated rise in productivity.

**programme music**   Music which paints a scene or tells a story. Among early examples are the violin concertos by Vivaldi called *The Four Seasons*, but it was in the 19th century, with the increased resources of the symphony orchestra, that composers most widely and effectively gave musical expression to literary and other extra-musical ideas. The concert overture and the symphonic poem proved to be ideal vehicles for this, and in many cases (such as in Smetana's cycle of symphonic poems, *Má Vlast* (1874–9, My Country), they embodied nationalistic ideals and aspirations. The capability of music to convey a 'programme' without the aid of a written commentary is severely limited, but its illustrative powers have been proved many times. ▷ **classical music; overture; symphonic poem**

**progressive education**   A term sometimes used to denote teaching which places greater emphasis on the wishes of the child. It usually involves greater freedom of choice, activity, and movement than traditional forms of teaching. Progressive education has been pioneered in certain schools such as Summerhill and Dartington Hall, UK, but its influences have spread to other schools, particularly in the primary sector. The term is no longer as fashionable as it was a few years ago.

**proletariat**   In radical and socialist philosophy, a term coined to denote the working class, ie those who live by their labour and do not own property. It is particularly important in Marxist and communist ideology, though it has no distinctive meaning from 'wage labour'. ▷ **communism; Marxism; radicalism**

**proportional representation** Any system of voting designed to ensure that the representation of voters is in proportion to their numbers. There are many voting methods, none of which achieves perfect proportionality. In the *list system* the number of candidates on a party's list who are elected depends on the proportion of votes they receive in national elections. In the *single transferable vote*, votes are cast in multi-member constituencies and an ordered preference for all the candidates is expressed on the ballot paper; votes are then transferred from one candidate to another

*Ballot paper for proportional representation*

until someone gains enough to be elected. Proportional representation comes close to meeting the democratic principle of majority government; examples can be found in most West European countries (but not the UK). The case against it is that it does not in fact produce majority party government, but unstable coalitions, and breaks the bond between MPs and their constituencies. ▷ **coalition; democracy**

**Protestantism** Expressions of Christian faith originating from the 16th-century Reformation as a protest against Roman Catholicism. It became the established religion of England under Queen Elizabeth I. Common characteristics include the authority of scripture, justification by faith alone, and the priesthood of all believers. The original groupings were those who followed Luther, Calvin, and Zwingli, and the term now embraces most non-Roman Catholic or non-Orthodox denominations. There are many doctrinal differences, but in recent decades there has been a marked communal interest in church unity. ▷ **Anabaptists; Baptists; Calvinism; Congregationalism; ecumenism; Lutheranism; Nonconformists; Orthodox Church; Presbyterianism; Reformation**

**psychiatry**   A branch of medicine concerned with the study, diagnosis, prevention, and treatment of mental and emotional disorders. The subject includes a range of sub-specialities, such as *child psychiatry, forensic psychiatry* (the study and treatment of patients who have broken the law), and *psychotherapy*. The range of conditions treated by psychiatrists is wide, and includes patients suffering from psychoses (in which there is a loss of contact with reality), neuroses (in which anxiety plays a major component), eating disorders, disorders of dependence, mental retardation, and sleep disorders. ▷ **psychonalysis; psychosis**

**psychoanalysis**   The theory and clinical practice of a form of psychology which emphasizes the unconscious aspects of the mental life of an individual. The treatment, pioneered by the Austrian psychoanalyst Sigmund Freud (1856–1939), is a form of therapy which attempts to eliminate conflict by altering the personality in a positive way. Freud introduced ideas concerning the use of the study of dreams as a way of understanding people's deeper emotions; he emphasized the introspective study of the self and, with colleagues such as Alfred Adler (1870–1937) and Carl Jung (1875–1961), advanced ideas about normal and abnormal psychological processes. A distinction needs to be clearly made between psychoanalysis and **psychotherapy**, which is a broader subject, including such other techniques of intervention as group psychotherapy and family psychotherapy. ▷ **psychology**

**psychology**   The science of mental life — a succinct definition used in 1890 by US psychologist William James (1842–1910). There are many branches and facets to the subject, notably developmental psychology, which studies the emergence of thought and behaviour in children; educational psychology, which studies the way children learn and the problems they encounter; occupational psychology, which studies people in their work environment; physiological psychology, which studies the processes in brain and body underlying behaviour; and abnormal psychology, which studies the nature of abnormal psychological states. Contemporary psychology has seen a particular revival of interest in cognitive processes (such as memory, attention, perception, and intelligence), with new interpretations using concepts from communication theory, information processing systems, control systems, and computer systems for the organization and representation of knowledge. The application of psychological methods pervades many aspects of everyday life. These methods are used  for example  in the study of learning  the assessment of food preferences, the investigation of attitudes, opinions, and prejudices, the design of work and leisure environments, personnel selection and management, counselling, and therapy. ▷ **behaviourism; cognitive psychology; mentalism; psychoanalaysis**

**psychosis** A psychiatric term with a variety of uses. It is most clearly used when referring to psychiatric illnesses in which there is a loss of contact with reality, in the form of delusions or hallucinations. But it is also used as an indication that a psychiatric illness is severe rather than mild or moderate in its impact on the individual. In addition, psychoses can be illnesses in which there is a qualitative change in the emotions; illnesses in which there is regression to immature forms of behaviour; and situations where there is marked withdrawal and a lack of relating to others. ▷ **neurosis; psychiatry**

**psychotherapy** ▷ **psychoanalysis**.

**public debt** The total amount of government borrowings, both short-term, such as treasury bills, and long-term bonds; also known as the *government debt* or the *national debt*. The total UK public debt in the late 1980s was over £197 thousand million, whilst that of the USA was over $2850 thousand million. ▷ **national accounts**

**public enterprise** ▷ **private enterprise**.

**public sector** ▷ **private sector**.

**public sector borrowing requirement (PSBR)** The amount of money a government needs to raise in a financial year by borrowing. The need results from tax revenues and other income being less than the total expenditure budgeted by the various government departments. The balance has to be borrowed — in other words, there is a budget deficit. This occurred in the UK in the 1970s and early 1980s, but the sale of state-owned enterprises and general economic growth led to a budget surplus in the late 1980s. In contrast, the USA Federal budget showed a huge deficit throughout the period. Reducing PSBR has been seen, in the UK, as an important means of reducing money supply, and thus a way of keeping inflation under control. ▷ **budget; inflation**

**Quakers** ▷ **Friends, Religious Society of**.

**quantum field theory** ▷ **quantum mechanics**.

*q*

**quantum mechanics** A system of mechanics applicable at distances of atomic dimensions ($10^{-10}$m or less), and providing for the description of atoms, molecules, and all phenomena that depend on properties of matter at the atomic level. In 1900, the study of electromagnetic radiation emitted by objects on account of their temperature (*blackbody radiation*) led German physicist Max Planck to the idea that light is composed of photons — minute packets (*quanta*) of light. Light, thought to be wave-like, thus appeared to behave like particles. In 1923 French physicist Louis de Broglie suggested that matter particles may in turn behave like waves, and that particles such as electrons have a wavelength associated with them. The development of quantum mechanics applicable to particles moving at high speed was due to British physicist Paul Dirac in 1928, and is known as **relativistic quantum mechanics**. The final development of quantum theory, incorporating the creation and destruction of particles  took place during the 1940s and is called **quantum field theory**.

The wave-like nature of electrons and other particles is expressed by wave-functions, the most fundamental way of describing either simple particles or other more complicated quantum systems.  Particles such as electrons are no longer considered as point-like objects, but are spread out in a way governed by wave-functions. Quantum mechanics necessarily means dealing with a probabilistic description of nature, and thus contrasts with classical mechanics, in which the precise properties of every object are in principle calculable. The attributes of quantum systems have measurable values which are distinct and separate from each other. For example, the energy of an electron in an atom does not have a continuous spectrum of values, but only allows certain values; the energy is said to be *quantized*. When an electron in an excited atom jumps from one possible energy state to another of lower energy, a quantum of light is emitted. Measurements on quantum states will give one of the possible values, with a probability controlled by the wave-function. ▷ **mechanics; uncertainty principle**

**quarantine**  A period during which people or animals suspected of carrying a contagious disease are kept in isolation. Originally quarantine was an attempt to prevent the spread of plague in the 14th century: ships arriving at port were kept isolated and offshore for 40 days. Later the principle was applied to many infectious diseases, and the time shortened to relate to the incubation period of the particular infection. The practice is now rarely used in human illness: possible infected suspects are merely kept under medical supervision at home or in hospital. It is still applied to dogs and other animals imported from overseas to the UK as a defence against the spread of rabies; a six-month period is normal. ▷ **preventive medicine**

**racism**  An ideology that claims to explain an alleged inferiority of certain racial or ethnic groups in terms of their biological or physical characteristics. Racist beliefs have been used to justify genocide, chronic poverty, and the maintenance of systems of inequality (such as South African apartheid). *Racial discrimination* takes place when someone is treated in a particular way because of their race or ethnicity. The term is usually understood to mean negative discrimination — that is, treating people in a way which will disadvantage them in relation to other social groups (eg with reference to housing or employment). Negative racial discrimination is illegal in most modern societies, though often difficult to prove in a court of law. ▷ **affirmative action; apartheid; ethnicity; ideology; segregation**

**radicalism** Any set of ideas, normally of the left but not exclusively so, which argues for more substantial social and political change than is supported in the political mainstream. What is radical is a matter of judgment, and so the term is very widely applied. There are radical parties which are left of centre in most countries, but their policies vary enormously, ranging from moderate to violent revolutionary. There may also be right-wing radicals, as in the case of fascism and Nazism. Outside politics, the term refers to any approach which offers a fundamental challenge to established traditions or ideas, such as in the arts or scientific research. ▷ **fascism; left wing; right wing**

**radioactive waste** A by-product of the many processes involved in the generation of nuclear power. Despite nearly 30 years of commercial nuclear power generation, there is no widely accepted solution to the problem of radioactive waste disposal. Three levels of waste are produced: low, intermediate, and high. *Low-level* and *intermediate-level* waste is generally buried in pits: at Drigg, adjacent to the Sellafield nuclear complex in the UK, and in abandoned salt mines in Germany. *High-level* waste is in the meantime generally stored in stainless steel tanks, and continually cooled. One possibility for long-term storage is vitrification (solidification in glass), to reduce the volume of waste. Proposals exist for the burial of high-level waste either under the sea-bed or deep underground on land. The production and storage of radioactive waste is a major international environmental issue, with strong opposition from such pressure groups as Greenpeace. ▷ **hazardous substances; nuclear reactor; waste disposal**

**radio astronomy** ▷ **astronomy**.

**radiocarbon dating** A method for measuring the decay of the radio-active isotope 14C in organic material up to 100000 years old, developed in 1948–9 by US chemist Willard Libby (1908–80). Living animals and plants take in carbon, which contains some radioactive carbon14. When the organism dies, it stops taking in carbon, and as the carbon14 decays, its proportion to the total amount of carbon decreases in a way which is directly related to the time elapsed since death. Using samples principally from wood and charcoal, the technique revolutionized archaeological dating across the world. ▷ **archaeology; isotopes**

**rainforest** The vegetation type found in wet equatorial regions and other areas of high rainfall. Tropical rainforests display a great diversity of plant and animal species, a closed canopy layer which allows little light to reach the forest floor, and rapid cycling of nutrients within the forest. Despite the luxuriant growth of these forests, when cut down the soils are relatively infertile, because most of the nutrients are in the vegetation, and soils are

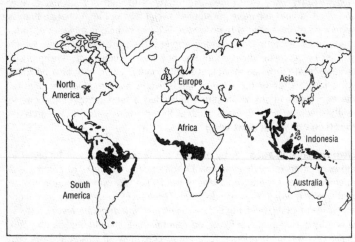

*The distribution of rainforests worldwide*

rapidly washed away. Many of the trees have considerable commercial value (eg mahogany, teak), and large areas are being cleared. Deforestation is also occurring to create new agricultural areas (cattle ranching) and industry (mining). The United Nations Food and Agricultural Organization estimates that about 100 000 sq km/62 000 sq ml are cleared each year. This rate of disappearance is alarming many conservationists, because of the extinction of unique plant and animal species. Tropical rainforests also play an important role in the global climate system which could be disrupted by clearance. ▷ **conservation; environment**

**Rastafarianism** A religious movement from the West Indies, followed by about one million people. It largely derives from the thought of Jamaican political activist Marcus Garvey (1887–1940), who advocated a return to Africa as a means of solving the problems of Black oppression. When Haile Selassie was crowned Emperor of Ethiopia in 1930, he came to be viewed as the Messiah, with Ethiopia seen as the promised land. Rastafarians follow strict taboos governing what they may eat (eg no pork, milk, coffee); ganja (marijuana) is held to be a sacrament; they usually wear their hair in long dreadlocks; and they cultivate a distinctive form of speech. ▷ **Black Consciousness; religion**

**rationalism** ▷ **empiricism**.

**Realism**  In art criticism, a term (used especially with a capital R) referring to the deliberate choice of ugly or unidealized subject-matter, sometimes to make a social or political point. Realism with a small 'r' is often used rather vaguely as the opposite of 'abstract'. More generally, in literature and art, the term refers to an approach which advocates that work should appear true to life. ▷ **abstract art; Naturalism; Surrealism**

**Rebaptizers** ▷ **Anabaptists**.

**recession**  An economic situation where demand is sluggish, output is not rising, and unemployment is on the increase. Not as severe a downturn as a depression, it is usually identified when gross domestic product declines for two successive quarters. The recession of 1980–2 gave rise to very high levels of unemployment throughout the Western world. ▷ **depression; gross domestic product; reflation; trade cycle**

**recycling**  Putting waste substances back into productive use, a procedure advocated by many conservationists. It is a means of reducing

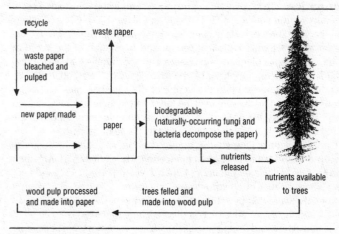

*The recycling of paper*

the demand on non-renewable resources, and of preventing problems of pollution and waste disposal. Examples include the pulping of waste paper to make recycled paper, the existence of bottle banks to collect used glass, and the smelting of metals from scrap. In the UK about 62% of lead is recycled. Incentives for recycling can be provided by government subsidies or by a deposit tax on containers. A distinction should be drawn with **reuse** — for example, returning milk bottles so that they can be used again. ▷ **conservation; non-renewable resources; pollution; waste disposal**

**referendum** A device of direct democracy whereby the electorate can pronounce, usually for or against, some measure put before it by government; also known as a **plebiscite**. The word has two plurals: **referenda** is the more formal and conservative usage, but **referendums** is nowadays more common. In some countries a petition of sufficient voters can put an issue to a referendum. Most commonly referendums are held on constitutional changes, rather than on government policy. In the UK there have been consultative referendums in recent decades in relation to British membership of the Common Market (1975) and devolution in Scotland and Wales (1979). Some people opposed their use, on the grounds that they undermined the sovereignty of Parliament. ▷ **democracy; parliament**

**reflation** In economics, government action designed to stimulate an economy which is in a period of recession. Strategies include increasing government spending, lowering taxes, and reducing interest rates. ▷ **interest; recession**

**Reformation** The Protestant reform movements in the Christian Church, inspired by Martin Luther (1483–1546), John Calvin (1509–64), and others in 16th-century Europe. It was a complex phenomenon, with various factors common to all reforms: a Biblical revival and translation of the Word of God into the vernacular; an improvement in the intellectual and moral standards of the clergy; emphasis on the sovereignty of God; and insistence that faith and scriptures are at the centre of the Christian message. Non-religious factors aiding the spread of the Reformation included the invention of the printing press; the political, social and economic uncertainties of the age; and a general feeling of revival caused by the Renaissance.

In Germany, Luther's 'ninety-five theses' (1517) questioned the authority of the Church and led to his excommunication. The Lutheran Church then spread rapidly, in Switzerland under Ulrich Zwingli (1484–1531) and later under Calvin, neither of whom allowed any form of worship or devotion not explicitly warranted by scripture. The doctrine of the priesthood of all believers and the importance placed on preaching the Word of God led to an educated clergy, and decentralized church communities were better able to prevent abuse of ecclesiastical privilege. In England, Henry VIII declared that the king was the supreme head of the English Church, and appropriated

Church property; in 1549 the Book of Common Prayer, embodying Reformation doctrine, was published, and under Elizabeth I a strong anti-papal stance was taken. In Scotland, under the influence of Calvin and the leadership of John Knox, the Presbyterian Church of Scotland was established in 1560, and remains the national Church. The Reformation also took root as Lutheran and Reformed Churches in France, Scandinavia, Czechoslovakia, Hungary, Romania, and Poland. ▷ **Anglican Communion; Christianity; Protestantism**

**reformism** Any doctrine or movement that advocates gradual social and political change rather than revolutionary change; most commonly applied to socialism. The underlying premise is that democratic procedures provide the most suitable means through which to build social change. ▷ **revolution; social democracy; socialism**

**reincarnation** The belief that following death, some aspect of the self or soul can be reborn in a new body (human or animal), a process which may be repeated many times. This belief is fundamental to many Eastern religions, such as Hinduism and Buddhism. Alleged past-life regressions, where a hypnotized person appears to 'remember' past lives, have recently fuelled Western interest in reincarnation, although such cases may only represent the person trying to meet the implied demands of the hypnotist. ▷ **Buddhism; Hinduism**

**relativism** Any philosophical position which maintains that there are truths and values, but denies that they are absolute. The Greek philosopher Protagoras (fifth century BC) argued that all truth is necessarily relative: to say that something 'is true' is always a shorthand way of saying that it 'is true for a particular circumstance', where the circumstance might be an individual, society, or conceptual framework. From an anthropological point of view, the relativistic view has several interpretations — in particular, that different societies have fundamentally different views about values, or that there are no absolute values valid for all societies. ▷ **epistemology; ethics**

**relativistic quantum mechanics** ▷ **quantum mechanics**.

**relativity** ▷ **general relativity; special relativity**.

**religion** A concept which encompasses a widely varying set of traditions, practices and ideas, and defies any single definition. Some religions involve the belief in and worship of a god or gods, but this is not true of all. Christianity, Islam, and Judaism are theistic religions, while Buddhism does not require a belief in gods, and where it does occur, the gods are not considered important. There are theories of religion which take it to be a wholly human phenomenon, without any supernatural or transcendent origin and point of reference, while others argue that some such reference is the essence of the matter. Several other viewpoints exist, and there are often boundary disputes regarding the application of the concept. For example, debate continues as to whether Confucianism is properly to be considered a religion; and some writers argue that Marxism is in important respects a religion. ▷ **apologetics; Baha'i; Buddhism; Christianity; cult; deism; fundamentalism; God; Hare Krishna movement; Hinduism; Islam; Jainism; Jehovah's Witnesses; Judaism; millenarianism; mysticism; Pentecostalism; sect; Shinto; Sikhism; theology**

**Renaissance** The revival of classical literature and artistic styles at various times in European history; the word is from French, meaning 're-birth'. Such renaissances occurred in the eighth and ninth centuries, in the 12th century, and from the fourteenth to the sixteenth centuries. The first, or *Carolingian* (named after Emperor Charlemagne the Great (742–814)), centred upon the recovery of classical Latin texts in cathedral schools. The second was marked by the foundation of universities, and the rediscovery of Aristotle's ethical and philosophical works. The third was notable for the development of naturalistic works of art, the study of ancient Greek authors, above all Plato, and the critical study of Christian texts. It is this last revival which many historians have thought marked the beginnings of modern times. The period saw the rise of secular states and values. There were many new institutions, such as permanent embassies and spies, standing armies, and regular taxation. Above all, the period witnessed a fundamental change in attitudes  illustrated by the rejection of clerical authority  the study of pagan (as opposed to Christian) sources of knowledge, and the introduction of secular values into works of art. ▷ **classicism**

**renewable resources** Resources with a yield which may be used without danger of exhaustion, such as solar power, wave power, wind energy, and hydroelectric power, most of which are directly or indirectly due to solar energy. Some renewable resources (eg crops, timber, fish) can be sustained in the long-term only through careful management, so that they are not overexploited (eg overcropping, overgrazing) or misused in the short-term. ▷ **alternative energy; non-renewable resources**

**Representatives, House of** ▷ **House of Representatives**.

**republic** A form of state and government where, unlike a monarchy (which is hereditary), the head of state and leader of the government is periodically appointed under the constitution. It thus covers most modern states, and in this respect the term has lost something of its earlier meaning and appeal as an alternative to systems where political power was hereditary.

Republics now vary considerably in form, ranging from liberal democratic states to personal dictatorships. ▷ **dictator; liberalism**

**retail price index**   An economic guide which shows changes in the *cost of living* in the UK from month to month. It is based on the shop prices of a range (a 'basket') of essential goods. ▷ **index-linking; standard of living**

**re-use**   ▷ **recycling**.

**revolution**   A long-term change of regime in a country followed by a major reconstitution of the political, social, and economic order. The emphasis is on complete change, though continuities have been a feature of almost all major revolutions. This is notable in Marxism, which not only advocates social and political change by revolution, but also how revolution comes about. Revolutions are normally viewed as involving violent over-throw and the use of force, but this is not a necessary condition. In this respect, it can be distinguished from the sudden overthrow of a ruler by force in a *coup d'état*. Famous revolutions include the French Revolution of 1789 and the Russian Revolution of 1917. ▷ **reformism**

**rhetoric**   The spoken and written language of persuasion. Rhetoric has had a chequered history. In the classical and medieval world, it was a formal branch of learning concerned with the techniques and devices required to persuade or convince an audience. Leading early analysts included Aristotle (fourth century BC), Cicero (first century BC), and Quintilian (first century AD), who developed theories of successful speech-making. Subsequently it came to signify elaborate and pompous language, which is nonetheless empty and insincere. In recent years, however, there has been a renewed interest in its role in interpersonal and mass communication, as attention has focused on the rules and conventions that enable language and other sign systems to convey meaning, and to present a message in the most effective way. ▷ **semiotics**

**ribonucleic acid**   ▷ **DNA**.

**right wing**   One end of the political continuum, originally identifying those who supported the institutions of the monarchy during the French Revolution. In the 19th century the term was applied to those who were conservative in their view, supporting authority, the state, tradition, property, patriotism, and institutions such as the Church and family. Those on the right were strongly opposed to socialism. In the 20th century, while the right is still associated with such a position, it has also developed a radical, non-conservative side. On the one hand, this has been associated with extreme nationalism (fascism), and, on the other, with attempts to reverse what are viewed as socialist developments. ▷ **centre, the; conservatism; left wing; New Right; socialism**

**RNA** ▷ **DNA**.

**Rococo**   In art history, the period following the late Baroque in European art and design; the word is from French *rocaille*, meaning 'rock-work'. It flourished especially in France and Southern Germany about 1700–50, until superseded by the Neoclassical taste spreading from Rome. Whereas Baroque was dramatic and powerfully theatrical, Rococo sought effects of charm and delicacy on a small scale — surface effects rather than bold masses. It was therefore most successful as a style of interior decoration. The greatest Rococo painter was the Frenchman Antoine Watteau (1684–1721). ▷ **Baroque; classicism**

**Roman Catholicism**   The doctrine, worship, and life of the Roman Catholic Church. A direct line of succession is claimed from the earliest Christian communities, centring on the city of Rome, where St Peter (claimed as the first bishop of Rome) was martyred and St Paul witnessed. After the conversion of the Emperor Constantine in the fourth century, Roman bishops acquired something of the authority and power of the emperor. Surviving the fall of Rome in the fifth century, the Church was the only effective agency of civilization in Europe, and after the 11th-century schism with the Byzantine or Eastern Church, it was the dominant force in the Western world, the Holy Roman Empire. The Protestant Reformation inspired revival and reform, the most dramatic reforms being enacted by the two Vatican Councils of the 19th and 20th centuries. The Second Vatican Council (1962–5) signalled a new era, with a new ecumenical spirit pervading the Church. Great emphasis was placed on the Church as the 'people of God', with the laity being given a much more active part in liturgy (eg the Mass being said in the vernacular instead of Latin).

Doctrine is declared by the Pope, or by a General Council with the approval of the Pope, and is summarized in the Nicene Creed. Scripture and the tradition of the Church are both accepted as authoritative. Principal doctrines are similar to those of mainstream Protestant and Orthdox Churches — God as Trinity, creation, redemption, the person and work of Jesus Christ, and the place of the Holy Spirit — the chief doctrinal differences being the role of the Church in salvation, and the nature of the sacraments. Ancient traditional practices, such as the veneration of the Virgin Mary and the Saints, are still regarded as valuable aids to devotion. At the other extreme, Roman Catholic priests in South America, preaching liberation theology, have assumed a political role. The hierarchy of the Church includes cardinals, bishops, priests, and several minor and religious orders. The organization of the Church is controlled by the Vatican, an independent state in Rome which, under the direction of the Pope, implements Church policy, and administers property and finance. In 1990, there were over 995 million Catholics worldwide — the largest membership of any religion. ▷ **Christianity; God; Reformation; theology; Trinity**

**Romanticism**   A large-scale movement of the mind in the late 18th–early 19th centuries, which affected the whole of human understanding and experience. The Renaissance made humanity the measure of the universe; Romanticism placed individuals at the centre of their own world. This was partly due to the work of philosophers, but it was the imaginative writers of the time who effectively liberated the subjective impulse. Among the more important writers associated with Romanticism are: in England, Wordsworth, Coleridge, Blake, Keats, Shelley, and Byron; in Germany, Goethe, and Schiller; and in France, Rousseau, and Hugo. In the visual arts, likewise, Romanticism refers to an attitude of mind, rather than a style. The range of subjects greatly expanded, some being chosen for their heightened emotional qualities, such as death-bed scenes, horrific disasters, or exotic appeal. Its features include a cult of nostalgia, a yearning for 'long ago and far away', the treatment of lost causes, and Egyptian, Greek, and medieval revivals. Leading Romantics include the English artists Turner and Constable and the Spanish artist Goya. Music between about 1810 and 1910 also displayed the dominance of subjective emotion over objective detachment. The period saw the growth of the symphony orchestra, the expansion of the main musical genres (symphony, opera, concerto, etc), and the emergence of new genres (such as the concert overture). Composers were able to express a response to literature and the other arts. National styles began to assert themselves, such as in Czechoslovakia and Russia. Major Romantic composers include Berlioz, Chopin, Liszt, Mahler, Verdi and Wagner. ▷ **art; classical music; literature; programme music**

**Salvation Army**   A non-sectarian Christian organization founded in the East End of London in 1865 by William Booth (1829–1912), dedicated to ministering to the poor and needy. It retains a military-style structure and evangelical atmosphere, and its members, both men and women, wear distinctive uniform. It is now established in over 80 countries. ▷ **Christianity; evangelicalism**

**sanctions**   In international law, penalties imposed by one state against another. Apart from war, they include such acts as the withdrawal of economic aid and the cancelling of cultural and sporting agreements. Examples from recent history include the sanctions imposed by Britain against Rhodesia (now Zimbabwe) following that country's unilateral declaration of independence in 1965, and the widespread use of sanctions against South Africa during the 1980s, in opposition to that country's policy of apartheid. ▷ **apartheid; boycott; embargo**

**scepticism** or **skepticism** A philosophical tradition which casts doubt on the possibility of human knowledge. An extreme version maintains that one is never in a position to have justified beliefs about anything — including the truth of scepticism! Less extreme versions are directed at particular sources of knowledge, such as perception, memory, or reason. ▷ **philosophy**

**scientific method** The procedures which scientists use in order to arrive at conclusions and to formulate scientific laws. The traditional view is that this is an inductive process, with observation leading to hypotheses which are then experimentally tested under rigorously controlled conditions. However, a number of philosophers of science have criticized this view as unreal — unrelated to the way in which scientists actually work. They point out that the formulation of hypotheses is as often as not a matter of inspired personal guesswork, which cannot be subjected to predictable and controlled procedures. On the other hand, the subsequent formulation and investigation of the hypotheses does seem to be a stage which can proceed in an objective and systematic way. ▷ **induction**

**secondary picketing** ▷ **picketing**.

**Second World** ▷ **Three Worlds theory**.

**secretary of state** The title of most UK government ministers who preside over a department, as distinct from junior ministers. It has increasingly replaced the title of **minister**, although formally there is now little to distinguish them except that secretaries of state are normally in charge of larger departments. In the USA, the term refers to the head of the state department in charge of foreign affairs, a senior member of the administration. ▷ **cabinet**

**sect** A separately organized group, usually religious, which rejects established religious or political authorities, and claims to adhere to the authentic elements of the wider tradition from which it has separated itself. It is distinctive and exclusive, claiming to possess true belief, correct ritual, and warranted standards of conduct. Membership is voluntary, but the sect accepts or rejects persons on the basis of some test of worthiness, and membership takes precedence over all other allegiances. It maintains rigorous standards of conduct and demands intense personal involvement. All major religions have produced a wide range of sects throughout their history. ▷ **religion**

**segregation** The cultural, political, and typically geographical separation of one group of people from another. It is often based on perceived ethnic or racial divisions, an extreme example being apartheid (literally 'separateness') in South Africa, where physical segregation between Whites and Blacks has been most apparent (eg in public transport, washrooms, housing, sport) and enshrined in law. It also characterized the period of Black slavery in the USA, generally being associated with the exploitation of poorer ethnic groups by a politically dominant elite. Housing ghettoes and other forms of social separation in inner cities provide an example of segregation arising from economic and political (rather than legal) inequalities. ▷ **apartheid; ethnicity; racism**

**select committee**   Members of a legislature whose task is to inquire into matters that come within its competence, usually as prescribed by the government. Two main types may be distinguished. An *ad hoc* committee normally ceases to exist when its task is completed (the name is from Latin, meaning 'for this' — in other words, the committee has been formed for a particular purpose). A *permanent* or *standing* committee is not restricted in this way; it meets regularly to investigate particular policy areas or the actions of government departments. Select committees vary in their power and influence across political systems; membership is usually based on party composition in the legislature. An example is the Senate committee set up to investigate the Watergate affair. ▷ **legislature; Watergate**

**semantics**   The study of the meaning-system of a language. The word *meaning* has itself many meanings, and semantic approaches vary widely. In one view, meaning is the relationship between language and the external world (*referential* or *denotative* meaning), and semantics enquires into the precise relationship between a word and the concept it stands for. In another, it involves the mental state of the speaker, as reflected in a range of personal and emotional overtones (*affective* or *connotative* meaning). In a third, it refers to the social context in which language is used, and from which it derives part of its significance (*contextual* meaning). In a fourth, it refers to the sense relations which link words and phrases, by which we know, for example, that some words have the 'same' meaning (eg *car, automobile*), some have 'opposite' meaning (eg *single, married*), and some have an 'included' meaning (eg *banana*, included within *fruit*). Within linguistics, it is useful to distinguish between *lexical* meaning (the 'dictionary meaning' of a word), and *structural* meaning, which a form derives from its position and function in the grammatical system of the language. ▷ **linguistics; semiotics**

**semiology**   ▷ **semiotics**.

**semiotics**   The study of signs, sign systems, and the social production of meaning; also known as **semiology**. Semiotics recognizes a large number of systems which people use to communicate meaning — written and spoken language, gestures, touch, dress, dance, film, etc. The meaning is largely produced by relationships and differences between individual signs, organized in codes, rather than by simple reference to external reality. To determine the meaning of a particular sign, such as the word *hot*, it is not enough to point to something that is hot; reference needs to be made to other words which relate to it, such as *warm, cool, lukewarm,* and so on, and which help to give 'hot' its meaning. Facial expressions, gestures, and other signs need likewise to be interpreted in a systematic way. ▷ **communication theory; linguistics; semantics**

**Senate**   The upper house of the US Congress, consisting of two Senators from each State (100 in all), chosen by the people to serve for six years; a third are chosen every two years. It has powers of 'advice and consent' on presidential treaties and appointments. Much of its work is done through committees rather than on the floor. It is presided over by the US Vice-President, who can cast the deciding vote if there is a tie. ▷ **Congress; House of Representatives**

**separatism**   The demand for separation by a particular group or area from the territorial and political sovereignty of the state of which they are a part. Examples of separatist movements are the Basques in Spain and the Tamils in Sri Lanka. Separatism is associated with claims for the right to political independence and self-rule, and is often connected with discrimination against minorities. ▷ **devolution; home rule**

**sequestration**   ▷ **bankruptcy**.

**serialism**   A method of composing music in which a series (or 'row' or 'set') of different notes is used, in accordance with certain strict practices, as the basis of a whole work. The most common type is 12-note serialism, in which the 12 pitches of the chromatic scale are re-ordered to form one of a possible 479001600 different series. This can then be presented vertically as chords, or horizontally as melodic lines, or as a mixture of both; it can be used backwards (*retrograde*), or with the intervals inverted (*inversion*), or in both retrograde and inversion; it can also be transposed to any other pitch. Thus, 48 versions of a single series are possible, and these provide all the pitch material for the composition. The Austrian composer Arnold Schoenberg (1874–1951) arrived at 12-note serialism in 1923, as a means of structuring music written without a key (*atonal* music); and his method was adopted, in very different ways, by several other composers. ▷ **classical music; modernism**

**service industry**   An industry which does not manufacture a product, but provides a service. It is a fast-growing sector in most Western nations, representing a higher proportion of gross domestic product and employment than the manufacturing industry. Activities include banking and other financial services, tourism, hotels, and catering. The expression 'post-industrial society' refers to a situation where relatively few people are engaged in manufacturing. ▷ **gross domestic product**

**set**  In mathematics, a well-defined class of elements — in other words, a class where it is possible to tell exactly whether any one element does or does not belong to it. We can have the set of all even numbers, as every number is either even or not even, but we cannot have the set of all large numbers, as we do not know what is meant by 'large'. The study of the mathematical and logical laws governing sets is called **set theory**.

**Seventh Day Adventists**  ▷ **Adventists**.

**sexism**  A set of preconceived assumptions about the 'proper' roles, attitudes, and characteristics (especially physical) that men and women have, typically working to the advantage of men over women. Examples include the views that 'a women's place is in the home', or that men are 'naturally aggressive'. Sexism can be identified by behaviour, speech, and the written word, and is criticized most strongly by feminists. In language, it can be illustrated by the use of male pronouns to include female persons, as in 'Each student should pick up his work by tomorrow'. The avoidance of such 'sexist language' (eg by using a plural form, such as 'Students should pick up their work...', or using two pronouns, such as 'his or her work...') has been a noticeable feature of linguistic change since the 1970s. ▷ **chauvinism; feminism; gender**

**shadow cabinet**  ▷ **cabinet**.

**shares**  Certificates of part ownership of a company, which represent equal amounts of money invested in the company. Companies limited by shares receive their funds from investors when they are first set up, and these funds are taken in exchange for share certificates. Each share represents a vote at a General Meeting of the company, and control of the company is in the hands of whoever owns more than 50% of the shares. A share also entitles the owner to a share of the profits, if there are any. ▷ **stocks**

**Shinto**  The native religion of Japan, so named in the eighth century to distinguish it from Buddhism, from which it later took many features. It emerged from the nature-worship of Japanese folk religions, and this is reflected in ceremonies appealing to the mysterious powers of nature for benevolent treatment and protection. By the eighth century, divine origins were ascribed to the imperial family, and in time became the basis for State Shintoism and its loyalty and obedience to the Emperor. In 1945, State Shinto lost its official status. ▷ **Buddhism**

**shop steward**   A part-time trade union official who represents the union members at their place of work. Shop stewards look after the needs of their members in negotiations with management and in union meetings at local and national levels. Originating in the various departments ('shops') of engineering factories, the post is now found in a wide range of industries. ▷ **trade union**

**shuttle diplomacy**   A form of international negotiation in which senior diplomats, often from a mediating nation or the United Nations, travel frequently between the various countries involved. Recent examples of shuttle diplomacy include the efforts of US secretary of state Henry Kissinger (1923–   ) to bring about peace between the Arab states and Israel in the 1970s, and those of US secretary of state Alexander Haig (1924–   ) between Britain and Argentina at the time of the Falklands War (1982). ▷ **summit diplomacy**

**Sikhism**   A religion founded by the Guru Nanak (1469–1539) in the Punjab area of N India. Under his leadership and that of his nine successors, Sikhism prospered. It is called a religion of the gurus (spiritual teachers), and seeks union with God through worship and service. God is the true Guru, and his divine word has come to humanity through the ten historical gurus. The line ended in 1708, since when the Sikh community itself is called guru. The Adi Granth, their sacred scripture, is also called a guru. The so-called 'five K's' are basic aspects of Sikh identity: *kangha* (a comb), *kach* (short trousers), *kirpan* (a sword), *kara* (a steel bracelet), and *kes* (the hair and beard remaining uncut). Sikh beliefs focus on the unity of God and the brotherhood of man, and reject the caste system. The Sikh understanding of life is closely related to preserving the territory of the Punjab, with a separatist movement seeking an independent state. The siege by Indian troops of the Sikh Golden Temple at Amritsar in 1984 during which a Sikh fundamentalist leader was killed, led to the revenge assassination of Indian prime minister Indira Gandhi later that year. In 1990, there were over 18 million Sikhs worldwide. ▷ **religion**

**Sites of Special Scientific Interest (SSSIs)**   Areas in the UK originally designated by the government's Nature Conservancy Council for the purposes of conservation. They include the country's best examples of particular wildlife habitats, interesting geological features, and habitats for rare plants and animals. In return for compensation, management agreements may be made between the council and site landowners to protect them. Nevertheless, many have been lost or damaged. ▷ **conservation; habitat loss**

**slander**   ▷ **libel**.

**Social and Liberal Democratic Party**   ▷ **Liberal Party; Social Democratic Party**.

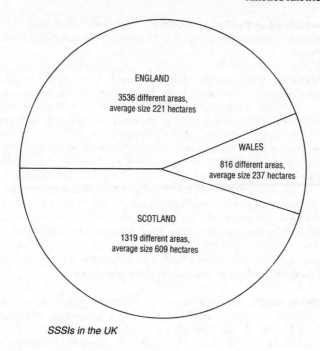

ENGLAND

3536 different areas,
average size 221 hectares

WALES

816 different areas,
average size 237 hectares

SCOTLAND

1319 different areas,
average size 609 hectares

*SSSIs in the UK*

**social democracy** A section of the socialist movement which emerged in the late 19th century, and which advocates achieving social change through reformist rather than revolutionary means. Social democrats accept and work through existing state structures, although such movements may contain radical left-wing sections. Some political parties that have adopted the social democratic label in the latter part of the 20th century are, however, moderate centrist parties. ▷ **centre, the; reformism; Social Democratic Party; socialism**

**Social Democratic Party (SDP)** A UK political party formed in 1981 by a group of four politicians: David Owen (1938–  ), Shirley Williams (1930–  ), Roy Jenkins (1920–  ), and Bill Rogers (1928–  ). They were known as the 'gang of four' — an allusion to the four politicians who held power in China during the Cultural Revolution of the 1970s. They broke away from the Labour Party primarily over disagreements on policy and the degree of influence exerted on policy by the trade unions. Although espousing socialist principles, the party was a moderate centrist one. The SDP formed an electoral pact with the Liberals in 1981, but despite some early electoral successes failed to break the two-party 'mould' of British politics. It merged with the Liberal Party in 1988 becoming the **Social and**

**Liberal Democratic Party**, although a small faction, led by David Owen, continued in existence as the SDP until 1990. ▷ **Labour Party; Liberal Party**

**socialism** A wide-ranging political doctrine which first emerged in Europe during industrialization in the 18th century. Most socialists would agree that social and economic relationships play a major part in determining human possibilities, and that the unequal ownership of property under capitalism creates an unequal and conflictive society. The removal of private property or some means of counterbalancing its power, it is held, will produce a more equal society where individuals enjoy greater freedom and are able to realize their potential more fully. A socialist society will thus be more cooperative and fraternal. Possibly the major division within socialism is between those who believe that to bring it about revolution is necessary, and those who believe change can be achieved through reforms within the confines of democratic politics. There are also differences as to how far capitalist production needs to be eradicated to bring about a socialist society. ▷ **anarchism; Fabian Society; Labour Party; Maoism; Marxism; reformism; revolution; social democracy**

**social science** A general term describing a number of disciplines, such as sociology, economics, political science, and geography, which have explored various aspects of society (eg social structure, the market, power, and spatial relations) through methods which are conventionally understood to be objective and 'scientific'. Research involves data collection and analysis in order to test hypotheses or models. Mathematical analyses are now commonplace in some areas, such as demography and social mobility studies. Nevertheless, there is debate over whether these disciplines are 'scientific', in the same way as the natural and physical sciences, given that they are measuring patterns of human behaviour rather than the organic or inanimate material of the natural and physical world. ▷ **economics; political science; sociology**

**social security** In the UK, the provision of financial aid by the state to reduce poverty. It consists of a wide range of benefits, covering such matters as housing and child allowances, which are available to those in need. In the USA, it is a tax on wages and salaries which is imposed in order to pay for retirement benefits, disability insurance, and hospital insurance. The tax is an important part of all federal revenues (around 40%) and is the equivalent of British national insurance. ▷ **insurance; poverty trap; welfare state**

**sociology** The study of patterned social behaviour which makes up a social system or society, a term originally coined by French social theorist Auguste Comte (1798–1857). Sociologists study the structure of social relationships as these are modified as a result of social interaction, and thereby seek to explain the development of new institutions or new types of society. Modern sociology has a number of key theoretical approaches which try to account for social structure and social change. While they differ in very important respects, they all share the belief that they can 'get behind' the surface appearance of everyday life, to reveal its complexity and interest. Any aspect of society can be examined sociologically, but there have emerged certain areas of study that have gained most attention, such as the family, gender, the media, science and technology, medicine, crime, social class, and systems of inequality. ▷ **class; functionalism (sociology); social science**

**Solidarity**   An organization established in Poland in 1980 to coordinate the activities of the emerging independent trade union following a long period of industrial unrest, notably in the Lenin shipyard in Gdansk. Its full name was the National Committee of Solidarity (*Solidarność*, in Polish), and its first president was Lech Walesa (1943–   ). Solidarity organized a number of strikes in early 1981 for improved wages and conditions, and became a force for major political reform. It attempted to seek reconciliation with the Polish government through proposing a council for national consensus, but suffered continuous harassment and was rendered largely ineffective by the declaration of martial law in 1981 and by being made illegal. It remained underground, but came back into the political arena in mid-1988. Following its success in the 1989 elections, Solidarity entered into a coalition government with the communists, with one of its members eventually becoming prime minister, and Walesa becoming president. ▷ **communism; trade union**

**sonata**   A musical composition, usually for keyboard (harpsichord, piano, organ) or for another instrument with keyboard. The main Baroque type, however, was the trio sonata for two solo instruments (usually violins) and continuo (the bass line of the composition, played by a harpsichord or organ, plus a cello or viola da gamba). This is exemplified in works by Purcell and Handel, and is normally in four or more movements. The classical sonatas of Haydn, Mozart, and Beethoven are nearly all in three or four movements — a model adopted by many 19th–20th-century composers, including Schubert, Chopin, and Brahms. ▷ **Baroque; classical music**

**sonnet**   A poem of 14 lines, with a structural balance between the first eight lines (*octave*) and the last six (*sestet*); the name is from Italian *sonnetto*, meaning 'little song'. Introduced in 13th-century Italy, the sonnet has remained one of the most popular and adaptable of all poetic forms. A variety of metrical and rhyme schemes may be employed. Famous English practitioners include Shakespeare, Milton, and Wordsworth; but the form is found in many languages. ▷ **literature**

**special education**   The provision of education for children who have special educational needs. They may be pupils who suffer from some kind of physical or mental handicap, who have learning or emotional difficulties, or whose needs cannot otherwise be catered for within the normal provision. In many cases the pattern is to provide special schools, but the trend in some countries has been for such children to be taught in ordinary schools.
▷ **dyslexia; mainstreaming**

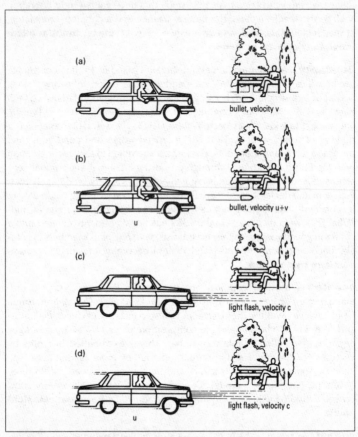

*Special relativity – In (a) a bullet with velocity v is fired from a stationary car; in (b) a car is moving with velocity u, with a similar bullet fired in the same direction as the motion of the car; as seen by an observer, the bullet has velocity u + v. In (c) a flash of light sent by a stationary car is measured by an observer as c, the standard velocity of light; in (d) a flash of light is sent from a car moving at velocity u; the observer measures the velocity of the flash and finds that it too is c, not c + u. The velocity of light is always the same.*

**special relativity** A system of mechanics applicable at high velocities (approaching the velocity of light) in the absence of gravitation. It was presented in 1905 by German mathematical physicist Albert Einstein (1879–1955). Its fundamental postulates are that the velocity of light is the same for all observers, no matter how they are moving; that the laws of physics are the same in all inertial frames; and that all such frames are equivalent. On this basis, no object may have a velocity in excess of the velocity of light; and two events which appear simultaneous to one observer need not be so for another. The system gives laws of mechanics which reproduce those of 'common sense' mechanics at low velocities, and is well supported experimentally, especially in particle physics. Generalized special relativity, incorporating gravitation, is called **general relativity**. ▷ **clock paradox; general relativity; quantum mechanics**

**Stalinism** A label used pejoratively outside the USSR to refer to the nature of the Soviet regime under Joseph Stalin between 1929 and 1953. It refers to a monolithic system, tightly disciplined and bureaucratic, with the party hierarchy having a monopoly of political and economic power. It also involves the total subservience of society and culture to political ends, suppression of political opponents, and the promotion of an individual above the party. ▷ **communism; Trotskyism**

**standard of living** The level of welfare achieved by a nation or group — usually measured in terms of food, clothing, housing, and other material benefits. There has been a considerable long-term rise in living standards in the West, particularly since 1945; but the same has not been true of the poorer developing nations. A simple measure for comparative purposes is gross national product per head of population. This shows a very fast rate of growth in Western Europe and the USA, and a very wide gap between the richest nations and the poorest. ▷ **developing countries; gross domestic product; poverty trap; retail price index**

**statute** ▷ **Act of Parliament**.

**stereotype** An image, conception, or belief which exaggerates, over-simplifies, and thus distorts the characteristics of people and their behaviour. For example, one group might consider another to be backward, belligerent, sexy, or arrogant. Relatively powerless ethnic groups, in particular, tend to be subject to racialist stereotypes. Such stereotypes often gain credence among people who have little or no direct experience of the groups to which they are applied. ▷ **ideology; racism; sexism**

**still life** In art, the representation of inanimate objects, such as books, candles, cooking utensils, musical instruments, fruit, flowers, etc. Still life was painted in antiquity; in Western Europe it flourished above all in the

Netherlands in the 17th century. Some still lifes are obviously symbolic (such as the painting of a skull); others seem to be demonstrations of painterly skill. ▷ **art**

**stock exchange**  A building where stocks, shares, and bonds are traded. The London Stock Exchange is located in the City of London near the Bank of England. Until 1986, business was carried out on 'the floor of the House', ie in the Stock Exchange itself. Individuals and institutions wishing to buy or sell securities would contact a stockbroker, who would place the order with a jobber (a trader on the floor). In 1986 the distinction between brokers and jobbers was abolished, and a computerized system was introduced for share trading. Firms are now brokers/market-makers; they may buy and sell on their own account as well as act as agents for others. The London Stock Exchange has some 5000 individual members and over 300 member firms. Most capital cities in the West have a stock exchange, Wall Street in New York City being the largest. ▷ **stock market; stocks**

**stock market**  The system of buying and selling stocks and shares; also, a building or electronic network in which these transactions take place (the *stock exchange*). A stock market 'crash' refers to a situation when the prices of stocks fall dramatically, resulting in many bankruptcies. The most famous case was the Wall Street crash of 1929; a less dramatic crash also occurred in October 1987 in most world stock markets. ▷ **stock exchange; stocks; shares**

**stocks**  A term which in general refers to financial assets. In accountancy, stocks are physical items held in storage, ie materials or goods for sale. In business and finance, the term refers specifically to securities or documents having a value. These may be shares in a company or loans to governments or companies. ▷ **shares**

**structuralism**  A theory which attempts to define the general properties of cultural systems, including language, mythology, art, and social organization; the approach derives from the work of the Swiss linguist Ferdinand de Saussure (1857–1913) and the French anthropologist Claude Lévi-Strauss (1908–  ). The fundamental thesis is that individual terms or phenomena can be understood only in relationship to other elements of the same system, and that each system is built up using a limited set of contrasts or oppositions. The impact of structuralism on literary criticism has been especially significant, since by redefining the relationship between language and world as cultural rather than natural, structuralism undermines traditional conceptions of meaning, and exposes the ideology built into our assumptions and values. ▷ **ideology; linguistics; semiotics**

**subsidy**   A payment or concession made by a government to a private body, in order to further a public objective. For example, a subsidy might be given to a transportation company to enable a particular road or rail network to be completed. Subsidies are also sometimes given to bodies which would be unable to survive without them, such as theatres and art galleries.

**summit diplomacy**   A term first used in the 1950s for negotiations between heads of state and governments with the intention of resolving disagreements; also known as **summitry**. It was regarded as a means of making progress when traditional methods of diplomacy were proving to be less effective. Since the 1960s it has been applied to any special meeting between national leaders, usually following lengthy diplomatic nego-tiations, with a symbolic and formal content. ▷ **shuttle diplomacy**

**summitry**  ▷ **summit diplomacy**.

**supernatural**  ▷ **paranormal**.

**supply and demand**   A basic economic concept relating to the way market forces work. 'Supply' is the amount of a product which producers are willing to provide. 'Demand' is the amount of that product which consumers want to buy. According to the principle of supply and demand, the price of the product will move to the level where the quantity demanded by purchasers equals the quantity that suppliers are willing to sell. ▷ **market forces**

**Surrealism**   An important movement in modern art and literature which flourished between the Wars, mainly in France; the name is from French, meaning 'over' or 'intense' realism. The first Surrealist manifesto of André Breton (1924) proposed the replacement of 19th-century Realism by the three related means of humour, dream, and counter-logic (the absurd). This initiative was taken up by many artists and writers, and the term is now used to describe the heightened or distorted perception and registration of reality, by whatever means. The basic idea was to free the artist from the demands of logic, and to penetrate beyond everyday consciousness to the 'super-reality' that lies behind. Freud's theory of the subconscious was appealed to, and many pictures by Dali, Magritte, and others seek to recreate the fantasy world of dreams. Objects are taken out of their normal context, their scale drastically changed, or they are represented as made of an inappropriate material, such as Dali's melting watches. In literature the movement is illustrated by the poetry of Aragon and Eluard the plays of Ionesco and Beckett, and the novels of Genet and Burroughs. Spanish film director Luis Buñuel guaranteed its impact on the cinema. Advertising since about 1960 has been indebted to the images of Surrealism, usually rendered by trick photography. ▷ **Dada; modern art; Realism**

**Symbolism**   The belief that ideas or emotions may be expressed in terms which make them communicable, whether in words, music, graphics or plastic forms. Several 19th-century authors aimed to create a world in their writing which goes beyond direct experience and makes contact with the subconscious mind. In English, they include Coleridge, Blake and Poe, and in French a number of poets, such as Baudelaire, Mallarmé, Verlaine and Rimbaud, who came to be known as Symbolists. Their influence on subsequent art, literature, and aesthetic theory has been far-reaching. The modern novel as well as poetry and drama is often heavily symbolic; the visual arts and the cinema likewise employ sophisticated 'coding' techniques. ▷ **Realism**

**symphonic poem**   A single-movement orchestral work in which a composer seeks to express the emotional, pictorial, or narrative content of a poem, story, painting, etc. It was developed by Hungarian composer Franz Liszt (1811–86) from the programmatic concert overture, and taken up by other Romantic composers. The Austrian composer Richard Strauss (1864–1949) preferred the term *Tondichtung* ('tone poem'). ▷ **classical music; overture; programme music; Romanticism**

**symphony**   An orchestral work originating in the 18th century, although the term had been used earlier with different meanings. The classical symphony of Haydn, Mozart, Beethoven, and Schubert was mostly in four movements: a fast movement; a slow movement; a minuet or scherzo; and a finale. In the 19th century the structure was varied a good deal, and programmatic or descriptive intentions were often present, as in the five-movement *Symphonie Fantastique* of Berlioz. The example of Beethoven's Ninth Symphony, which used solo singers and chorus, was followed by many composers, including Mahler. Sibelius's structural innovations led eventually to a single-movement symphony (No. 7, composed in 1924), while other composers (eg Shostakovich) have either modified the Romantic structure to serve their expressive purposes or, like Stravinsky, sought to restore the older symphonic styles. ▷ **classical music; Romanticism**

**systematics**   The classification of organisms into a hierarchical series of groups which emphasizes their presumed evolutionary interrelationships. The main categories of modern classifications are (in order of increasing generality): species, genus, family, order, class, phylum (animals), division (plants), and kingdom. For example, the lion is a member of the species *Panthera leo* belonging to the genus *Panthera* belonging to the cat family (*Felidae*), ultimately a member of the animal kingdom. ▷ **taxonomy**

**tactical voting**   Casting one's vote in an election for a candidate with the best chance of defeating another candidate who would otherwise be the most likely to win. This generally occurs where the candidate of one's choice is highly unlikely to be successful, or where preventing a particular candidate from being elected is of greater importance. ▷ **democracy**

*t*

**tariff**   A tax placed on goods imported into a country. Its aims are to prevent too many imports entering the country, and to raise revenues for a government. If tariffs become too strict, there will be a rise in smuggling. ▷ **free trade; import quotas**

**tautology**   In everyday use, needless repetition — saying something twice, when once would do. Ordinary definitions and mathematical equations have both been deemed tautologies by some 20th-century philosophers. In modern logic, the term is used for a statement which is true because of the way it is formally constructed. For example, 'Either A is B or A is not B' is a tautology. The statement is formally true, even when A is replaced by 'black' and B by 'white'. ▷ **logic**

**taxation**   The means by which a government raises money to finance its activities. *Direct* taxes are paid by individuals (eg income tax, national insurance contributions) and companies (eg corporation tax). *Indirect* taxes are those levied on goods and services (eg value-added tax, sales tax). The taxation rules frequently change, in response to government policy and needs, and changes are generally announced in a budget statement. In the past, tax has been levied on many things, including windows and jockeys. ▷ **black economy; budget; excise tax; income tax; tax haven; VAT**

**tax haven**   A country or area where rates of taxation are especially low; also called a **tax shelter**. Companies or individuals may choose to reside there to avoid paying high rates of tax in their own home country. Examples include the Isle of Man, the Channel Isles, and some West Indian countries. ▷ **taxation**

**taxonomy**   The theory and practice of describing, naming, and classifying organisms. It is divided into *alpha taxonomy*, the description and designation of species typically on the basis of their form and structure; *beta taxonomy*, the arrangement of species into hierarchical systems of higher categories; and *gamma taxonomy*, the study of the evolutionary relationships between groups (*taxa*) and of variation within and between populations. ▷ **systematics**

**technology**   The use of tools, machines, materials, techniques, and sources of power to make work easier and more productive. Industrial technology began 200 years ago with the introduction of power-driven machines, the growth of factories, and the mass production of goods. Whereas science is concerned with understanding how and why things happen, technology deals with making things happen; it can be subdivided into many specializations, such as medical, military, and nuclear. Technology has helped people to gain control over nature, and so build a civilized world. Undesirable side-effects include increased pollution and loss of jobs as a result of automation. ▷ **automation; productivity**

**telecommunications**   The transmission of data-carrying signals, often between two widely-separated points; it includes radio, telegraphy, telephones, television, and computer networks. Telecommunications in the modern sense began in the 19th century, with railway telegraph lines introduced in the 1840s. Telephones for commercial use were introduced in the 1870s, and radio telegraphy in the 1890s. During the 20th century, first radio (from the 1920s) and then television (from the 1950s) became important for communication over distance. In 1962 the US Telstar 1 satellite was launched to relay communications signals; however, this had a low orbit, and so could be used for only a short part of each day. Now large numbers of *geostationary* satellites provide day-long international links for telephony and television transmissions, carried by high frequency radio waves (microwaves). The use of optical fibre links in telephone cables enables hundreds of simultaneous conversations to be transmitted. ▷ **mobile communications**

**terrorism**   Coercive and violent behaviour undertaken to achieve or promote a particular political objective or cause, often involving the overthrow of established order. Terrorist activity is designed to induce fear through its indiscriminate, arbitrary, and unpredictable acts of violence, often against members of the population at large. It may be 'official', as under Stalin, or 'unofficial', as employed by various opposition or underground movements. Such movements are usually minority groups (such as the IRA) who feel there are no other means available to them of achieving their objectives. Terrorism may be confined to a specific territory or may have an international dimension, as seen in hijackings and hostage-taking. ▷ **activism; Lockerbie disaster**

**tertiary education**   Education which follows that received in a secondary school or equivalent institution. It is often used to refer to further and higher education, but in the UK it can also refer to attendance at a **tertiary college**, which is a college for all those over 16 wishing to pursue academic or vocational courses. ▷ **further education**

**Thatcherism**   The name given to the policies, style, and content of the Conservative administration during the 1980s under prime minister Margaret Thatcher (1925–   ) — used chiefly by her political opponents and by the media. Its concerns included the use of monetarist policies to control inflation, the weakening of trade unions, the strengthening of the role of market forces in the economy, and an emphasis on law and order. Criticisms were directed chiefly at the personal and centralized style of government adopted by Mrs Thatcher herself, and for its apparent neglect of disadvantaged groups within society. ▷ **conservatism; monetarism; New Right; privatization**

**theist**   Someone who believes in a single divine being, transcendent and personal, who created the world and, although involved with and related to the creation, is distinct from it. Theism is a feature of Jewish and Islamic as well as Christian faith, and contrasts with both deism and pantheism. ▷ **agnosticism; atheist; deism; God; pantheism**

**theology**   Literally, the science of the divine, or of discourse about God. In Christianity, it is understood as the systematic critical clarification of the historical beliefs of the Church. It has two main divisions. *Natural theology* studies whatever can be known about God from nature or by reason alone. *Revealed theology* studies whatever can be known only through the self-disclosure of God — such as in the Bible. ▷ **apologetics; Christianity; God**

**think tank**   A colloquial name for a group of people brought together in order to develop new ideas and offer expert advice. These bodies are often appointed as a consultative body by a government at national level, but will also be found in such fields as industry, scientific research, and the arts. ▷ **policy unit**

**Third World**   ▷ **Three Worlds theory**.

**Three Age System**   The chronological division of Old World prehistory into three successive ages of *Stone*, *Bronze*, and *Iron*. The Stone Age has also been subdivided into the *Palaeolithic* (*Old Stone Age*), characterized by chipped stone, and the *Neolithic* (*New Stone Age*), characterized by polished stone tools. There is also the term *Mesolithic* (*Middle Stone Age*), covering the five millennia following the end of the last glaciation, and *Chalcolithic* for the *Copper* or earliest Bronze Age. ▷ **archaeology**

**Three Worlds theory**   A theory that sees the world as being divided into three main blocs of countries, defined by their economic status. These are the developed capitalist economies (the **First World**), the developed communist countries (the **Second World**), and underdeveloped countries (the **Third World**), covering most of Latin America and recently independent African and Asian states. The Third World countries tend to adopt a position of neutrality, thereby dividing the world politically in three. The large number and diversity of Third World nations makes an adequate definition impossible: the concept includes the oil-rich countries alongside the poorest countries. Some (including the United Nations) recognize a 'Fourth World', of the 25 poorest nations. ▷ **capitalism; communism; developing countries**

**Tiananmen Square**   The largest public square in the world, covering 40 ha/98 acres and lying before the gate to the Imperial Palace in central Beijing (Peking). It was here that the People's Republic was proclaimed in September 1949. In June 1989, it was the scene of mass protests by students and others against the Chinese government, crushed by troops of the Chinese Army with an undisclosed number of dead.

**totalitarianism**   In its modern form, a political concept first used to describe the USSR's communist regime and Italy and Germany's fascist regimes during the period between the two World Wars. It is difficult to distinguish from related concepts such as 'authoritarianism' and 'dictatorship', but certain common features can be identified. These relate to the use of power and the means of government employed by the leadership, which claims exclusive rights to govern, usually on behalf of the party and its ideology. Furthermore, all aspects of social, political, industrial, military, and economic life are controlled or permeated by the state apparatus — 'total' control. Political opposition is suppressed, and decision making is highly centralized. ▷ **authoritarianism; communism; dictator; fascism**

**trade cycle**   The repeated pattern of peaks and troughs in an economy; also called a **business cycle**. A boom may be followed by a recession, perhaps also by a depression, then by a recovery, and then by another boom. Trade cycles vary greatly between periods and countries, and are not usually as predictable as the term 'cycle' suggests. However, notable fluctuations in economic growth can often be seen over periods of seven or eight years, and much longer trends have also been identified, in such areas as growth rates and unemployment. The major problem for governments is how to even out economic activity and maintain continuous growth. ▷ **boom; depression; recession**

**Trades Union Congress (TUC)**   A voluntary association of trade unions in the UK, founded in 1868. It meets annually in September to decide policy, and representation at the Conference is based on one delegate per 5000 members. Very large unions therefore have considerable voting power — 'the block vote'. There are over 80 affiliated unions, representing some 10 million individual union members. The role of the TUC is to develop systematic relations with the government and the Confederation of British Industry, to represent the interests of its members on national councils and commissions, and to help settle disputes between members. It also has representation on the Council of ACAS and on the Manpower Services Commission. ▷ **ACAS; trade union**

**trade union**   An association of people, often in the same type of business, trade, or profession, who have joined together to protect their interests and improve their pay and working conditions. The trade union movement developed in the early years of the 19th century, growing rapidly after the repeal of the Combination Acts (which had declared unions illegal) in 1824–5. In 1834, six Dorset labourers were sentenced to transportation to Australia for attempting to press for higher wages; these have become famous as the 'Tolpuddle Martyrs'. Since then, unions have played an important role in industrial relations. They have developed in all Western nations over the last 150 years. They are often organized into branches, with local 'shop' representation in the form of a shop steward. The Transport and General Workers Union (TGWU) is Britain's largest trade union, with members drawn from many industries and trades. ▷ **ACAS; industrial action; shop steward**

**transplantation**   The transfer of an organ or tissue from one person to another. Unless the recipient is an identical twin, such a graft sets up an immunological reaction which may destroy the transplanted tissue. This reaction results from the introduction of foreign protein to the recipient. It may be partially or completely controlled by the use of drugs, and is less severe in closely related persons. Tissues that have been transplanted successfully are bone marrow, undertaken for leukaemia, and the kidney and heart, carried out for severe kidney and heart failure. The cornea in front of the eye may also be transplanted, but is a special case as it does not set up any immunological reaction in the host. Corneas can be stored in banks, and used to treat blindness when this results from damage to the front of the eyes.

**treasury**   The department of a government or (in the USA) firm which is in charge of finance. It includes the provision of capital, borrowing, the short-term deposit of surplus funds, and foreign exchange dealing. In UK government terms, the **Treasury** is the name of the department responsible for managing the nation's finances, headed by the Chancellor of the Exchequer, who is responsible to the Prime Minister (the First Lord of the Treasury). It operates through the central bank to manage the government's monetary policy. In the USA, it is known as the *Department of Treasury*, and elsewhere usually as the *Ministry of Finance*. ▷ **Chancellor of the Exchequer**

**tribunal**   An official body exercising functions of a judicial nature. In the UK, tribunals frequently deal with matters where the citizen is in conflict with a government department. They tend to be specialized, governing such issues as employment rights, mental health, and taxation. ▷ **arbitration; legislature**

**Trinity**  A distinctively Christian doctrine that God exists in three persons, Father, Son, and Holy Spirit. The unity of God is maintained by insisting that the three persons or modes of existence of God are of one substance. The doctrine arose in the early Church because strictly monotheistic Jews nevertheless affirmed the divinity of Christ (the Son) and the presence of God in the Church through the Holy Spirit. The functions of the persons of the Trinity, and the relationship between them, has been the subject of much controversy, but the trinitarian concept is reflected in most Christian worship. ▷ **Christianity; God**

**Trotskyism**  A development of Marxist thought by Russian revolutionary leader, Leon Trotsky (1879–1940). Essentially a theory of permanent revolution, Trotskyism stressed the internationalism of socialism, avoided coexistence, and encouraged revolutionary movements abroad. However, this conflicted with Stalin's ideas about the development of socialism, and having been expelled from the Soviet Union in 1929, he was eventually assassinated. Trotskyism has since inspired other extreme left-wing revolutionary movements, but they are factionally divided, and have little support ouside some Western capitalist states. ▷ **communism; Marxism; Militant Tendency; Stalinism**

**twelve-tone music**  ▷ **serialism**.

**twin paradox**  ▷ **clock paradox**.

*u*  **uncertainty principle**  In quantum theory, a fundamental limit on the precision of simultaneous measurements, irrespective of the quality of the measuring equipment used; stated in 1927 by German physicist Werner Heisenberg (1901–76), and thus often called the **Heisenberg uncertainty principle**. If an attempt is made to measure simultaneously the position and momentum of a particle, there will always be a level of uncertainty in the values obtained. This is a consequence of the wave description of matter. The principle may be interpreted as a result of disturbance to a system due to the act of measuring it. ▷ **quantum mechanics**

**unicameral system**  ▷ **bicameral system**.

**urbanization**  The process whereby an increasing proportion of the population of a region or country live in urban areas, particularly a country's largest urban settlement. It is characterisitic of economically advancing nations, where it is occurring at a much faster rate than it did historically in the developed (Western) world. Urbanization is linked to industrialization. ▷ **migration**

**utopianism**   A political philosophy distinguished by its belief in an ideal future state of global social harmony. The name derives from the imaginary state described in Thomas More's *Utopia* (1516). Utopians work to establish the basis for the utopia of the future. It has taken many forms, such as anarchism, and other radical forms of collective social action. ▷ **anarchism; political science**

**VAT**   The abbreviation for **value-added tax**, a tax levied upon certain products or services as a percentage of their value (17.5% in 1991). The customer pays the tax on top of the basic price. In the UK, VAT was introduced in 1973 as a replacement for purchase tax. ▷ **excise tax; taxation**

**vegan**   ▷ **vegetarianism**.

**vegetarianism**   The practice of eating a diet devoid of meat. People who follow a diet containing animal protein from dairy products and eggs are known as **ovo-lacto-vegetarians**. Those who shun all animal foods are known as **vegans**. People become vegetarians for a variety of ethical, ecological, and religious reasons. The vegetarian diet may be healthier than that of the omnivore, since it is likely to contain less fat and more fibre. There are few nutritional disadvantages in being vegetarian, the only possible problem being in the low levels and low availability of iron in vegetable foods. Veganism, however, does pose problems, with low dietary intakes of available calcium, iron, and zinc, and little or no dietary intake of vitamin $B_{12}$, which is never found in plants. Vegans overcome the latter problem by taking vitamin $B_{12}$ tablets, or by eating fermented foods where the bacteria provide the $B_{12}$. ▷ **vitamins**

**vertical thinking**   ▷ **lateral thinking**.

**vicious circle**   A faulty method of reasoning, in which A is being used to prove or define B, at the same time as B is being used to prove or define A. An everyday example of the frustration that comes from vicious circle reasoning can be found in some dictionaries: you look up a word, say *deficient*, and it tells you the meaning is 'inadequate'; you then look up *inadequate* and it tells you the meaning is 'deficient'. More generally, the term is used to describe a problematic situation where a proposed solution makes the original problem worse. ▷ **logic**

**visibles**   ▷ **invisibles**.

**vitamins**   Organic substance present in minute quantities in natural foods that are essential for health, classified as either *water soluble* or *fat soluble*.

## MAIN TYPES OF VITAMIN

| Vitamin | Chemical name | Deficiency symptoms | Source |
|---|---|---|---|
| **Fat soluble** | | | |
| A | retinol (carotene) | night blindness; rough skin; impaired bone growth | milk, butter, cheese, egg yolk, liver, fatty fish, dark green vegetables, yellow/red fruits and vegetables, especially carrots |
| D | cholecalciferol | rickets; osteomalacia | egg yolk, liver, fatty fish; made on skin in sunlight |
| E | tocopherols | multiple diseases produced in laboratory animals; in humans, multiple symptoms follow impaired fat absorption | vegetable oils |
| K | phytomenadione | haemorrhagic problems | green leafy vegetables, beef liver |
| **Water soluble** | | | |
| $B_1$ | thiamin | beri-beri, Korsakov's syndrome | germ and bran of seeds, grains; yeast liver, milk, cheese, eggs, green leafy vegetables, pulses, yeast |
| $B_2$ | riboflavin | skin disorders; failure to thrive | |
| $B_6$ | pyridoxine | dermatitis; neurological disorders | liver, meats, fruit, cereals, leafy vegetables |
| | pantothenic acid | dermatitis; neurological disorders | widespread in plants and animals; destroyed in heavily-processed food |
| | biotin | dermatitis | liver, kidney, yeast extract; made by microorganisms in large intestine |
| $B_{12}$ | cyanocobalamin | anaemia; neurological disturbance | liver, kidney, milk; none found in plants |
| | folic acid | anaemia | liver, green leafy vegetables, peanuts, cooking and processing can cause serious losses in food |
| C | ascorbic acid | scurvy | blackcurrants, citrus fruits, other fruits, green leafy vegetables, potatoes; losses occur during storage and cooking |

When absent from the diet or present in insufficient amounts, they result in specific abnormalities.

**vivisection**   The practice of dissecting live animals for experimental purposes. The research includes experiments which study the effects of new drugs, food additives, cosmetics, and a wide range of chemicals on the body tissue and behaviour of such animals as guinea pigs, rabbits, rats, and monkeys, as an alternative to using human subjects. Such research is now strictly controlled by legislation in most Western nations, but nonetheless provokes considerable public opposition in some countries, including the use of violence against scientists and research organizations by animal rights extremists.

**vocational education**   Education which is aimed at the preparation of students for their present or future employment. Often undertaken in colleges of further education, it can also take place on the job in the workplace itself. A wide range of vocational qualifications is usually available, some from chartered award-giving institutions, others from professional organizations — such as, in the UK, the system of National Vocational Qualifications (NVQs). In addition, pre-vocational education is available for pupils of school age, and also for 16- to 19-year-olds in colleges, who wish to acquire work experience and explore the nature of different careers before making their choice. ▷ **further education**

**war**   A military conflict between two states, or, in the case of civil war, between different groups within a state. International war is subject to international law, and wars can be either lawful or unlawful. There have been a series of treaties since the 18th century covering the conduct of war, largely designed to prevent 'unnecessary suffering', or action that has no military advantage. The use of more overtly ideological wars and modern weapons have made it more difficult to regulate the conduct of war (eg greater difficulty in protecting civilians from aerial bombardment). Today the main source of international law on war or the use of force is the United Nations Charter, notably article 2(4). Distinctions are also now drawn between *conventional warfare*, which does not involve the use of nuclear weapons, *nuclear warfare, chemical warfare*, and *biological warfare*. A *guerrilla war* is conducted by non-regular forces, often avoiding direct engagement, designed to make a state ungovernable prior to a seizure of power. ▷ **nuclear weapons**

*W*

**Warsaw Pact**   The countries which signed the East European Mutual Assistance Treaty in Warsaw in 1955: Albania, Bulgaria, Czechoslovakia, East Germany, Hungary, Poland, Romania, and the USSR. Albania withdrew in 1968. The pact established a unified military command for the armed forces of all the signatories. All members were committed to giving immediate assistance to any other party which is attacked in Europe. It was a communist response, in part, to the formation of NATO by the West. The Pact began to lose its identity and purpose after the events in Eastern Europe which commenced in 1989. ▷ **communism; Iron Curtain; NATO**

**waste disposal** The disposal of waste from domestic, industrial, and agricultural sources; a major environmental concern. Methods commonly used include burial in landfill sites and at sea, incineration (sometimes for power generation), and the production of refuse-derived fuel pellets which can be used as an energy source. Care is needed with the disposal of toxic and hazardous substances to ensure that pollution of water, air, and land is avoided, and to prevent the build-up of methane, an inflammable gas. It is possible to recover this landfill gas as an energy source. An alternative to the disposal of some waste is recycling (eg of paper and glass). ▷ **hazardous substances; pollution; radioactive waste; recycling**

**watercolour** Any form of painting in which the pigment is mixed with a water-soluble medium such as gum arabic. Watercolour was used in ancient Egypt and China, and medieval manuscripts were illuminated with water-based paint. The great masters of watercolour were all English, including Thomas Girtin (1775–1802), John Cotman (1782–1842), and J M W Turner (1775–1851). ▷ **art**

**Watergate** A political scandal which led to the first resignation of a president in US history (Republican Richard Nixon, in office 1968–74). The actual 'Watergate' is a hotel and office complex in Washington DC, where the Democratic Party had its headquarters. During the presidential campaign of 1972, a team of burglars was caught inside Democratic headquarters, and their connections were traced to the White House and to the Committee to Re-elect the President. Investigations by the Washington Post, a grand jury, and two special prosecutors revealed that high officials who were very close to President Nixon were implicated, and that Nixon himself was aware of illegal measures to cover up that implication. A number of officials were eventually imprisoned. Nixon himself left office when it became clear that he was likely to be impeached and removed. ▷ **Irangate**

**welfare state** A system of government whereby the state assumes responsibility for protecting and promoting the welfare of its citizens in such areas as health, income maintenance, unemployment, and pensions. A comprehensive system was established in the UK following World War II, funded out of national insurance contributions and taxation. Such systems may be universal in coverage or subject to some form of means testing. In recent years concern has been expressed about the proportion of the budget consumed by welfare services, with those on the political right claiming that welfare provision decreases self-reliance and freedom of choice. ▷ **National Health Service; poverty trap; social security**

**West Bank**   A region of the Middle East lying to the west of the River Jordan and the Dead Sea. It is part of the former mandate of Palestine, administered by Jordan between 1949 and 1967. It was seized by Israel in the 1967 War, and remains under Israeli occupation, administered as the district of Judea-Samaria. The area includes Old (East) Jerusalem, as well as Bethlehem, Jericho, Hebron, and Nablus, and has been a focus of territorial aspirations by the Palestine Liberation Organization. It has been the scene of an uprising (or *intifada*) against the Israelis since early 1988, during which time schools and many shops have been closed. ▷ **Gaza Strip**

**women's liberation movement**   A broad cultural and political movement initiated by women to improve their social position by freeing themselves from the constraints and disadvantages of a society said to be dominated by men. 'Women's lib' has very strong roots in the USA and Europe, and has been 'politicized' especially by radical feminists who claim the continued existence of 'patriarchy' (ie male dominance) in capitalist societies. ▷ **feminism; sociology**

**work-to-rule**   ▷ **industrial action**.

**World Bank**   The generally used name for the **International Bank for Reconstruction and Development**, a bank founded in 1945 to finance development in the poorest countries. The bank is affiliated to the United Nations, and based in Washington DC. ▷ **developing countries; International Monetary Fund**

**World Council of Churches**   An inter-denominational Council of over 200 Churches, formed in Amsterdam in 1948. Originating in the ecumenical movement of the early 20th century, its main task is to seek the unity of the Church. It comprises most of the main-line Christian denominations with the exception of the Roman Catholic Church, with which, however, it keeps close contact. Its headquarters is in Geneva, and its ruling body, a representative Assembly, meets every six or seven years. ▷ **Christianity; ecumenism; religion**

**writ**   A written document, issued by a court, which commands someone to do or not do something. It is the first stage in legal proceedings. The best-known form of writ is the *summons*, which requires a person to appear in court on a certain day. The term has a broader meaning in some jurisdictions. ▷ **injunction**

**Zeebrugge disaster**   A major shipping disaster which took place in March 1987 outside the Belgian ferry port of Zeebrugge (pronounced **zee**-*bru-guh*). The Townsend Thoresen ferry, *Herald of Free Enterprise*, foundered just outside the harbour, with the loss of 193 lives. The accident resulted from the main car deck doors having been left open to the sea. An official inquiry held four crew members and the ferry's operators to have been at fault in events leading to the capsize, and several recommendations to ensure future safety were made.

### Spring Signs

Aries, the Ram
*21 Mar-19 Apr*

Gemini, the Twins
*21 May-21 Jun*

Taurus, the Bull
*20 Apr-20 May*

### Summer Signs

Cancer, the Crab
*22 Jun-22 July*

Leo, the Lion
*23 July-22 Aug*

Virgo, the Virgin
*23 Aug-22 Sep*

### Autumn Signs

Libra, the Balance
*23 Sep-23 Oct*

Scorpio, the Scorpion
*24 Oct-21 Nov*

Sagittarius, the Archer
*22 Nov-21 Dec*

### Winter Signs

Capricorn, the Goat
*22 Dec-19 Jan*

Aquarius, the
Water Bearer
*20 Jan-18 Feb*

Pisces, the Fishes
*19 Feb-20 Mar*

*Signs of the Zodiac*

**Zionism**   The movement which sought to recover for the Jewish people its historic Palestinian homeland after centuries of dispersion. The modern movement arose in the late 19th century with plans for Jewish colonization of Palestine, and under Theodor Herzl (1860–1904) also developed a political programme to obtain sovereign state rights over the territory. Gaining support after World War I, its objectives were supported by the British Balfour Declaration in 1917, as long as rights for non-Jews in Palestine were not impaired. After World War II, the establishment of the Jewish state in 1948 received United Nations support. Zionism is still active, as a movement encouraging Jews living outside of Israel to immigrate to and take an interest in the Jewish state. ▷ **Judaism**

**zodiac**   A zone of fixed stars, approximately 16 degrees in width, which marks the apparent courses of the Sun, Moon, and planets (apart from Pluto) about the Earth. Early astronomers projected patterns on to this area of sky, creating 12 groupings or constellations. It is important to distinguish between constellations — rather ill-defined star groups of variable size — and *signs*, an idealized version occupying equal 30-degree segments. On the 21st of each month (approximately) the Sun appears to change sign, moving in the sequence Aries, Taurus, Gemini, Cancer, Virgo, Libra, Scorpio, Sagittarius, Capricorn, Aquarius and Pisces. The disposition of the planets within the signs of the zodiac furnishes important information to the astrologer, who believes that each differentially influences the character and behaviour of those born under them. ▷ **astrology**

# Index of Proper Names